THE WORKPLACE REIMAGINED

In the wake of the pandemic, many employers continue to allow their employees to work from home, but much of the workplace remains governed by strict structural norms such as shifts, schedules, attendance, and leave-of-absence policies that determine when and where work is performed. In *The Workplace Reimagined*, Nicole Buonocore Porter explores how these workplace norms marginalize people with disabilities and workers with caregiving responsibilities. Using COVID-19 as a lens to illustrate how entrenched workplace norms are often not inevitable or necessary, Porter theoretically and practically reconceptualizes the workplace to end the stigmatization of these employees and helps readers understand the value of accommodating all workers. This book is timely, eye-opening, and will help us realize a workplace in which we account for the reality, precarity, and diversity of all our lives and bodies.

NICOLE BUONOCORE PORTER is Professor of Law and Director of the Martin H. Malin Institute for Law and the Workplace at Chicago-Kent College of Law, Illinois Institute of Technology. As an expert in employment discrimination and disability law, Porter has authored or coauthored five books and more than 45 law review articles and essays.

The Workplace Reimagined

ACCOMMODATING OUR BODIES AND OUR LIVES

NICOLE BUONOCORE PORTER
Chicago-Kent College of Law, Illinois Institute of Technology

CAMBRIDGE
UNIVERSITY PRESS

CAMBRIDGE
UNIVERSITY PRESS

Shaftesbury Road, Cambridge CB2 8EA, United Kingdom

One Liberty Plaza, 20th Floor, New York, NY 10006, USA

477 Williamstown Road, Port Melbourne, VIC 3207, Australia

314–321, 3rd Floor, Plot 3, Splendor Forum, Jasola District Centre, New Delhi – 110025, India

103 Penang Road, #05–06/07, Visioncrest Commercial, Singapore 238467

Cambridge University Press is part of Cambridge University Press & Assessment, a department of the University of Cambridge.

We share the University's mission to contribute to society through the pursuit of education, learning and research at the highest international levels of excellence.

www.cambridge.org
Information on this title: www.cambridge.org/9781009347426

DOI: 10.1017/9781009347440

First published 2023

A catalogue record for this publication is available from the British Library.

A Cataloging-in-Publication data record for this book is available from the Library of Congress

ISBN 978-1-009-34742-6 Hardback
ISBN 978-1-009-34746-4 Paperback

This book is for my family, for their unwavering support and encouragement. And it's also for all workers everywhere who struggle to balance their jobs with the rest of their lives.

Contents

Preface

My early scholarly work addressed two separate workplace law issues—disability discrimination and discrimination against women with caregiving responsibilities. After several years, I began seeing the similarities between these groups of employees; specifically, both groups of employees are subordinated because they cannot comply with the rigid workplace norms regarding *how* the job is performed or *when* and *where* the job is performed. If they seek modifications to these stringent workplace norms, they are stigmatized for doing so—what I call "special treatment stigma." Their employers might refuse to provide accommodations, but even if they do, they might look at these employees less favorably, and that will often have workplace consequences such as lower pay, derailed or denied promotions, and sometimes even termination. Moreover, accommodated employees are often resented by their coworkers, either because the coworkers believe the accommodations place unfair burdens on them, or because the coworkers wish they had the same accommodations.

Over the years, I've explored many solutions for ending the subordination that these groups of workers experience. But in doing so, I've come to realize that the only solutions that can work to end this subordination are solutions that protect all workers. If we accommodate everyone, special treatment stigma should disappear. Accommodations will no longer be seen as preferential treatment; instead, they will simply be seen as doing the work in a different way.

Furthermore, accommodating everyone recognizes the reality that all employees, at times, will need some form of workplace accommodations. Older workers and pregnant workers (in addition to people with disabilities) might need modifications to how the job tasks are completed (such as heavy lifting). Most workers will have periodic needs for short leaves of absence or flexible schedules for a variety of reasons. And of course, all workers get sick. As COVID-19 has taught us, we want those workers to stay home without penalty.

Accordingly, this book explores how we might reimagine the workplace in a way that accommodates all of our bodies and all of our lives.

Acknowledgments

I would like to thank my husband, Bryan Lammon, for his support throughout the long journey of writing this book. I would also like to thank my former law school, University of Toledo College of Law, for their financial support while I began writing the book. And I want to thank my current law school, Chicago-Kent College of Law, for their summer research support that allowed me to complete the book.

Several colleagues and friends have supported my work during my career, and countless conversations with these scholars helped me to think through the concepts and ideas this book addresses. At the risk of leaving someone out (and in no particular order), I want to thank Rebecca Zietlow, Joseph Slater, Rachel Arnow-Richman, Doron Dorfman, Ann McGinley, Michelle Travis, Brad Areheart, Stephen Befort, Laura Kessler, and Deborah Widiss. Finally, I want to thank all of the scholars whose work has inspired me and helped to create this book.

1

Introducing a Workplace Reimagined

I INTRODUCTION

Before the COVID-19 global pandemic, employers were often reluctant to allow their employees to work from home. And courts routinely refused to require employers to do so. Their rationales varied but often came down to an inability to imagine how employees could successfully work from home. How could they work in teams? How could they be adequately supervised? How could they interact with clients or customers? Yet when the global pandemic forced millions of employers to close their doors and millions of employees to work from home, the unimaginable became not only imaginable but very successful. In fact, the work-from-home experience during the pandemic has led many employers to adopt policies that will allow employees to work from home permanently.[1] This book is ultimately about just this type of reimagining of the workplace. If we can reimagine *where* work is done, then maybe we can also reimagine *how* and *when* work is done.

At a broader level, this book is primarily about two groups of employees that seemingly have very little in common—employees with disabilities and workers with caregiving responsibilities. Despite the obvious differences between these groups of employees, their common bond is that both are subordinated in the workplace because they often cannot comply with the ideal worker norm of most workplaces.[2] Both often need variations or modifications to either *how* the job is done or *when* and *where* the job is done. This need for modifications creates two types of disadvantages in the workplace. The first are workplace consequences, which might include refusal to hire, refusal to provide the accommodations that are necessary to perform the job (thereby leading to termination), or refusal to promote or advance these workers. But even if employers grant these groups of workers the requested

[1] *See, e.g.*, Katsabian 2021.

[2] Albiston 2010. Professor Joan Williams coined the phrase "ideal workers" to refer to what employers expect (and even demand) from their workforce. Williams, JC 2001.

accommodations so that they can meet the workplace requirements, the second disadvantage that might result is the resentment of coworkers that happens when some employees receive special benefits in the workplace. I refer to both of these disadvantages collectively as "special treatment stigma."[3] I have spent many years thinking about how to eliminate this stigma.

The only solutions that will avoid special treatment stigma are those that accommodate *everyone*—all of our *bodies* and all of our *lives*. If everyone has the right to a reimagined workplace, special treatment stigma should disappear.[4]

But there is another (and perhaps equally compelling) reason to allow everyone access to a reimagined workplace; that is, because everyone, at times, will fail to live up to the ideal worker norm and will need some type of modification to either how the job is done or when and where the job is done.

For instance, older workers and pregnant employees might need modifications to how the job tasks are completed, such as acquiring assistive devices or alternative methods of production to avoid heavy lifting. Child-free workers might have periodic times when they have caregiving obligations that conflict with the rigid time norms of most workplaces, such as caring for an adult loved one or someone else's child for whom they care deeply. And *all* workers occasionally get sick. As COVID-19 has taught us, we want those workers to stay home when they are sick without penalty. For all these reasons, the two reform proposals outlined in Chapters 8 and 9 are universal in nature—accommodating everyone.

The remainder of this chapter provides a brief introduction to some of the concepts and laws I address in subsequent chapters and gives the reader a sense of the rest of the book. But before proceeding, a couple of points about terminology and definitions. First, I most often refer to individuals with disabilities using "people first" language. For example, I might refer to a "person who uses a wheelchair" rather than a "wheelchair user." Most (though not all) people with disabilities find that people-first language properly places the emphasis on who they are as a person rather than defining them primarily through their disability.[5] Sometimes this people-first convention can get overly verbose or awkward, in which case I use phrasing that makes a sentence easier to read.

Second, what do I mean by caregiver? This is a complicated question and it is probably easier to explain what I *don't* mean. I am not referring to someone who gets paid to care for others, whether that's a nanny, day care worker, home health care worker, nursing home staff member, etc. We primarily think of "caregiver" as being synonymous with "parent," and in most instances, I *am* referring to the care work performed by parents. But I don't want to ignore all of the workers who are caring for

[3] Porter 2016b, at 96–105. I first coined the term "special treatment stigma" in Porter 2010a.

[4] Porter 2016b.

[5] Bagenstos 2009. However, a significant counter-trend has emerged, positing that people-first language ignores the identity aspect of disability and also ignores the fact that disability is often socially created. Schur et al. 2013, at 7; Moore 2019.

family members who are not their children—for example, grandparents caring for grandchildren, adult children providing care for their parents, one spouse caring for another spouse, etc.[6]

Moreover, even though much of the discussion in this book related to caregivers' experiences will be focused on women because women continue to perform the vast majority of the caregiving in this country, I recognize that men are also caregivers, sometimes even primary caregivers.[7] Thus, I am including men as caregivers in most of my discussions. The one circumstance in which I am only referring to women is with regard to pregnancy. I include pregnant women in my definition of "caregiver." This makes perfect sense when you think about the fact that pregnant women are, quite literally, caring for the baby growing inside their bodies.

Finally, someone suggested to me that I should not use the word "accommodation" because there is so much baggage associated with that word. The person who made this suggestion is not wrong, but the main purpose of this book is to take away the stigma associated with accommodations. Accordingly, although I will sometimes use "modifications" or other words that are synonymous with accommodation, I will continue to use and embrace the word "accommodation." I hope to demonstrate why the stigma surrounding this word is both wrong and unnecessary, and I can therefore reclaim the word accommodation, and take away its pejorative meaning.

II ALLIES IN WORKPLACE DISADVANTAGES

Workers with disabilities and employees with caregiving responsibilities face similar workplace disadvantages in two respects. The first is these groups' inability to consistently meet their employers' workplace expectations and norms. The second is the attendant "special treatment stigma" that follows from that inability or difficulty.

A *Inability to Meet the "Ideal Worker" Norm*

Both employees with disabilities and workers with caregiving responsibilities will occasionally have difficulty performing all of their assigned workplace tasks and/or meeting all of their employers' expectations. Some of the difficulty stems from not being able to perform some of the physical functions of the job or needing a variation in how the job tasks are performed. But more often, the difficulty results from the inability to consistently meet an employer's expectations regarding when and where work is performed. I call these latter expectations the "structural norms" of the workplace. Structural norms include employers' required hours, schedules,

6 Albiston & O'Connor 2016; Clarke 2011; Jacobs & Gerson 2004; Kessler 2001; Widiss 2021b.

7 *See generally* Williams, JC 2010.

shifts, attendance requirements, and policies related to leaves of absence and working from home.[8]

1 Physical Functions of the Job

The inability to consistently perform a job's required physical functions is more common for individuals with disabilities than for caregivers. But, as noted, given that my definition of "caregiver" includes pregnant women, and because some pregnant women will have difficulty performing some of the physical tasks of some jobs, this problem relates to both groups of employees. For instance, one difficulty that both individuals with disabilities and pregnant women sometimes have is lifting heavy objects.[9] Many occupations, especially those in the manufacturing or service industries, require employees to be able to lift large amounts of weight. Disabilities that might make heavy lifting difficult or impossible include back impairments, other musculoskeletal impairments, and impairments that directly affect strength or cause weakness. And one of the most frequent restrictions doctors place on pregnant women is to avoid heavy lifting.[10]

Another workplace requirement that both pregnant women and individuals with disabilities might struggle with is standing for an entire shift. Obviously, some jobs can only be performed while standing, but there are many jobs for which employers require standing when the job could be performed competently while sitting. For instance, a cashier at a grocery store could likely perform most of the job while sitting on a stool, and yet many grocery store employers require all employees to stand for an entire shift.[11] This means that individuals with disabilities and pregnant women who are unable to stand for an entire shift would be unable to perform the grocery store cashier position.[12]

2 Structural Norms of the Workplace

Even when an employee can perform the physical functions of the job despite a disability or pregnancy, it might be difficult for that employee to consistently meet their employers' expectations regarding the structural norms of the workplace.[13] As noted in Section II.A, structural norms refer to when and where work is performed, rather than the actual tasks of the jobs.

For example, some employees have difficulty working an assigned shift. Imagine an individual who has kidney failure and cannot work the assigned rotating shifts

8 Porter 2014c.
9 Porter 2020a.
10 Cox 2012, at 454.
11 Bornstein 2020.
12 Porter 2020a; Porter 2016a, at 250.
13 Albiston 2010.

because of his dialysis schedule. Or consider a single mother who cannot work the midnight shift because she has no one at home to care for her children.[14]

For some employees, the obstacle is strict attendance policies. For instance, an employee who has cancer might be fatigued or nauseous from the chemotherapy treatment she receives, which might cause her to occasionally miss work. Or imagine a mother whose husband frequently travels for work, forcing the mother to miss work when her small children are sick and cannot attend day care or need to be taken to the doctor.

Real-life cases of employees not meeting their employers' norms surrounding hours, shifts, and schedules are plentiful—I will discuss just a few. In the caregiving context, one woman with caregiving responsibilities was fired for refusing to work overtime. In *Upton v. JWP Businessland*, the plaintiff was a divorced single mother who was fired when she requested to work more manageable hours than the 14-hour, six-day-a-week schedule that her employer demanded.[15]

Other workers face termination for having too many absences because of pregnancy or because of their caregiving responsibilities. Some of the most troubling work–family conflict stories involve a caregiver having to make the impossibly unfair decision between leaving a child alone or losing her job. For instance, one woman's employment was terminated because her child was in a car accident and had to be taken to the hospital.[16] Another mother left her one-year-old and nine-year-old children home alone because the babysitter did not arrive on time and her employer had threatened termination if she did not report to work. While she was gone, the children died in a fire.[17] These are just a few of the negative (and even tragic) consequences that can occur when caregivers try to meet the ideal worker norm.

Examples in the disability context include one employee who had multiple sclerosis (MS) and asked if she could limit her overtime because her MS symptoms were exacerbated by working more than 40 hours per week; the employer refused and terminated her.[18] In a similar case, the plaintiff was a systems engineer working 60–80 hours per week. After he was diagnosed with hepatitis C, he requested an accommodation that would allow him to reduce his hours to 40 per week so he could get adequate rest and reduce his stress level. Although the employer accommodated him temporarily, the employer refused to accommodate him permanently, arguing that the accommodation was not reasonable. The court agreed, and the plaintiff lost his disability discrimination claim.[19]

[14] Albiston 2010.

[15] 682 N.E.2d 1357, 1358 (Mass. 1997).

[16] 9TO5, NAT'L ASS'N OF WORKING WOMEN, 10 THINGS THAT COULD HAPPEN TO YOU IF YOU DIDN'T HAVE PAID SICK DAYS: AND THE BEST WAY TO MAKE SURE THEY NEVER HAPPEN TO ANYONE, http://1000voicesarchive.org/resource/228/10things.pdf.

[17] Bernstein 2003.

[18] EEOC v. AT&T Mobility Servs., LLC, No. 10-13889, 2011 6309449, at *1, *13 (E.D. Mich. Dec. 15, 2011).

[19] Davis v. Microsoft Corp., 37 P.3d 333, 335, 337 (Wash Ct. App. 2002).

What all of these employees have in common is their inability to meet the ideal worker norm. Although the reasons for their failures are different—disability for some and caregiving responsibilities for others—they all must deal with the consequences of their failure to conform to the ideal worker norm.

B *Special Treatment Stigma*

Because these groups of employees often have difficulty meeting their employers' ideal worker norm, they sometimes seek workplace modifications. These might be formal requests for an accommodation because of a disability pursuant to the Americans with Disabilities Act (ADA) (which mandates such accommodations). Or employees might ask for schedule modifications for their caregiving obligations even when they have no legal right to those modifications. These requests for changes to how or when work is performed leads to "special treatment stigma." This stigma manifests itself in two distinct but related ways. First, having to provide accommodations to individuals in the workplace makes an employer assume it is more expensive or burdensome to employ such individuals than it is to employ workers who do not require accommodations. This belief, in turn, causes an employer to be reluctant to hire and promote these individuals. The second way special treatment stigma manifests itself in the workplace is by causing coworkers to resent accommodated employees. This resentment occurs for two possible reasons: (1) coworkers believe that the accommodation will require them to work harder or longer; or (2) the accommodation is something everyone wants, so coworkers resent the fact that others can receive a benefit they also covet.

1 Workplace Consequences

Many employers are reluctant to provide accommodations to employees who request them. Employers often see requests for accommodations as evidence that those employees just "can't cut it" in the workplace.[20] Even if the employer has a legal obligation to provide accommodations, this does not always lead to employers eagerly granting these requests. In fact, employers are often willing to provide informal accommodations to an employee until and unless the employee formally requests an accommodation, thereby signaling a possible legal obligation.[21]

For instance, in *Serendnyj v. Beverly Healthcare*, in attempting to prove that the employer was discriminating against her because of her pregnancy, the plaintiff pointed to the fact that before her pregnancy, other employees assisted her in performing more strenuous job duties, but after she became pregnant and asked for the same assistance, the employer refused. The court stated that there was a

[20] Williams, JC 2010, at 49.

[21] *See, e.g.*, Bagenstos 2009, at 56.

material difference between requesting and receiving assistance from other employees and forcing those employees to give assistance as an accommodation. The former, the court said, was completely voluntary and was given in a spirit of teamwork, but if the employer granted the plaintiff's request, the assistance by the coworkers would be mandatory and maybe against their wishes.[22]

Further evidence that employers dislike having to provide accommodations is the fact that the ADA has not noticeably improved the employment rates of individuals with disabilities. Scholars have argued that the reason for this is because employers are resistant to having to provide accommodations to individuals with disabilities, so they simply do not hire them in the first place. As most lawyers know, it is far easier for an employer to defend a failure-to-hire claim than it is to defend a termination claim. Therefore, anything that arguably increases the costs of employing an individual or makes it more difficult for the employer to fire an employee might incentivize the employer to not hire the individual in the first place.[23]

2 Coworkers' Resentment

The second way in which accommodated employees experience special treatment stigma is because of coworker resentment. Coworkers are often resentful when individuals with disabilities or workers with caregiving responsibilities are given deviations from workplace rules or any other kind of "special treatment" in the workplace. One reason for this resentment is that these coworkers might be required to bear some of the burden of their coworkers' accommodations. They might be required to work harder or longer or to vary their working hours in order to accommodate schedule changes for individuals with disabilities and workers with caregiving responsibilities. For instance, consider some common accommodations given to employees with disabilities: job restructuring, providing part-time or modified work schedules, providing leaves of absence, and reassigning individuals with disabilities to vacant positions. In all of these cases, the accommodation would have *some* effect on other employees. Job restructuring, for example, might require other employees to perform tasks that the disabled employee cannot perform, and these tasks might be physically arduous, such as heavy lifting. Part-time or modified work schedules and leaves of absence could cause other employees to have to work longer or different hours to make up for the absences of the disabled or caregiving coworker.[24]

Even when accommodations do not directly burden non-disabled coworkers, those coworkers might nevertheless resent the accommodated employees because those employees are receiving the types of workplace benefits that many

[22] 656 F.3d 540, 549 (7th Cir. 2011).

[23] *See, e.g.*, Bagenstos 2009, at 117, 134; Porter 2010a at 379.

[24] *See generally* Chapter 6, *infra*.

coworkers covet, such as schedule flexibility, reduced hours, or work-from-home arrangements.[25]

In the disability context, the resentment is greater if the coworkers think that the accommodated employee does not have a "true" disability under the ADA. This has become a more significant problem after the ADA Amendments Act was passed in 2008. It greatly expanded the protected class under the ADA. Thus, if coworkers see someone obtaining a coveted accommodation and the coworkers do not think that the employee is "truly disabled" or deserving of the accommodation, the resentment might be worse.[26]

Similarly in the caregiving context, accommodating caregivers is likely to create tension between those caregivers and their coworkers. Coworkers argue that accommodating caregivers unduly privileges those who become parents while requiring non-parents to work longer hours to pick up the slack for their caregiving coworkers. Many studies indicate that employees without primary caregiving responsibilities would often prefer to work fewer hours and therefore resent the fact that only parents are allowed to work less.[27]

To sum up, the inability of employees with disabilities and workers with caregiving responsibilities to consistently meet their employers' expectations, and the stigma that follows from that inability, is the problem explored in this book. As for solutions, before we can explore where the law should go, we need to understand where the law is right now. The next section explains the current protections in the United States for employees with disabilities and workers with caregiving responsibilities.

III APPLICABLE LAWS

Despite some of the similar experiences shared by employees with disabilities and workers with caregiving responsibilities, the applicable laws offer quite different protections. Individuals with disabilities are covered by the ADA.[28] Discrimination based on caregiving responsibilities is covered (if at all) by Title VII's[29] prohibition on sex discrimination, the Pregnancy Discrimination Act (PDA),[30] and the Family and Medical Leave Act (FMLA).[31] As is discussed in the next section and in later chapters, despite these statutory protections, patterns of discrimination "among work, disability, and gender persist."[32]

[25] Porter 2016a.
[26] Porter 2016a.
[27] Arnow-Richman 2003, at 392.
[28] 42 U.S.C. § 12101 *et seq. see also* Albiston 2010, at 103 (noting that the ADA appears to have more promise than Title VII because it requires reasonable accommodations).
[29] Title VII of the Civil Rights Act of 1964, 42 U.S.C. § 2000e.
[30] 42 U.S.C. § 2000e(k).
[31] 29 U.S.C. §§ 2601-2654.
[32] Albiston 2010, at 79.

A *The Americans with Disabilities Act*

Individuals with disabilities are entitled to reasonable accommodations if needed to perform the essential functions of their positions. Although scholars and courts dispute the breadth of the accommodation mandate, at least in theory, the accommodation obligation can be very broad. For instance, employers could be required to eliminate non-essential or marginal functions of a job if the employee with a disability cannot perform those functions. Or the employer might be required to allow an employee to work different hours or a different schedule. Employers might also be required to modify the physical aspects of the job or provide assistive devices that would allow the employee to perform the essential functions of the position.[33] The statutory limit on providing accommodations is that the accommodation cannot cause an "undue hardship" on the employer, which is defined as "significant difficulty or expense."[34]

Despite these legal obligations, many employers refuse to accommodate their employees' disabilities, and if the disabled workers sue, they often lose. In the first eighteen years after the ADA was passed, employees often lost their ADA claims because courts determined they did not fall into the ADA's protected class. The Supreme Court and lower federal courts had interpreted the ADA's definition of disability very narrowly, leading to plaintiffs having their ADA claims dismissed in over 90 percent of cases.[35] Even after the ADA was amended in 2008 to dramatically expand the definition of disability, there are signs indicating that employees are not faring much better on the merits of their cases, especially when the accommodation sought is a change to the employer's structural norms.[36] In other words, even though employers are technically obligated to accommodate their disabled employees, they often don't and courts rarely force them to.

B *Caregiver Protections: FMLA, Title VII, PDA*

Workers with caregiving responsibilities are not entitled to accommodations in the workplace. In fact, they are entitled to very few benefits. In certain circumstances, workers with caregiving responsibilities are entitled to leaves of absence under the FMLA; however, this entitlement is fairly limited. The FMLA's caregiving provisions only cover absences to care for an employee's spouse, child, or parent who has a serious health condition. The statute does nothing to address the routine caregiving obligations most parents have, such as when babysitters or nannies are sick, schools are closed, a parent's presence is needed at school, or children have routine

33 42 U.S.C. §§ 12111(9)(A)-(B), 12112(b)(5)(A).

34 42 U.S.C. § 12111(10)(A).

35 Colker 2005, at 79.

36 Albiston 2010; Porter 2014b, at 70–81.

medical appointments. Furthermore, the coverage of the FMLA is limited. It only covers employers who have 50 or more employees and only applies to employees who have worked for their employer for one year and who have worked at least 1,250 hours in the prior year. Finally, the FMLA only requires the employer to provide unpaid leave, making it difficult (if not impossible) for many caregivers to take advantage of their right to leave.[37]

Other than this limited entitlement to leave under the FMLA, there is no protection for workers with caregiving responsibilities. Although Title VII protects against sex discrimination (in addition to discrimination based on race, color, religion, and national origin), it only prevents employers from discriminating based on sex or sex plus another characteristic, such as the fact that a woman is a parent. Thus, if an employer refused to hire a woman because she was the mother of young children and the employer assumed (with no evidence) that her status as a mother meant she would not be committed to her job, she should have an actionable claim. However, Title VII does not impose upon employers an affirmative obligation to provide accommodations that would help caregivers balance their work lives and home lives. In other words, Title VII protects only caregivers who are able to perform as "ideal workers" (often because they can afford full-time nanny care or have a stay-at-home spouse).[38] It does nothing to protect what I call "real workers" – those caregiving employees who work hard and are good at their jobs but still occasionally need variations of the default structural norms of the workplace in order to attend to all the routine obligations that arise when caring for children or other family members who are ill, injured, or disabled.[39]

Finally, there is limited protection for pregnant employees under the PDA. The PDA was an amendment to the definition section of Title VII. It simply states that the terms used in Title VII – "because of sex" or "on the basis of sex" – include:

> because of or on the basis of pregnancy, childbirth, or related medical conditions; and women affected by pregnancy, childbirth, or related medical conditions shall be treated the same for all employment-related purposes, including receipt of benefits under fringe benefit programs, as other persons not so affected but similar in their ability or inability to work.[40]

Thus, the PDA only protects women who are pregnant or recovering from childbirth and leaves women (and caregiving men) without coverage for the rest of the child's life. Moreover, the PDA only requires an employer to treat pregnant employees as the employer would treat other employees who are similar in their inability to work. Thus, if a small employer not covered by the FMLA does not provide leaves of absence for short-term illnesses or injuries, it would not have to

[37] 29 U.S.C. §§ 2611(4)(A), 2611(2)(A), 2612(a)(1)(C); 2612(c); 2614(a)(1).
[38] Albiston 2009, at 1154.
[39] Porter 2010a, at 370–80; *see also* Kessler 2001, at 407.
[40] 42 U.S.C. § 2000e(k).

provide leave for a pregnant woman who just gave birth.[41] As discussed in Chapter 3, the legal landscape has arguably improved with the Supreme Court's 2015 decision in *Young v. United Parcel Service, Inc.*,[42] but the fact remains that, even when pregnancy accommodations are required, they will only protect women during pregnancy and for the recovery period immediately after. The PDA cannot help caregiving employees after the first six to eight weeks after the child's birth. And of course, the PDA cannot help those caregivers who are caring for adult family members. In sum, workers with caregiving responsibilities are rarely entitled to accommodations that would help them balance their work lives and home lives.

IV THE SOLUTION: REIMAGINING THE WORKPLACE

The solution is to reimagine the workplace. Reimagining the workplace will require a change of attitude as well as new laws that will dismantle employers' entrenched structural norms. In other words, we need to change minds and change workplaces.

A *Changing Minds*

First, we need to change the way employers and employees think about the accommodations given to employees with disabilities and workers with caregiving responsibilities.[43] This change in attitude involves two inter-related ideas. The first is that we need to eliminate the "us versus them" mentality. Because caregiving and/or having a disability are very common and often inevitable, this dichotomy does not reflect reality. The number of two-earner and single-parent families has dramatically increased in the past few decades. And as the population ages, even non-parents might suddenly be called upon to provide care for a sick or disabled spouse, partner, parent, or other adult family member. Furthermore, with the broadened definition of disability after the ADA Amendments Act in 2008, many workers who do not identify as disabled will likely find themselves with a medical condition that would qualify as a disability and might need accommodating. Thus, because all of us are likely to need accommodations at some point in our working lives, we all benefit from having workplace structures that can accommodate the needs of caregivers and individuals with disabilities.[44]

The second part of changing attitudes is recognizing that, even for those rare employees who never need accommodations in the workplace, there are still compelling reasons to support those who do. In Chapter 7, I demonstrate that we all benefit from working together to help our coworkers. Society benefits when

[41] Porter 2010a, at 376.

[42] Young v. United Parcel Serv., Inc., 575 U.S. 206 (2015).

[43] Emens 2021.

[44] *See* Chapter 7, *infra*.

caregivers can successfully balance work and caregiving responsibilities. And society also benefits when people with disabilities are able to remain employed and independent, rather than having to rely on public support. Employers benefit too, through increased loyalty and decreased attrition.

B *Changing Workplaces*

The second part of reimagining the workplace involves making workplaces more accessible for employees with disabilities and workers with caregiving responsibilities. However, if we only accommodated these two groups of employees, special treatment stigma would persist. Accordingly, my proposed solutions for reimagining the workplace include *all* employees, rather than only protecting the two groups of employees that are the primary focus of this book. In other words, even though I can justify protecting *only* employees with disabilities and/or caregiving responsibilities, I recognize that the best way to destigmatize accommodations is to provide them to *all* employees.

So, what does a reimagined workplace look like? First, it recognizes that bodies and brains come in all shapes, sizes, abilities, and different ways of performing various tasks. Second, it recognizes that virtually all workers will sometimes need modifications to one or more of these workplace norms: 40+ hours, mandatory overtime, 9–5 schedule, few or no absences, and always performed at the employer's place of business (as opposed to remote work). Accordingly, a reimagined workplace allows *all* employees to benefit from the ability to perform job tasks in a different way and to have access to some measures of workplace flexibility.

The first part of my proposed reform addresses a workplace benefit all employees need: reasonable attendance requirements. There is no right in this country to any paid time off. Many employers have very draconian attendance policies, where more than seven absences in an entire year (for any reason) can result in termination. This makes life very difficult for employees with caregiving responsibilities who often must miss work because their child is sick, the caregiver is sick, or the school or day care is closed. Of course, this is also difficult for employees who have disabilities or get sick with the cold, flu, or more recently, COVID-19. As we have experienced during the pandemic, when employees are required to go into work when they are sick (or risk termination), everyone is harmed.[45] Although FMLA would cover some of the absences mentioned here, it wouldn't cover all of them. Plus, almost 40 percent of the workforce is not covered by FMLA, and FMLA leave is unpaid leave.[46]

Accordingly, in Chapter 8, I propose a reform that would (among other things) provide *all* employees with up to 10 days of job-protected absences, regardless of the

[45] Bakst et al. 2020.

[46] *See generally* Chapter 8, *infra*.

reason for the absence. Because it would supplant employers' policies on sick leave, personal leave, bereavement leave, as well as short-term FMLA leave, employers would no longer have to scrutinize the reason for the absence, and administering leave would become dramatically easier and cheaper. And because all employees would be entitled to the paid days off, regardless of the reason for their absence, there would be no reason for non-disabled and/or non-caregiving employees to resent their coworkers.

Of course, paid leave is not the only accommodation that employees might need. Accordingly, the second part of my proposed reform is a universal accommodation mandate. This proposal would allow *all* employees to request accommodations in the workplace and would protect those employees against retaliation for making such requests. Employers would be obligated to provide those accommodations unless the employer could demonstrate that the accommodation would cause an undue hardship. The undue hardship defense under the ADA is fairly stringent—employers can only deny an accommodation if it causes significant difficulty or expense.[47] This stringent undue hardship test would apply for workers who *need* an accommodation to be able to perform the essential functions of their job (whether because of disability, pregnancy, advanced age, etc.). It would also apply to workers who *need* the accommodation in order to meet unavoidable caregiving obligations.[48] However, if a requested accommodation is not strictly necessary, the employer would still have to grant it if it did not cause an undue hardship, but the undue hardship test would be easier to meet for the employer. Employers would not be required to provide the requested accommodation if it causes anything more than a *de minimis* expense.[49]

The hope is that, because employers will be considering many more accommodation requests, they will realize two things: (1) many accommodations are easy to provide and cost little or nothing;[50] and (2) it is often more efficient to restructure the workplace rather than providing individual accommodations. Using our experience with working from home during the pandemic as an example, many employers have realized that work-from-home arrangements can be very successful and have restructured their workplaces to allow all eligible employees to work from home after the pandemic, without those employees having to make individual accommodation requests. This is the type of reimagining the workplace that I hope my book will inspire.

[47] 42 U.S.C. § 12111(10)(A).

[48] I realize this seems like a very vague standard. In Chapter 9, I provide enough detail to hopefully alleviate any concerns about ambiguity.

[49] This is the standard for religious accommodations under Title VII. Trans World Airlines, Inc. v. Hardison, 432 U.S. 63 (1977). *See generally* Porter 2016b.

[50] Colker 2005; Harris 2007, at 6; Hoffman 2011, at 1543; Lin 2021; O'Brien 2005, at 119; Pendo 2002; Schartz 2006b; Schur et al. 2014, at 612; Shinall 2020; Stein 2003; Wendell 1996.

Through the combination of these reforms, not only will disabled and caregiving employees receive needed accommodations that allow them to remain gainfully employed, but all employees will benefit from a reimagined workplace that is more accepting of our varied bodies and our varied lives. And once employers are accommodating a larger percentage of their workers, those accommodations will stop being seen as "special treatment" and will instead be seen as simply a different way to perform the job.

V THE STRUCTURE OF THE BOOK

The next three chapters of this book describe the workplace experiences of the two groups of employees that are the primary focus of this book. Chapter 2 provides an overview of caregiver discrimination in the workplace, starting with the historical context before moving to the laws designed to alleviate some of the tension between work and family, yet ultimately describing how those laws have proved wholly inadequate in ameliorating what I call the "caregiver conundrum." Chapter 3 provides a background to disability discrimination in the workplace. After a brief history, this chapter explains and explores the shortcomings of the main legal protection for individuals with disabilities, the ADA. Chapter 4 then moves beyond broad generalizations and explores intersecting identities that affect the experiences of workers with caregiving responsibilities and people with disabilities.

The second part of the book, which includes Chapters 5 and 6, describes the problem that faces both groups of employees. Chapter 5 discusses the entrenchment of structural norms, demonstrating that employers are very wedded to their default rules and policies regarding hours, shifts, and schedules, and explores why this entrenchment persists. Chapter 6 describes in detail the effects of "special treatment stigma" for both individuals with disabilities and workers with caregiving responsibilities.

The third part of the book (Chapters 7–9) turns to the solutions—how we go about reimagining the workplace. Chapter 7 provides the theoretical support and practical justifications for the reimagination that takes place in Chapters 8 and 9. Chapter 8 begins with an examination and critique of other reforms that have been suggested throughout the years before turning to the first part of the reform—tackling time off by mandating 10 days of paid time off for all workers. Chapter 9 provides the second part of the reform—a universal accommodation mandate with a unique two-tiered undue hardship defense, designed to ameliorate special treatment stigma while simultaneously reimagining the workplace. Chapter 9 also discusses logistics of the proposal and addresses anticipated criticisms. Throughout the book, I use our experience with COVID-19 as a frame for understanding how employers' stringent norms and policies harm everyone while also demonstrating the possibility of reimagining those norms.

2

The Caregiver Conundrum

I INTRODUCTION

What is the caregiver conundrum? Simply put, it is the difficulty caregivers face when trying to balance their caregiving responsibilities with their work responsibilities. Caregivers face conflicts both at work and at home. In many cases, these conflicts create serious hardships on the caregivers and their loved ones.[1] The reason many caregivers feel this conflict is because of entrenched workplace policies and practices that make it difficult to balance work and family. Specifically, I am referring to workplace policies that demand long hours, rigid schedules, and shifts that are not compatible with family life; along with strict attendance policies, stingy or non-existent leaves of absence policies, mandatory and frequent travel, mandatory overtime, and the requirement to relocate.[2]

These policies define most jobs, especially the good jobs, such as full-time manufacturing jobs and high-level executive or professional jobs.[3] This set of workplace norms has been defined many ways. Michelle Travis calls it the full-time, face-time norm.[4] Joan Williams refers to this as the ideal worker norm,[5] which is the term that seems to have gotten the most traction. The employees who are the most successful at meeting these norms are those employees (almost always men) who have someone at home (usually a stay-at-home spouse) to perform all of the family related care.

But for caregivers who do not have a stay-at-home spouse, and who do not have the means to delegate (or an interest in delegating) all or most of their childcare responsibilities, occasionally their work suffers because the laws of physics prevent them from being in two places at once. These caregivers are what I call "real"

1 Porter 2010a.
2 Porter 2010a.
3 Williams, JC 2001, at 16.
4 Travis 2005, at 16
5 Williams, JC 2001, 16.

workers. Real workers are the caregivers who are often talented and efficient employees but either do not put in as many hours as their non-caregiver counterparts or violate their employers' attendance policies because they have children (or other family members) who need some care. These are the parents to whom "life happens," and they are left juggling too many balls, which inevitably leads to one or more of those balls falling to the ground.[6]

Who are these real workers? They are single moms, married moms, moms with enough money for good day care, moms with barely enough money for substandard day care, and even some dads. They are all races, religions, ages, gender identities, and sexual orientations. They appear throughout the income spectrum. (I discuss some of the intersectional effects of these problems in Chapter 4.) These real workers are (mostly) women who feel the stress of trying to manage everything and often feel like quitting. They are the caregivers who feel guilty for being just "good enough" and who frequently allow themselves to be marginalized via reduced hours or part-time work schedules, because society has taught them that they are not worthy of equal wages. They are, after all, not "ideal" workers. This chapter describes the difficulties facing these "real" workers, beginning with the history of the relationship between work and caregiving responsibilities (which is primarily the history of women's relationship with paid work). It then describes the caregiver conundrum before turning to a brief survey of our current laws, which provide too little protection to working caregivers.

II HISTORY OF WOMEN IN THE (PAID) WORKFORCE

Before I begin the brief description of the history of women in the workplace, a couple of disclaimers are in order. First, I am not a historian. Thus, this description is a summary of what has been written by other scholars. Second, in the interest of time and space, I am painting with a broad brush. I recognize that there are race and class (and many other) differences that are relevant to the historical account of women in the workplace, but I have reserved a more detailed and nuanced discussion of these differences for Chapter 4.

Before the nineteenth century, men and women worked together in their homes and farms. Inhabitants of small and large farms raised much of their own food. Both men and women were "stay-at-home" parents, so to speak, although neither fathers nor mothers cared for children full time. Running the household required the full-time work of both parents and often the children as well. Men and women did different tasks, but both were considered valuable and indispensable to the family's survival.[7]

The physical separation of home and work did not occur until the turn of the nineteenth century with the commercial and industrial economy separating market

6 Porter 2010a.

7 Williams, JC 2001, at 35.

work and family work both geographically (factories separate from homes) and temporally (preset workday separate from work done at home at all times of the day).[8] Over the nineteenth century, the US census moved from defining women performing labor in the home as productive workers to classifying the same women performing the same work as non-productive dependents, along with children and individuals with disabilities. So despite the fact that caregiving and managing a home used to be considered productive work, the advent of the industrial age caused much of women's work to become invisible and less valuable.[9]

This is when the breadwinner dad and stay-at-home mom model began.[10] In her work, Joan Williams discusses this domesticity, which assumed that women were not inferior but simply different from men. They were equally important in their distinctive domestic sphere. They were valued for their ability to teach their children middle-class values and to provide support to their husbands after long days in the rough business world.[11] Although many women went to work during World War II, most of those women were expected to happily return to the home after the war ended, to allow the men who had served in the war to have their jobs back. Of course, this story assumes white, middle-class women. As discussed in Chapter 4, lower-income and/or women of color have historically combined work and family out of necessity.

The ideal worker norm, which persists today, developed during the period where employers provided high wages and generous benefits in exchange for complete control over their employees and their working hours. This bargain worked at one time because breadwinner husbands were provided a sufficient wage to support their families and therefore, their wives could take care of the home and children, which freed up the men to be ideal workers.[12]

By the last half of the twentieth century, when women began entering the workforce in larger numbers, the ideal worker norm was already firmly entrenched. These workplace norms, which included the standard 40-hour workweek, mandatory overtime, travel and relocation expectations, and lack of leave for parenting, were common features of many jobs.[13] As will be discussed in the next section, these norms have contributed to the caregiver conundrum.

Despite the difficulties many women face balancing work and family, women are present in the workforce in record numbers.[14] Some mothers work out of necessity, either because they are single mothers or because stagnant wages for men (especially

[8] Williams, JC 2001, at 46.
[9] Albiston 2010.
[10] Albiston 2009, at 1119.
[11] Williams, JC 2001, at 38, 50.
[12] Albiston & O'Connor 2016, at 10.
[13] Albiston 2010, at 66.
[14] Jacobs & Gerson 2004. There has been a dip in those numbers courtesy of COVID-19. Porter 2021. Hopefully, that will be a temporary dip.

blue-collar men) mean that women will also have to work to make ends meet. Specifically, in 2014, 26 percent of kids live with a single parent.[15] And 59.6 percent of married couples have dual earners.[16] Of course, many women work because they want to, because it contributes to their identity and purpose in life.

III CAREGIVER CONUNDRUM DESCRIBED

Regardless of whether mothers are working out of necessity or by choice, the caregiver conundrum is experienced by most women who are balancing work and caregiving responsibilities. The following discussion is undoubtedly a simplistic version of the problems that contribute to the caregiver conundrum, but it should suffice for our purposes. I divide the problem caregivers face in the workplace into three categories: (1) those caregiving workers who feel stretched thin and stressed out, wishing there were more hours in the day to devote to work and/or their families; (2) those caregiving workers who either are not working enough hours or earning enough money to make ends meet or whose career advancement is stalled because of their caregiving responsibilities; and (3) those caregivers who manage to perform as "ideal workers" but still suffer from workplace marginalization because their employers are operating under erroneous assumptions about the competence and commitment of caregivers in the workplace.

A *Not Enough Time and/or Flexibility*

Many caregivers, especially those with young children, simply do not have enough time or flexibility to comfortably balance their work responsibilities and their home responsibilities.[17] Most workplaces still follow the 40-hour workweek. Many require overtime (whether compensated or not). And many workplaces have very stringent attendance policies and offer very little flexibility.[18] In 2000, 26.5 percent of men worked more than 50 hours per week and 11.3 percent of women did (up from 5.2 percent in 1970).[19]

One quick reminder: Although much of this chapter is discussing caregivers who are caring for minor children, it's important to remember that a great many caregivers are caring for elderly and/or disabled family members. As the population ages, the number of workers who are caring for their parents is growing.[20] And many,

[15] Widiss 2021b.
[16] Jacobs & Gerson 2004.
[17] Albiston & O'Connor 2016, at 55.
[18] Bakst et al. 2020.
[19] Jacobs & Gerson 2004.
[20] Albiston & O'Connor 2016, at 16.

many workers are caring for *both* children and adult loved ones, earning the moniker the "sandwich generation."[21]

For those workers who are putting in more than 40 hours per week, it is easy to see how they might feel stressed, guilty, and ultimately unhappy, even if they love their job. When I was a practicing attorney, one of the female partners who was a mentor to me confessed that when her children were younger, she employed three nannies in order to cover the hours she needed. Two of the nannies were needed just to cover the regular weekday hours, as this attorney frequently worked 11- or 12-hour days. The third nanny would fill in for either of the first two nannies as needed and was available on weekends as needed. Although she was not complaining when she told me this, it made me very sad (and frankly, as a new attorney with one child and another on the way at the time, it made me very nervous). I remember thinking that it was sad that she spent so many hours away from her kids. And I also remember thinking that most workers cannot afford to hire three nannies. For those of us who use commercial day care centers (for infancy to kindergarten) and school plus after-school care (for elementary school ages), most close at 6:00 (and sometimes 5:30). And many workers do not have a backup if the child is too sick to attend day care or school or if the school or day care closes because of snow days, in-service days, regular breaks, or a global pandemic.

Dual-earner families should arguably be able to make long-hour schedules work if one spouse goes into work very early and leaves early enough to pick up the kids while the other spouse takes the kids to day care/school before work and then works later in the evening. Such a schedule assumes that both spouses are willing to contribute equally to the needs of the family, and yet we know that women are still responsible for the vast majority of this "second shift."[22] Moreover, such a schedule assumes that both spouses work for employers that are willing to let them adjust their schedules (flex time) to meet the needs of their families. Many employers do not allow such flexibility. Finally, single moms (and sometimes dads) who must work long hours are really in a bind.[23] Unless they have family members nearby who are willing and able to help (an increasingly less common scenario), they will struggle to find adequate care for their children.[24]

Even if workers are rarely required to work overtime, 40 hours per week is still a difficult schedule for many caregivers, especially single moms. When you add in lunch breaks and commute time, 40 hours per week often translates into 10-hour days or longer. As many scholars have noted, both parents (or one single parent) working 10+ hours per day is not great for kids.[25] In addition to not having much time with their kids, such a schedule leaves very little time for everything else that goes into managing a household—grocery shopping, cooking meals, cleaning,

[21] Clarke 2011, at 1267–68; Jacobs & Gerson 2004.
[22] Hoschild & Machung 2012.
[23] Albiston & Fisk 2021.
[24] Jacobs & Gerson 2004; Widiss 2021a, at 2189–90.
[25] Jacobs & Gerson 2004; Williams, JC 2001.

laundry, paying bills, home and yard maintenance, car maintenance, managing the kids' schedules, and keeping up on medical and other necessary appointments, not to mention the mountain of paperwork that goes along with many of these tasks.

Because this long-hour schedule makes balancing work and family difficult, employees who are primary caregivers might request a variance from it, by requesting to work part-time or reduced hours. (Side note: Many people refer to any reduced-hours schedule as "part time" but because part time is usually thought of as "half time," it is not an accurate description in many cases. For instance, many lawyers who are primary caregivers will request an 80/80 arrangement, which is 80 percent of their regular salary to work 80 percent of the billable hour quota. But because the regular billable hour quota will often require an average of 50–60 hours per week, 80 percent of the billable hour quota will often require around 40 hours per week. It is ridiculous to call this arrangement "part time.")[26] Employers will sometimes grant requests to work part-time or reduced hours. But this does not always mean that the problem is solved. Employees who request and receive such modifications are stigmatized by those accommodations in a couple of different ways. I call this "special treatment stigma," and although the concept is discussed at length in Chapter 6, a brief description here is warranted.

First, employees who are granted a reduced-hours or part-time schedule might experience the resentment of their coworkers. This might be caused by the fact that the coworkers feel like they will have to work harder to make up for the reduced hours of the caregiving employee. Or resentment might be caused by the fact that the coworkers wish *they* could work reduced hours. Maybe the coworker is not a caregiver but is taking college courses part time and would benefit from being able to work fewer hours, but because she does not have caregiving responsibilities, she is not afforded this opportunity.[27]

The second way employees are stigmatized by reduced-hours or part-time work (when it's allowed) is because the employer treats them differently (read: worse) because of it. They are almost always paid an hourly rate that is much less than what their full-time counterparts receive, even when they are doing the exact same type of work. These workers might be put on the (official or unofficial) "mommy track" where they are no longer considered for advancement. Or their supervisor might simply treat them differently, seeing them as more committed to their families than their jobs. When new and interesting assignments arise, the supervisor is likely to pass up the employee who is working less than full time.[28]

Despite the negative effects from being granted reduced hours, these caregivers might nevertheless be better off than those employees who are not allowed to work

[26] Porter 2006; *see also* Cox 2022.

[27] Arnow-Richman 2003, at 392; Jones 2014.

[28] Albiston & O'Connor 2016, at 37; Cox 2022; Hochschild 1997; Jacobs & Gerson 2004; Kaminer 2004; Williams, JC 2001.

reduced hours. Not being formally allowed to work less doesn't mean that caregiving employees will miraculously be able to meet the long-hour norms of their workplaces. Unless someone has a stay-at-home spouse, family who can babysit, or enough money for exceptional nanny care, they will often not be able to work as many hours as their non-caregiving counterparts. In these cases, there are almost always career consequences. For professional employees, if they work fewer hours than is expected, they will likely experience lower (or no) raises and bonuses, or stalled career advancement. As just one example, lawyers often have very high billable hour quotas that require working much more than 40 hours per week. If the lawyer misses that quota because of caregiving responsibilities, she might be denied a bonus and/or a raise, and when it comes time for her promotion to partnership, it is likely that promotion will be delayed or denied based on her failure to meet the billable hour quota.

The situation is obviously worse for caregivers who work for employers with overly stringent attendance policies. If these workers violate these attendance policies, they might be disciplined or terminated.[29] Some employers allow as few as six to eight absences in an entire year regardless of the reasons for the absences. Absent FMLA protection (discussed shortly and in Chapter 8), the employer's authorized absences have to cover sick days for the worker, sick days for the worker's child(ren), appointments (doctor, dentist, orthodontist, etc.), conferences at school, performances at school, caring for a sick parent or partner, etc. Many caregivers find it difficult, if not impossible, to meet their employers' very strict attendance policies, and hence, may find themselves making the impossibly unfair choice between keeping their jobs and doing what is required to care for their families.[30]

In Arlie Hochschild's book, *The Time Bind: When Work Becomes Home and Home Becomes Work*, she studied a real-life corporation for several years, interviewing hundreds of employees regarding their work/life balance issues. Several troubling stories emerged from her study. One woman talked about a particularly bad winter when one of her sons had the chicken pox and the other son contracted pneumonia and was put in the hospital. When this employee called her supervisor to ask for some time off so she could stay with her son in the hospital, her supervisor refused. She took sick and vacation days anyway and was disciplined for doing so. In another example, a single mother's son needed surgery but because she had already used up her sick and vacation days, she waited six months to schedule her son's surgery so she could arrange a day off. Her son's doctor threatened to press child abuse charges against the mother for postponing the surgery. In another single-parent example (this time a single father), the father's coworkers covered for him each night during 15-minute extensions of his 30-minute break so that he could drive home and put his 10-year-old daughter, who was home alone, to bed. When his

[29] Bakst et al. 2020, at 9 (employee terminated for missing work because eight-month-old child had pneumonia).

[30] Bakst et al. 2020.

supervisor discovered this practice, the supervisor put a stop to it. The fourth example involved a supervisor threatening to fire a mother who left work to care for a daughter with a dangerously high fever.[31]

The common thread between all of these scenarios is sick children. In fact, nine out of ten examples of work–family balance crises that came up in Hochschild's interviews with hourly working parents involved sick children.[32] It should be noted, however, that Hochschild's study took place before the passage of the Family and Medical Leave Act (FMLA). Presumably, some of these absences would (or at least should) be excused under the FMLA but, as discussed later, the FMLA would not protect the workers in all of these stories.

The reader might be surprised to hear about these stringent (and even cruel) attendance policies. But they do exist, and often in larger numbers than most people realize. In one recent study, 66 percent of the largest employers studied had stringent attendance policies, affecting 18 million employees. Under these policies, employees accrued points for every absence regardless of the reason with very few absences leading to termination.[33]

Related to stringent attendance policies is a general lack of flexibility with respect to when and where work is performed. This refers not only to those caregivers who would prefer to work from home some or all of the time (a topic that has taken on renewed significance since the beginning of the COVID-19 pandemic) but also those caregivers who are willing and able to work full time (or even overtime) but need a little flexibility with respect to *when* those hours are performed.[34] Although flexible hours are not possible for all positions, and although more employers are increasingly offering flextime, it remains the case that there are still *many* workers who have little to no flexibility in their hours. Accordingly, if the only time they can get their child into the doctor overlaps by one hour with their scheduled shift, they cannot take that hour off and put in the extra time earlier or later in the day (or during a lunch break). Instead, they have to take it as a partial-day absence, which implicates the aforementioned problem with overly stringent attendance policies.

Even employees who technically have the right to a flexible schedule will often experience disgruntled supervisors if they are not at work when the supervisor expects them to be there. Because the supervisor already might perceive the employee as less committed (especially if she recently returned from maternity leave), the absence will confirm his perception of her lack of commitment. Sociologists call this confirmation bias, and it has a pernicious effect on the advancement of workers who occasionally need flexibility with respect to their hours of work. Once the employee's absence becomes salient to the supervisor, he will

[31] Hochschild 1997, at 163–64.
[32] Hochschild 1997, at 163–64.
[33] Bakst et al. 2020, at 1, 8.
[34] Dowd 1989.

most likely remember it and consider it when it's time for him to evaluate her or consider her for promotion.[35]

Finally, although not directly related to hours, caregivers in some careers are disadvantaged because of expectations of travel and/or relocation. Because working mothers are overwhelmingly still the primary caregivers of their children, frequent travel obligations for work put an increased strain on their families. This is especially true for single parents. But even some married women avoid travel obligations either because their spouses object to it, or they feel too guilty to leave their spouses and children fending for themselves. These days, many more jobs require travel, so a caregiver who is unwilling to travel or puts limitations on travel will likely find job and promotion opportunities limited.[36]

Similarly, many women are not in a position to relocate because of their families, and especially their spouse's career. While this trend is changing slightly, it is still the case that many more women leave their jobs, homes, and communities to follow their husbands for his job than the reverse. A workplace that creates a norm of being willing and able to relocate in order to achieve success will inevitably discriminate against female caregivers.[37] When I was an in-house lawyer for a manufacturing company, some of the manufacturing plants used an evaluation scoring system for salaried employees of 1–5, with 5 being the highest. Employees who were excellent employees but who were unable or unwilling to relocate could not score above a 4. The top score (5) was reserved for only those employees who were willing to relocate. These kinds of policies are common and will often have adverse career effects on women with caregiving responsibilities.

B *Not Enough Money/Advancement*

For many years, when scholars discussed the problems facing workers with caregiving responsibilities, they were often referring to professional/managerial workers who, as discussed, do not have adequate time to balance both work and their families. But as many have rightly noted, there are other workers who are not complaining about working too many hours, because they are not working *enough* hours.[38]

These workers would prefer to work more hours, not less, and they are often stuck in low-paying jobs with little chance for advancement. If they are working part time, it is not by choice, and they often must cobble together two or more part-time positions in order to make ends meet. This is especially true of single parents. The number of involuntary part-time workers in the United States had doubled since 2007.[39]

35 Hampson 2017, at 1116; Selmi 2000, at 752; Williams, JC & Segal 2003, at 96.
36 Albiston 2010, at 66; Arnow-Richman 2003, at 355.
37 Williams, JC & Bornstein 2006.
38 Clarke 2011, at 1268; Jacobs & Gerson 2004; Selmi & Cahn 2006, at 8.
39 Albiston & O'Connor 2016, at 14; *see also* Jacobs & Gerson 2004.

To make matters worse, recently we have seen an uptick in the number of employees working in the contingent workforce, where they not only don't get enough hours, but they often don't know when their next shift will be until days or sometimes hours before the shift is scheduled to start. These employees are called precarious workers, and their work arrangements make it difficult for them to arrange childcare for their children, especially if some of their shifts are during non-standard hours.[40]

Some of what these workers need, such as better and subsidized day care, more job security, and better pay is beyond the scope of this book. Although I have written about the pay gap and day care elsewhere,[41] I am not focused on that here for reasons discussed in Chapters 8 and 9. But it is important to remember that the workers I am describing in this sub section (the workers who are not working *enough* hours) have something in common with the workers who are working too many hours—both sets of workers often are living with very stringent attendance policies and no flexibility with respect to *when* and *where* they work.[42] Employers' entrenched time and schedule norms can and do affect both caregivers who are working too much *and* those who are not working enough.

C *Stereotypes about Working Mothers*

Some women with caregiving responsibilities are able to meet their employers' stringent time norms, either because they have a stay-at-home spouse (which is relatively rare), or because they have the luxury of reliable day care arrangements. This luxury might be the ability to afford to pay three nannies or having nearby and available family members who can help out when the unexpected happens (sick kids, school closures, etc.). And yet, these workers might still suffer discrimination because their supervisors make decisions based on stereotypes—most prominently, that women with caregiving responsibilities are less competent and less committed. This book is not really focused on these workers because they are the "ideal workers" that most employers want and expect. In other words, because they can perform as "ideal workers," they usually do not *need* any accommodations that would trigger special treatment stigma. But because so much has been written about the stereotypes against caregivers that can cause their marginalization in the workplace, I briefly describe this problem here.

First, some scholars have discussed studies that demonstrate hiring discrimination against mothers. These studies ask study participants to evaluate two fictional candidates whose resumes are identical except for the fact that one is a mother and the other is not.[43] The study participants favor the candidates who are not mothers.

[40] Albiston & Fisk 2021; Albiston & O'Connor 2016, at 4; Williams, JC 2010.

[41] Porter 2010b; Porter & Vartanian 2011c.

[42] Jacobs & Gerson 2004; Travis 2009a.

[43] Schoenbaum 2007.

Second, several studies involving stereotypes about family caregivers in the workplace demonstrated that women without children are rated high in competence, but mothers are rated low in competence. Thus, once a woman has a baby, she might find herself perceived more as a low-competence caregiver than the high-competence businesswoman she was before the baby. This often leads to more menial assignments and being passed up for promotions or more interesting work.[44]

And third, women who are caregivers also sometimes experience "benevolent stereotyping," where a manager might not consider mothers for jobs that would require travel or overtime, assuming that this is in the mother's best interests. But even if this stereotypical decision is meant to be helpful, it deprives the woman of the ability to make her own decisions about combining work and family.[45]

Some well-known cases illustrate the problem with these stereotypes. In one case, the plaintiff was a school psychologist who was told by her supervisors that it was impossible to do her job well with little children at home. She was denied tenure based on the assumption that she would not continue to work hard once she obtained tenure.[46] In another case, the vice president for the employer repeatedly asked the plaintiff "how her husband was managing given she was not home to cook for him, how work was going in light of her new child, and whether she could perform her job effectively after having a second child." The vice president told her that he preferred "unmarried, childless women because they would give 150% to the job."[47]

Although discrimination based on stereotypes is not the principal topic of this book, these cases demonstrate that for some women, being an "ideal worker" still might not be good enough. But turning our attention back to "real workers," who do not have several layers of backup childcare and sometimes miss work when kids get sick or schools close, let's explore the laws that might possibly protect them.

IV LACKLUSTER LAWS

Even though many caregivers need workplace flexibility to attend to unavoidable caregiving obligations, the law does very little to provide that needed flexibility.

A *Title VII Only Protects "Ideal Workers"*

Title VII of the Civil Rights Act of 1964 prohibits discrimination based on race, color, religion, national origin, and relevant here, sex.[48] The most common way of proving discrimination under Title VII is the comparator method, where the

44 Williams, JC & Segal 2003, at 90.

45 Williams, JC & Segal 2003, at 91, 95–96.

46 Back v. Hastings on Hudson Union Free School District, 365 F.3d 107, 114–15 (2d Cir. 2004).

47 Santiago-Ramos v. Centennial P.R. Wireless Corp., 217 F.3d 46, 51, 55–58 (1st Cir. 2000).

48 42 U.S.C. § 2000e-2(a).

plaintiff demonstrates that she was treated differently than a similarly situated person in a different protected class. So imagine that a mother who is a lawyer is denied promotion to partner, but the male attorneys who are at the same level are promoted. If the evidence demonstrates that the male attorneys bill more hours and therefore bring more money into the firm (either because they don't have children or they do but their wives do the majority of the caregiving), she will likely lose her claim. Basically, women who are caregivers are only going to win their claims if they have assimilated to the male ideal worker norm. In other words, in the context of this example, the mother-lawyer would need to have billed as many hours as the male attorneys who were promoted in order to have a valid claim using the comparator method.[49]

Alternatively, working mothers might be successful under Title VII if there is evidence of the types of stereotyping that was discussed previously. As Joan Williams and others have demonstrated, managers often have "loose lips" when it comes to women who are pregnant or who are mothers, meaning that they make explicitly discriminatory comments about them. Sometimes the comments demonstrate outright animus—"I don't think mothers belong in the workplace; they belong at home so I'm going to terminate Sally once she returns from maternity leave." Or sometimes, these comments are more subtle but nevertheless represent the types of stereotypes identified, such as a supervisor assuming that the working mother will be less committed to the workplace (or work fewer hours, refuse to travel, etc.) once she has had children and therefore takes an adverse employment action against her because of that stereotypical assumption.[50]

One final claim a caregiving employee might bring under Title VII is a disparate impact claim. This claim does not require that the plaintiff prove that the employer intentionally discriminated against her. (To be clear, a claim based on a stereotyping argument is still an intentional discrimination claim even though the decision-maker is unlikely to admit to (or even be aware of) having a discriminatory motive.) Instead, a disparate impact claim requires that the plaintiffs prove that a neutral policy or practice has a disproportionate effect on a protected class. Here, the protected class is women. In an ideal world, these claims should be enormously successful. Many employers' policies regarding hours, overtime, attendance, and not allowing leaves of absence or work-from-home arrangements will have a disproportionate effect on women because of their caregiving responsibilities.[51]

However, despite a few successful cases,[52] these claims are hard to bring for several reasons. First, it is difficult to compile the requisite statistics to show that the policy disproportionately affects women. This is especially the case with small

49 Williams, JC & Segal 2003, at 104.

50 Williams, JC & Segal 2003, at 104.

51 Travis 2005, at 37–39

52 Albiston 2009, at 1145.

employers, or employers who do not employ many women who are caregivers. Second, the disparate impact claim requires the plaintiff to point to a specific policy or practice that has caused the disparate impact. This should be easy—the plaintiff could point to a policy that does not allow flextime, arguing that such policy disproportionately affects women with children because they more often need flexible arrangements to fulfill their caregiving obligations. Inexplicably, however, courts often refuse to see the entrenched norms regarding when and where work is performed as "policies" or "practices"—instead, they simply see these norms as the way work is structured.[53] I agree with scholars such as Michelle Travis who argue that courts are erroneously applying the law when they do this, but it remains a serious impediment to bringing these disparate impact claims. The third obstacle for bringing a successful disparate impact claim is challenging the employer's defense to these claims. Even if the plaintiff can show that a policy or practice (such as refusal to offer flextime) disproportionately affects women, the employer can assert a defense by proving that the policy or practice is job related and consistent with business necessity.[54] Despite the plethora of evidence that flexible workplace policies can be (and are) good for businesses, courts will often refuse to look at that evidence and will instead base their decision on the "common sense" proposition that employers' norms regarding hours, schedules, and shifts are clearly supported by business necessity. The entrenchment of these norms blinds courts to seeing that work could be structured in a different way.[55]

B *The PDA's Narrow Protection*

Before women are mothers, they are often pregnant. And for many pregnant women, this is when discrimination begins. The Pregnancy Discrimination Act (PDA) was passed in 1978 as an amendment to Title VII after the Supreme Court held that discrimination based on pregnancy was not "sex" discrimination.[56] The PDA states

> The terms "because of sex" or "on the basis of sex" include, but are not limited to, because of or on the basis of pregnancy, childbirth, or related medical conditions; and women affected by pregnancy, childbirth, or related medical conditions *shall be treated the same for all employment-related purposes … as other persons not so affected but similar in their ability or inability to work.*[57]

Pregnancy discrimination in the workplace arises in three different circumstances. First, in some cases, there is explicit bias against pregnant women. This is another area where we see examples of "loose lips." In one case, the manager made comments

53 Albiston 2009, at 1146; Kessler 2001, at 414; Travis 2005.
54 42 U.S.C. § 2000e–2(k); Travis 2005.
55 Travis 2005.
56 General Electric Co. v. Gilbert, 429 U.S. 125 (1976).
57 42 U.S.C. § 2000e(k).

such as: "Oh my god, she's pregnant again." And "you're not coming back after this baby."[58] In these cases, the discrimination claim is more likely to succeed.

Second, some pregnant women will need modifications to the job's tasks either because the job is especially physically rigorous or because the pregnant woman's doctor has placed her on restrictions, often related to lifting heavy weight. This accommodation issue is a bit complicated, and because it shares features with accommodations under the ADA, I discuss it in more detail in Chapter 3. For now, it's sufficient to point out that these accommodation claims are not easy to win.

The third issue that arises with respect to pregnancy is related to time off, either during the pregnancy (for routine medical treatment or because of non-routine complications, such as bedrest) or for the period after the baby is born. As will be discussed in the next section, the FMLA applies to absences related to pregnancy. But the FMLA only covers employers who have 50 or more employees, whereas the PDA (as an amendment to Title VII) covers employers with 15 or more employees. So there are millions of pregnant women who will be covered by the PDA but not by the FMLA. In those cases, the italicized language in the statute just quoted—"shall be treated the same for all employment-related purposes . . . as other persons not so affected but similar in their ability or inability to work"—raises the question of when leave has to be given, which is based on when employers give leave to other employees who have medical issues that take them out of work for a similar period of time as pregnant women after childbirth.

When I was a practicing lawyer, I prepared employee handbooks for some smaller employers. When I would ask about maternity leave, often they had never had an employee who needed it. My follow-up question was usually whether they had ever had an employee who needed a leave of absence for other reasons, maybe a surgery or a broken leg (assuming the job could not be performed with a broken leg). Often these smaller employers only offered the employee with a broken leg two or three weeks of leave. Under the PDA, that means they would only have to provide a pregnant woman with two or three weeks of leave. As anyone who has had a baby knows, returning to work (especially in a physically rigorous job) two or three weeks after having a baby would be *very* difficult and, in some cases, dangerous.

Bottom line: The PDA provides *some* protection to pregnant workers but not nearly enough protection. Moreover, the caregiver conundrum continues after childbirth until the child is self-sufficient, which seems to be taking place later in life these days. Thus, it is easy to see how the PDA's protection is incomplete at best.

C *FMLA and Its Flaws*

The FMLA is discussed in depth in Chapter 8. Here, I will provide a brief summary. Enacted in 1993, the FMLA was considered a pretty big deal. With respect to

[58] Sheehan v. Donler Corp., 173 F.3d 1039, 1042-43 (7th Cir. 1999).

caregiving, it allows employees to take up to 12 weeks of leave per year for the birth or adoption of a child (including medical care while pregnant), and allows leave if the employee needs to care for a spouse, parent, or child with a serious health condition.[59] Prior to the passage of the FMLA, employers had no obligation to provide leave for caregiving and only for pregnancy under the circumstances mentioned.

Despite the benefits of the Act, it has been widely criticized, and for good reason. First, as noted, it only covers employers with 50 or more employees. Second, it defines eligible employees as only those who have worked for more than one year for the company and who have worked at least 1,250 hours in the past 12 months. These limitations mean that almost 40 percent of all employees are not entitled to FMLA leave. And as discussed in Chapter 4, these limitations are more pronounced for lower-income workers.[60]

Moreover, the FMLA only provides for unpaid leave, so many workers who are entitled to leave cannot afford to take it. Finally, with respect to caregiving, probably the biggest shortcoming of the statute is that it does not require employers to allow leave for routine childcare obligations. Employees have no federal right to miss work for their child's routine illnesses, school closures, sick babysitters, or any of the other parenting obligations that conflict with work.[61]

D *"Real" Workers Are Not Protected*

Although the aforementioned protections will help some caregivers who experience discrimination in the workplace, I believe these protections do not adequately protect what I call "real" workers.

First, these protections will not help a caregiver who violates her employer's attendance policy (or policy regarding overtime or shifts, etc.) because of her caregiving obligations. Imagine this scenario: a single mom works for an employer with a very stringent attendance policy where any more than seven absences in a year results in termination, regardless of the reason for the absence. (Of course, if the employee is eligible for FMLA leave, some absences would have to be excused, but the examples I use would not be valid FMLA absences.) Assume this employee uses an in-home caregiver because it is cheaper than commercial day care centers. And this employee does not have family in the area.

Imagine that this single mother accumulates seven absences by December 1 for the following reasons—(1) she had a 24-hour stomach virus; (2) her car broke down; (3) her furnace quit working (during winter) and she had to take off work to be available to get it replaced; (4) her young child woke up with a fever (that was

59 29 U.S.C. §§ 2601–2654. It also allows leave for an employee's own serious health condition, but that is not the topic of this chapter.

60 Porter 2010a, at 377–78.

61 Porter 2010a, at 378–79; Porter 2014d.

short-lived but still required her to miss one day of work); and (5)–(7) her caregiver has the flu. Her supervisor sends her discipline notices after absence two, four, and seven, reminding her of the attendance policy. In mid-December, her seven-year-old son wakes up vomiting. She hopes it's just a one-time thing, but he continues throwing up. She frantically calls a few friends to see if they are willing to watch her son, but either they are not available or they do not want her likely contagious son around their children (understandably). She cannot leave her seven-year-old son alone so she calls off work and is terminated. She is not protected by any of the laws I've discussed in this chapter.[62] (As an aside, although this is a tragic situation, it is less tragic than if she had left her seven-year-old home alone so she didn't miss work and something horrible had happened to the child. There are real-life stories of children dying in a house fire when a single parent left them alone to avoid getting terminated after the scheduled babysitter did not show.[63])

The Equal Employment Opportunity Commission (EEOC), who is charged with enforcing Title VII, agrees that the statute does not protect what I call "real" workers. In the EEOC's Caregiver Guidance that was released in 2007, it notes that employment decisions based on an employee's actual performance, such as missing work because of childcare problems, do not violate Title VII, even if the employee's deficiencies result from caregiving responsibilities.[64]

In addition to lacking protection from discipline as discussed previously, these laws also do not entitle a caregiver to any type of accommodation for her caregiving obligations. In other words, instead of waiting to be disciplined, imagine a caregiver proactively asks for some type of schedule modification. Maybe it is one afternoon off each week to take the child for medical treatment based on a chronic illness. (This should be covered by FMLA if she were eligible but remember that almost 40 percent of all workers are not eligible for FMLA leave.) Or maybe she asks for an exemption from mandatory weekend overtime because she does not have reliable day care on the weekends. Or she asks for one extra absence (before termination) when her nanny is sick with the flu and she can't find anyone else to watch her children. Regardless of whether the accommodation requested is feasible and reasonable, the employer is under no obligation to provide any of these accommodations.

There are some scholars who refute the claim that the law only protects ideal workers. It is true that there are certain situations where liability might result in the examples I've given. For instance, in the situation where the employer fires a female employee for accumulating more than seven absences in a year (or whatever number the employer allows), if there is evidence that the employer did not terminate a male employee who accumulated more than seven absences, she should

62 *See* Williams, JC 2001, at 172 (discussing these types of stories).

63 Bernstein 2003, at N1.

64 EEOC Enforcement Guidance 2007, at 16.

have a valid sex discrimination claim under Title VII. Or if the employer denies the single mom an accommodation to be exempt from mandatory overtime but allows another employee to skip mandatory overtime, she might have a valid discrimination claim. Joan Williams also points to cases where the employer *does* voluntarily provide some type of family-friendly arrangement and then takes an adverse employment action against the employee for using the arrangement.[65]

So yes, if an employer does not consistently follow its own stringent workplace structural norms, or it treats employees who take advantage of flexible workplace policies for caregiving differently than employees who use these policies for non-caregiving reasons, a valid claim might result. But this is quite different from what I am trying to achieve here—an affirmative obligation on the part of the employer to provide requested accommodations when real workers have mandatory caregiving obligations that conflict with their workplace obligations. The law currently does not provide this protection. In Chapters 7, 8, and 9, I propose that the law should provide such protection and I defend my proposal.

Despite this less-than-rosy picture of the current state of the law, there is some good news on the horizon. There has been a flurry of legislative activity at the state level, both with respect to leaves of absence and statutes that require employers to provide accommodations to pregnant women.[66] I do not want to minimize the importance of these acts but a full exploration of them is beyond the scope of this book.

V MEN, TOO

The caregiver conundrum does not just affect women. It also affects men. The common way we structure work and family means that men feel an enormous pressure to perform as ideal workers. And most of them do. Roughly one-third of fathers work 49 hours a week or more.[67] The history of domesticity put the breadwinner burden firmly on men's shoulders, causing anxiety about finances to be a permanent feature of masculinity. Although men are sometimes unhappy with the stress of the ideal worker norm, they usually feel as though they have no choice but to follow it.[68]

As Joan Williams has argued, domesticity hurts men, too.[69] Many dads want to be involved in the lives of their children but do not feel like they can. These dads suffer emotionally because of this (as do their children).[70] When men do try to break free from the ideal worker mold, they might suffer career consequences. First of all,

[65] Williams, JC & Segal 2003, at 128.
[66] Bornstein 2020, at 315; Widiss 2021b.
[67] Williams, JC 2001, at 18.
[68] Dowd 1989; Williams, JC 2001, at 41.
[69] Williams, JC 2010; *see also* Kessler 2001, at 420–21.
[70] Dowd 1989; Kaminer 2004, at 317–18; Malin 1994; Schultz & Hoffman 2006.

fathers who have wives who work make less than fathers whose wives do not work outside the home.[71] Second, working reduced hours for a male professional often signals a lack of ambition and can damage a man's long-term job security. Although part-time work is always taboo, it is an even greater taboo for men to admit that his top priority isn't work.[72]

In Arlie Hochschild's study discussed earlier, one male employee reported feeling hostility because he was pushing the boundaries simply by rarely taking work home and rarely working weekends. He believed his supervisors were watching him with an eagle eye. He believed that his superiors thought it was not acceptable for him to use his son as an excuse to leave work early.[73] Another male employee complained that the company did not seem to recognize that employees can have a rewarding career without becoming top managers—in other words, it is not everyone's goal to be a top manager. This man worried about not being considered a "serious player." He argued that the definition of serious player needs to be changed from its current definition, which is someone who has aspirations to go as high as they can in the company, often at the expense of their family. This employee stated: "[The company] needs to recognize serious players with serious families."[74] In another study, respondents reported "gendered expectations about who should care for their families,"[75] noting that "men who take leave suffer especially harsh stigmatization and penalties."[76]

One final way men are affected by the caregiver conundrum: If their wives are disadvantaged in the workplace, this obviously also affects the men through reduced family income.[77] The bottom line: Men also suffer when they try to balance work and family. Or put another way: The ideal worker norm harms everyone.

[71] Williams, JC 2001, at 74.
[72] Hochschild 1997, at 100.
[73] Hochschild 1997, at 119–20.
[74] Hochschild 1997, at 127.
[75] Albiston & O'Connor 2016, at 40.
[76] Albiston & O'Connor 2016, at 43; *see also* Grossman, Joanna 2004; Malin 1994; Williams, JC 2010.
[77] Crain 1991, at 1198.

3

People with Disabilities in the Workplace

I INTRODUCTION

This chapter discusses workers with disabilities, the other group of marginalized employees this book is exploring. People with disabilities have long suffered from exclusion and discrimination in the workplace. From the not-so-distant past where the onset of disability was considered synonymous with a complete inability to do any gainful activity,[1] to the passage in 1990 of the groundbreaking Americans with Disabilities Act (ADA) that ostensibly gave disabled employees the right to be free from discrimination in the workplace and elsewhere, we have witnessed so much progress, but we still have a long way to go.

This chapter focuses on the issues facing people with disabilities in the workplace. After a brief history of discrimination based on disability and the laws enacted to combat such discrimination, I turn to the two concepts that make the ADA different from other anti-discrimination statutes. First, unlike Title VII, which protects everyone based on race, color, sex, religion, and national origin, the ADA has a much more limited protected class.[2] Only those who meet the definition of disability—a physical or mental impairment that substantially limits one or more major life activities—are protected under the statute.[3] The definition of disability has been the subject of a great deal of debate and litigation. This chapter explores how we define and conceptualize "disability," from both legal and theoretical perspectives.

Second, this chapter addresses the other unique feature of the ADA—the right to reasonable accommodations.[4] This right also has been subject to a great deal of litigation and debate, again both legal and theoretical. After exploring this law and literature, I briefly address a unique subset of employees who might fall into both

1 Stein 2004a, at 167.
2 Areheart 2008, at 210; Colker 2005.
3 42 U.S.C. § 12102(1).
4 Dorfman 2019; Leonard 2005, at 12.

groups of employees this book is exploring (caregivers and people with disabilities)—pregnant women who need accommodations.

II HISTORY OF DISABILITY DISCRIMINATION

The treatment of people with disabilities in this country has a long and often tragic history. In the interest of space, this discussion only scratches the surface.

A *Early Days*

People with disabilities have experienced centuries of bias and stigma, and they have been the object of pity, disgust, and fear.[5] This stigma has led to their social and economic exclusion and marginalization. In the 1800s, people with disabilities were considered tragic and unable to contribute to society. Many were forced to undergo sterilization and were forced into institutions and asylums.[6]

The earliest definition of disability, used in social welfare legislation dating back to the Revolutionary War, is equated with an inability to earn a living.[7] This history continued up until World War I when the government provided rehabilitation services for veterans with disabilities in recognition of their service to the country. World War II veterans were able to put pressure on the government to provide even more rehabilitation services and vocational training.[8] But despite these advancements, many people with disabilities (especially those with mobility impairments) did not have access to public transportation, stores, office buildings, and many other places of public accommodation. Because of these barriers and discriminatory attitudes, many people with disabilities who had the ability and desire to work were shut out of the workforce.[9]

In the 1960s, disability rights advocates joined forces with other civil rights movements to demand equal access and opportunity for people with disabilities.[10] In the early 1970s, legislators finally started seeing disability as a civil rights issue and started seeing the disadvantage that flows from socially constructed barriers.[11]

B *The Rehabilitation Act*

The energized disability rights movement led to the passage of the Rehabilitation Act of 1973. This statute was the first legislation to address equal access and

5 Anderson 2000, at 115; Dorfman 2015.
6 Anti-Defamation League 2005; Schur et al. 2013, at 3.
7 Hahn 2000, at 168. Even today, many define disability to include someone who can't work. Dorfman 2022; Porter 2022.
8 Carey et al. 2020.
9 Anti-Defamation League 2005.
10 Anti-Defamation League 2005; Waterstone 2015a.
11 Anderson 2000, at 90.

opportunity for people with disabilities through the removal of architectural, transportation, and employment barriers.[12] The Act's primary sections related to employment included Section 501 (bars employment discrimination in the federal government), Section 503 (prohibits federal contractors from discriminating in employment against people with disabilities and requires these employers to take affirmative action to benefit people with disabilities), and Section 504, which prohibits entities who receive federal financial assistance from discriminating against people with disabilities.[13]

Section 504 was groundbreaking because it was the first legislation that treated disability as a civil rights issue rather than a social welfare issue.[14] Congress modeled Section 504 after Title VII of the Civil Rights Act of 1964.[15] Because it covered all institutions who receive federal financial assistance, it covered virtually all institutions of public education, most hospitals, and most other governmental entities. According to historians, Congress did not have a full understanding of how broadly Section 504 could be interpreted, and some speculate that Congressional staffers slipped Section 504 into the bill late in the process.[16] Despite the promise of Section 504, its potential was not fully realized until advocates pushed the Department of Health, Education, and Welfare (HEW) to issue regulations interpreting the Act. Regulations were drafted but not issued until 1977 when the Carter administration was confronted with demonstrations by disability rights organizations.[17] It was these regulations that provided important concepts, such as reasonable accommodations, that would eventually become pivotal for the ADA.

C *The ADA*

In the 1980s, disability rights advocates began to lobby for a broad civil rights statute for people with disabilities.[18] The ADA passed with overwhelming support in Congress and was signed by George H. W. Bush in 1990.[19] There are several stories told about why it received the support it did, especially among conservatives. One story is that several members of Congress had personal connections to or relationships with people with disabilities.[20] Another story is that proponents argued that the ADA would lead to more independence by increasing the employment rate of people with disabilities, which would save the government money by getting

[12] Wilcher 2018
[13] Wilcher 2018.
[14] Anderson 2000, at 94.
[15] Barry 2010, at 230; Colker 2005.
[16] Wilcher 2018.
[17] Colker 2005; Schur et al. 2013; Wilcher 2018.
[18] Anti-Defamation League 2005.
[19] Colker 2005.
[20] Anderson 2009, at 1279; McGowan 2000, at 33.

disabled people off welfare.[21] However, because there was a lack of a major public movement behind the statute, many people did not understand the ADA, which has led to problems when interpreting it.[22] Although there were protests and the famous "capitol crawl," these efforts did not resonate with the broader public (and as Laura Rothstein argues, the capitol crawl could not have influenced Congress because the Senate was already voting that day).[23] As Samuel Bagenstos reports, only 18 percent of the general public was aware of the ADA in 1990.[24] Michael Waterstone argues that the limited public awareness of the ADA was partly intentional to "operate a stealth campaign and minimize political resistance."[25]

The primary titles of the ADA include Title I, which covers all employers with 15 or more employees; Title II, which applies to discrimination by programs and services provided by governmental entities; and Title III, which applies to public accommodations—private businesses that are open to the public, such as stores, restaurants, hotels, movie theaters, entertainment and recreational venues, etc.[26] This book's focus is Title I.

D *Snapshot: Employment of People with Disabilities*

Despite the great promise of the ADA, there is a great deal of evidence that it is not working as intended, especially with respect to the employment rate of people with disabilities.[27] By most accounts, the employment rate of people with disabilities has not improved since the passage of the ADA, and may have even fallen.[28] In 2010, the monthly unemployment rate of people with disabilities was 14.8 percent compared to 9.4 percent of people without disabilities.[29] This is significant because unemployment rates do not include people who are not seeking employment, either because they are not interested in working or because their disabilities are too severe for them to work. These lower employment rates lead to people with disabilities having lower income levels; the poverty rates of people with disabilities are especially high in the United States.[30] Finally, among people with disabilities, more than 43 percent reported in 2010 that they experienced discrimination based on their disability.[31]

21 Bagenstos 2020, at 32; Colker 2005; Crossley 1999, at 634–35; Harris, J. 2020; Rothstein, 2019, at 296.
22 Anderson 2009, at 1280.
23 Rothstein 2019, at 299.
24 Bagenstos 2020, at 31.
25 Waterstone 2015b, at 840.
26 Porter 2013, at 535.
27 Colker 2007.
28 Schur et al. 2013, at 38.
29 Schur et al. 2013, at 39.
30 Schur et al. 2013, at 29.
31 Schur et al. 2013.

III DEFINING AND CONCEPTUALIZING DISABILITY

Unlike other anti-discrimination statutes such as Title VII, which protects all individuals from discrimination based on race, sex, religion, etc., the ADA defines a very specific protected class: people who have a physical or mental impairment that substantially limits one or more major life activities.[32] Individuals are also protected if they have a "record of" a disability or they are "regarded as" disabled, but these latter two definitions are not relevant for this project.[33] The definition of disability has been the subject of a great deal of litigation and debate. I turn to that next.

What qualifies as a disability? How do we know if someone has a disability? And who gets to define the boundaries of the definition of disability? If you asked 50 random people to define disability, you would likely get 50 different answers. And if you gave those same people a list of 20 impairments or medical conditions and asked them whether each one is a disability, for most of them, answers would vary. Some of these would be easy. If this list included blindness, deafness, an impairment that requires the use of a wheelchair, or someone missing a limb, most people surveyed would agree that all of these are disabilities.[34] But what about cancer? Diabetes? High blood pressure? Multiple sclerosis? Epilepsy? Asthma? Learning disability? HIV? Depression? Anxiety? Back or knee impairment? For all of these, and many more, it is unlikely there would be consensus. What's more: Even if you asked individuals who have those conditions if they perceive them to be disabilities, you would likely get very different responses. Some people with diabetes would not characterize themselves as having a disability, but others might. For things that we might refer to as "diseases" rather than sensory or structural impairments, few people would characterize them as "disabilities," even though they likely are under the ADA. And even some people who must use a wheelchair do not consider themselves disabled.[35]

On a more theoretical level, what is disability? Does it reflect our body's inability or difficulty in functioning compared to how we expect bodies to typically function? Is it a tragic occurrence that we should try to fix? Or is it an identity? Is it defined by its medical limitations? Or by how the person navigates their social environment? Scholars have spent many years discussing and debating these questions. This section briefly summarizes this discussion.

A *Conceptualizing Disability*

Beginning with the last set of questions, most scholars disagree with the primary way that the law has conceptualized disability, which is called the "medical model" of

32 Areheart 2008, at 210.

33 Porter 2013, at 535.

34 Linton 2007 (referring to these as "traditional" disabilities).

35 Porter 2022.

disability.[36] The medical model locates disability solely within the person who has the impairment, assumes that all impairments are bad, and seeks to fix or cure the disability. This model assumes that we would only look at the physical manifestations of the impairment in order to determine whether or not it constitutes a disability. Accordingly, this model is also very dependent on the medical profession to define the boundaries of disability. Because the medical model locates the disadvantage of disability solely in the person's body or mind, it makes it difficult to see disability rights as anything other than special treatment or charity. The medical model is also problematic because it stigmatizes people by defining them as less than normal.[37]

Instead of the medical model, most scholars favor what is called the "social model of disability," which distinguishes the "impairment" from "disability." An impairment might be biological,[38] but the resulting disability is socially created.[39] As Samuel Bagenstos notes, if you consider someone who uses a wheelchair because of paralysis and that person cannot get into the workplace because of stairs or cannot get to work because there is not a wheelchair lift on the bus, the paralysis "is very real. But . . . the social relations model posits, it is not her physical impairment that has disabled her: What has disabled her is the set of social choices that has created a built environment that confines wheelchair users to their homes."[40] An often-cited quote that helps people understand how the social model is different from the medical model is from disability scholar Simi Linton (who uses a wheelchair): "If I want to go to vote or use the library, and these places are inaccessible to me, do I need a doctor or a lawyer?"[41]

Although some argue that the social model does not necessarily lead to any specific policy prescriptions, there are benefits to thinking about disability using the social model. Most significantly, the social model encourages people to embrace their disability rather than disclaiming it. As noted by Doron Dorfman, the social model has helped empower people with disabilities by changing the way they think about themselves and their place within society and allowing them to form a common identity and establish a sense of community.[42]

36 Before the medical model was what some called the moral model, where disability was looked at as a moral failure and therefore undeserving of charity. Anderson 2000, at 88.

37 Bagenstos 2000, at 427; Crossley 1999, at 640, 651–52; Hahn 2000, at 169; Kafer 2013, at 5.

38 *But see* Areheart 2011, at 349 (arguing that even *impairment* is socially constructed in many situations).

39 Michael Oliver is credited for formalizing the social model of disability in Western academia. He used the "disability binary" to explain that impairment is separate from disability. Impairments can be located within the body, but the resulting disablement comes from inaccessible physical or structural barriers. Areheart 2011, at 350–51.

40 Bagenstos 2000, at 429.

41 Linton 2007, at 120.

42 Dorfman 2017, at 197; *see also* Eyer 2021.

This model also helps people realize the importance of building an accessible environment—both the physical environment and social structures. If the reason someone in a wheelchair cannot get into a building is because of the building's inaccessible features, then this is not the fault of the person's disability. The fault lies with the builder or owner of the building that failed to make it accessible.

To be clear, there are limits to the social model, as many scholars have acknowledged.[43] As Mary Crossley has stated, the "fundamental shortcoming of the social model—one which at least some of its proponents acknowledge—is that, by focusing on environmentally caused disadvantages, it ignores limitations inherent in bodily impairment."[44] Specifically, the social model tends to ignore that some disabilities cause real pain and real limitations.[45] It also does not work well for those with mental or developmental disabilities or those living with chronic illness.[46]

Accordingly, Doron Dorfman argues that we should embrace a more nuanced view of disability that manifests in the bio-psycho-social model of disability. This model considers not only the impairment and an inaccessible environment but also takes into account the actual lived experience of people with disabilities, including the pain that might accompany many disabilities.[47]

Doron Dorfman also critiques the social model because it has led many scholars to use disability as a metaphor to describe other types of disadvantages. These metaphors are used in everyday language, in the law, and in scholarship. Dorfman argues that there can be no disability without an impairment, and that using disability as a metaphor for disadvantage dilutes the lived experience of what it means to live with a disability.[48]

Despite these critiques of the social model, it remains true that inaccessible physical and social structures certainly make life with a disability more difficult. Accordingly, the social model has an important role in helping people to understand how society (through inaccessible physical and social structures) makes a disabled person's impairment more disabling.[49]

Other models, such as the cultural model, relational model, functional model, and human rights model, have been discussed in the disability literature,[50] although these other models tend to get more attention by disability studies scholars (rather than disability *law* scholars). For brevity's sake, this discussion will be very brief.

One such model was posited by disability scholar Alison Kafer. Critical of the social model's tendency to completely ignore the medical realities of many

[43] Ellis et al. 2019.
[44] Crossley 1999, at 657.
[45] Dorfman 2022; Linton 1998; Schur et al. 2013, at 11.
[46] Dorfman 2022.
[47] Dorfman 2022.
[48] Dorfman 2022.
[49] Crossley 1999, at 658
[50] Ellis et al. 2019.

disabilities, Kafer advances a hybrid political/relational model that builds on the social model. Kafer acknowledges that both the social and political/relational models share a critique of the medical model, but the social model distinguishes between disability and impairment, which Kafer doesn't find useful. This distinction erases the "lived realities of impairment" and overlooks the "often-disabling effects of our bodies."[51] As she states, people with chronic illness, pain, and fatigue note that "social and structural changes will do little to make one's joints stop aching or to alleviate back pain."[52] The social model can also marginalize disabled people who are interested in medical interventions or cures. Her model acknowledges the fact that disability is experienced in and through relationships (hence, the *relational* part) and frames disability as a direct refusal of the widespread depoliticization of disability (hence, the *political* part).[53]

Another model advanced by some disability studies scholars is the human rights model of disability, which is said to move beyond the social model.[54] The human rights model focuses on the inherent dignity of the human being. Theresia Degener argues that there are six primary differences between the social model and human rights model. First, the human rights model acknowledges the human dignity of disabled persons, regardless of whether these people have an impairment. Second, the human rights model goes beyond anti-discrimination by encompassing human rights, civil and political as well as economic, social, and cultural rights. As she explains, even in a society without barriers and discrimination, people with disabilities might need additional assistance. Third, while the social model neglects the fact that disabled persons might have to deal with pain, deterioration of quality of life, and early death, the human rights model acknowledges these life circumstances and demands they be considered. Fourth, the human rights model offers room for intersectionality, by considering all aspects of people's identity, rather than just their disability. Fifth, unlike the social model that is critical of policies for preventing disabilities, the human rights model offers a basis for assessment when prevention policies might be beneficial. Finally, the human rights model offers a road map to change the mutual reinforcing nature of disability and poverty. A human rights model sees people living in poverty not as objects of welfare and charity but as rights holders.[55]

These models are helpful for conceptualizing disability, but as several scholars have noted, the models do not necessarily tell us who ought to be able to claim the protection of our disability rights statutes.[56] (For instance, Alison Kafer acknowledges that the political/relational model is a site of questions rather than providing

[51] Kafer 2013, at 7.
[52] Kafer 2013, at 7.
[53] Kafer 2013, at 8–9.
[54] Degener 2016, at 2.
[55] Degener 2016.
[56] Samaha 2007.

the parameters of the definition of disability.)[57] Accordingly, the next section attempts to describe the variety of ways scholars, courts, and legislatures have attempted to define the ADA's protected class.

B *Defining Disability on the Spectrum: Narrow to Broad*

Turning from the theoretical to the legal, what are the outer limits of the definition of disability—that is, how broadly or narrowly should we define the ADA's protected class? This is another area where there is little consensus, with some favoring a narrow definition and therefore a smaller protected class under the ADA, where others favor a broader definition. Despite this disagreement, it is possible to reach somewhat of a consensus on the following terms used to define the contours of disability (from the narrowest definition of disability to the broadest): "traditional" disabilities, "truly disabled," "minority" or "civil rights" approach, and a "universal" approach.

At the narrowest definition, the ADA could be seen as covering only those individuals who have "traditional" disabilities. Although it is impossible to classify exactly what is or isn't a "traditional" disability, the list would likely include blindness, deafness, missing a limb, and impairments that require the use of a wheelchair. Some might also include intellectual disabilities. The late Paul Miller described "traditional" disabilities as "Jerry Lewis disabilities," referring to the well-known telethon hosted by Jerry Lewis.[58] I am unaware of any scholars who support such a narrow definition, although there is some evidence that courts and perhaps even a good portion of Americans think of disability in this narrow way.

A slightly broader definition of disability would limit protection to only those who are "truly disabled." Although most scholars do not support this still relatively narrow definition, it seems clear that many courts (especially before the ADA Amendments broadened the definition of disability in 2008) believed that the ADA's protected class should be limited to only those who are "truly disabled."[59] I discuss these court decisions more in the next section.

Moving along the spectrum toward a broader definition of disability, some advocate for what's alternatively called the "minority group" or "civil rights" approach to defining disability. This approach asserts that only *stigmatized* impairments should be considered protected disabilities under the ADA. Samuel Bagenstos advocates for this approach, although he doesn't use those specific words. Instead, he advocates for an approach that would target those who are subordinated or face systematic disadvantage because of their disabilities. In other words, if someone has a broken leg, they might not be able to do their job for a period of

57 Kafer 2013, at 10.
58 Miller 1998, at 776.
59 Bagenstos 2000, at 466; Barry 2010, at 251; Burgdorf 1997, at 536.

time and they might be terminated because of that, but they were not being targeted because of the *stigma* surrounding their impairment—having a broken leg is not stigmatizing.[60]

Finally, some scholars have advocated for what is called a "universal" definition of disability. Under this approach, anyone who experiences discrimination because of an impairment would be classified as having a disability that would entitle them to protection under the ADA regardless of whether or not the impairment has any limitation on any major life activity.[61]

The most well-known proponent of this approach is Robert Burgdorf, who was involved in drafting the ADA. Burgdorf makes an argument similar to the one I'm making in this book—that a limited protected class will cause those who receive protection under the Act to be stigmatized. As Burgdorf states "The ultimate goal is to provide equal opportunities for all Americans regardless of disability, not to identify a particular group of individuals who are entitled to some kind of special treatment."[62] Burgdorf recognizes that separating out those with more substantial limitations is common with social welfare programs (such as SSDI), but for anti-discrimination provisions, Burgdorf argues that everyone should be protected.[63]

This universal approach is criticized by some,[64] mostly by those who favor the minority group approach. For instance, Samuel Bagenstos argues that a universal definition threatens to deny people with more severe disabilities their lived reality. He notes that some people who have more severe disabilities are critical of protecting impairments that do not lead to stigma.[65]

One personal example of this mindset: When I first encountered disability law (first as a practicing attorney, and then as an academic), I often discussed the issue of how to define disability with my (now ex) husband. He has a visual impairment called Stargardt's disease that limits his vision to the point where he cannot drive a car or read normal-size font. He had a viscerally negative reaction to the idea of a broad definition of disability. When I would argue that cancer, diabetes, multiple sclerosis, and other impairments should be considered disabilities, he would vehemently disagree, stating that living with those impairments is not as limiting as his experience as a blind person. When I pushed him about how it harms *him* to have more people protected by the ADA (after all, protecting others doesn't take away *his* disability-based protection), part of his response was one of identity. He does identify as someone who has a disability. But more importantly, he had a fixed-pie mentality, which is a fairly common perspective. In other words, he believed that the benefits that accompany belonging to the ADA's protected class are limited (fixed pie), so if

[60] Bagenstos 2000, at 445, 476–84.
[61] Burgdorf 1997; *see also* Schur et al. 2013.
[62] Burgdorf 1997, at 526; *see also* Schur et al. 2013.
[63] Burgdorf 1997, at 583.
[64] Barry 2010.
[65] Bagenstos 2000, at 479; *see also* Dorfman 2022.

too many people are considered disabled, he might get less of that fixed pie. It's unclear what benefits he considered to be part of the fixed pie. The benefits of the ADA are freedom from discrimination (which can be applied expansively, as it is under Title VII) and the right to a reasonable accommodation if one is needed to allow a person to perform the essential functions of the job. It is this latter right or benefit that many people use as an argument in favor of a narrower definition under the ADA.[66] But as I discuss in the next section, there is little evidence that the accommodation provided to one person with a disability will limit or impede an accommodation provided to another employee. In any event, his concern is one that appears to be shared by the courts.

C *Rollercoaster Ride of the ADA Definition of Disability*

I use the rollercoaster metaphor to signal ups and downs. (Of course, depending on whether you like rollercoasters, whether up is good or bad is subjective.) I like rollercoasters, so I use the top of the hills to signify the law being favorable for people with disabilities.

1 The Courts' Narrowed Definition

As described in the history discussion, the ADA was passed in 1990 with the overwhelming support of Congress and the president. (The rollercoaster is at the top of a hill.) But despite the optimism of many when the ADA was passed, it was not long before courts began narrowly interpreting the definition of disability under the ADA.[67] Specifically, the Supreme Court issued a few decisions that made it dramatically more difficult for potential plaintiffs to prove that they have a disability and therefore are entitled to protection under the ADA. These decisions changed the way the ADA was interpreted.

For instance, in a trilogy of decisions, the Supreme Court stated that, when determining whether someone has a disability, courts should consider the ameliorative effects of mitigating measures. What are mitigating measures? These are things like medication or assistive devices that make the effects of a disability not as severe. In other words, if with the medication or assistive device the person does not have a "substantial limitation on one or more major life activities," then they will not be considered disabled.[68]

The examples are almost endless — eyeglasses that improve vision; medication that makes someone's depression not as severe; hearing aids that improve hearing;

66 *See, e.g.*, Barry 2010, at 220, 256; Selmi 2008, at 531.

67 Recall that the definition of disability is a "physical or mental impairment that substantially limits one or more major life activities." 42 U.S.C. § 12102(2).

68 *See* Sutton v. United Airlines, Inc., 527 U.S. 471 (1999); Murphy v. United Parcel Service, 527 U.S. 516 (1999); Albertson's, Inc. v. Kirkingburg, 527 U.S. 555 (1999).

diabetes that is controlled by regularly checking blood sugar, eating regular meals, and using insulin as needed; medication for epilepsy that eliminates or significantly lessens the frequency of seizures; anti-viral medications that treat HIV/AIDS; disease modifying treatment for multiple sclerosis; special orthotic shoes, knee braces, or back braces that improve structural impairments related to the knees or back; and so on.

The significance (and frankly, wrong-headedness) of this rule cannot be overstated. Take diabetes as an example. If an employee has diabetes and regulates his blood sugar through a closely monitored regimen of eating frequent and proper meals, testing blood sugar levels, and occasionally using insulin to regulate his blood sugar, he would not be disabled under the Supreme Court's jurisprudence because, in his mitigated state, his diabetes does not cause a substantial limitation on a major life activity.[69] But yet, think about how and when this employee completes these tasks that help control his diabetes? If he's a professional or managerial employee who works in an office, regulating his blood sugar would not be too difficult.

But imagine working on an assembly line, or as a nurse in the emergency room of a hospital, or as a cashier at a big box store, or a housekeeper or receptionist in a hotel, or a waitress. Those individuals do not automatically get breaks that are both frequent enough and appropriately timed to have the ability to engage in the tasks that would control their diabetes. Many hourly workers might only get one half-hour lunch, and maybe one 15-minute break. This is not enough to properly regulate blood sugar.[70] So these employees will need to ask their employers for an accommodation that would allow them to take more frequent breaks so that they can properly regulate their blood sugar. But here is where things get problematic (and quite circular): If the employer refuses to provide this accommodation, and the diabetic employee sued, in the pre-Amendments era, a court would likely hold that the diabetic employee was not disabled because, while properly managing his diabetes, he was not substantially limited in a major life activity. But if he was not considered disabled, he could not claim the protection of the ADA that would entitle him to a reasonable accommodation, which is the time needed to engage in this regimen. In sum, because he properly regulated his blood sugar, he would not be considered disabled, but if he was not considered disabled, he would not be entitled to the accommodation that would allow him to properly regulate his blood sugar.

One other Supreme Court case also led to a dramatic narrowing of the ADA's protected class. In *Toyota Motor Manufacturing v. Williams*,[71] the Court clarified

[69] Porter 2022.

[70] Keep in mind that a diabetic person's failure to properly regulate blood sugar can lead to the employee being light-headed, dizzy, and even passing out, which has in some cases led to the employee's termination. *See, e.g.*, Hutton v. Elf Atochem North America, Inc., 273 F.3d 884 (9th Cir. 2001).

[71] 534 U.S. 184 (2002).

the meaning of "substantially limits" and "major life activities" in the ADA's definition of disability. The Court held that if the claimed major life activity is "manual tasks," those tasks have to be of "central importance to most people's daily lives."[72] Moreover, "substantially limits" means "considerable" or "to a large degree." So, "to be substantially limited in performing manual tasks, an individual must have an impairment that prevents or severely restricts the individual from doing activities that are of central importance to most people's daily lives. The impairment's impact must also be permanent or long term."[73] Finally, the Court also stated that these terms need to be interpreted strictly to create a "demanding standard."[74]

Between the "mitigating measures" rule and the more stringent test for substantially limiting a major life activity, the ADA's protected class shrunk substantially. The lower courts dismissed many ADA cases, holding that the plaintiff did not have a disability and therefore cannot bring a claim under the ADA. And this happened regardless of how egregious or obvious the disability-based discrimination was. Some of the impairments that courts held were not disabilities included diabetes, cancer, AIDS, bipolar disorder, multiple sclerosis, monocular vision, epilepsy, cerebral palsy, intellectual disability, and many others. This led to a situation where 92 percent of all plaintiffs' cases under the ADA were dismissed before a trial.[75] (The roller coaster is at the bottom of the hill.)

2 The ADA Amendments Act of 2008

After this narrowed definition and the resulting dismissal of thousands of claims, Congress responded by amending the statute to bring the coverage of the ADA into line with the high expectations of the original statute. The ADA Amendments Act of 2008 ("Amendments" or "ADAAA") also enjoyed significant bipartisan support and was signed by George W. Bush in 2008. It went into effect on January 1, 2009.[76] (The rollercoaster is at the top of another hill.)

The Amendments did not change the basic definition of disability. Instead, the ADAAA added several "rules of construction" to help courts interpret the definition of disability. The full exploration of those provisions is unnecessary for this book's project. But I will summarize the highlights.

First, the Amendments make clear that Congress disagreed with the Supreme Court's decisions in *Sutton* and *Toyota*. Accordingly, even if an impairment is mitigated by medication or an assistive device (such as a hearing aid), we now

[72] *Id.* at 197.
[73] *Id.* at 198.
[74] *Id.* at 197.
[75] Stein 2003, at 92.
[76] Porter 2019a, at 389.

consider the person in their unmitigated state.[77] So if a person who is hard of hearing can hear well with a hearing aid, she would nevertheless be disabled if, without her hearing aid, she is substantially limited in the major life activity of hearing. Regarding the interpretation of "substantially limits," the Amendments make clear that the Court's "demanding standard" language in *Toyota* was incorrect, and therefore the Act should be interpreted broadly.[78] (Although, to be clear, what *substantially limits* actually means is still subject to a great deal of litigation and debate.)

Second, the Amendments broadened the definition of "major life activities." The new list of those activities includes (with additions in *italics*): performing manual tasks, seeing, hearing, *eating*, *sleeping*, walking, *standing*, *lifting*, *bending*, speaking, breathing, learning, *reading*, *concentrating*, *thinking*, *communicating*, and working.[79] In addition to that fairly broad list, Congress defined "major life activity" to also include the operation of "major bodily functions," including "functions of the immune system, normal cell growth, digestive, bowel, bladder, neurological, brain, respiratory, circulatory, endocrine, and reproductive functions."[80] These bodily functions basically track many of the impairments that lower courts had held were not disabilities under the original ADA, impairments such as diabetes (endocrine), HIV (immune system), cancer (normal cell growth), multiple sclerosis (neurological), high blood pressure (circulatory), etc.

Finally, the Amendments added a provision that states that if an impairment is substantially limiting when it is active, it is still considered substantially limiting even when it is in remission.[81] This is significant for impairments such as multiple sclerosis and cancer, which can be episodic or go into remission. If we combine this provision with the addition of the "major bodily functions" discussed previously, impairments such as cancer that is in remission and multiple sclerosis even when not experiencing a flareup would still be disabilities.

3 The Post-ADAAA Case Law

The case law after the Amendments is, on average, positive with respect to the definition of disability. In the first five years after the ADA was amended, research by me and other scholars indicated that the courts were basically following Congress's mandate to interpret the definition of disability broadly.[82] (The rollercoaster is maybe not at the very top of a hill but close.)

77 42 U.S.C. § 12102(4)(E)(i).
78 42 U.S.C. § 12102(4)(A).
79 Id.
80 42 U.S.C. § 12102(2)(B) (2012).
81 42 U.S.C. § 12102(4)(D).
82 Befort 2013; Porter 2014b.

As for the second five-year period after the Amendments (2014–18), the evidence is a little mixed. I studied the case law for this period in 2019. Basically, I read every case I could find from that five-year period that discussed the issue of disability. Of the 976 cases, I believe the vast majority of them were fairly and correctly decided. (To be clear, that does not mean that all of them found the plaintiff to have a disability; there are some cases where no reasonable interpretation of the law would allow someone to conclude that the person had a disability.)[83]

But I determined that 210 of those cases incorrectly held that the plaintiff was *not* disabled. This was a surprise, as were some of the opinions themselves. For instance, in a total of 88 cases, the courts were presumably unaware that the ADA had been amended at all because they failed to cite the amended statute or any of its provisions. Many of the plaintiffs in these cases had significant impairments that undoubtedly should have been considered disabilities.[84]

So where are we on the rollercoaster? Not as high as when the Amendments were first passed but certainly not at the bottom either. I have not conducted an in-depth review of the cases since 2019, but I plan to for the next five years (2019–23). As for where this rollercoaster ends up, we will just have to wait and see.

Although a background on the definition of disability is important for understanding the ADA's significance, this book is ultimately about accommodations, so I turn to that next.

IV REASONABLE ACCOMMODATION OBLIGATION

Other than the definition of disability, the reasonable accommodation obligation under the ADA has received more scholarly attention than any other issue. Scholars have spent decades conceptualizing, criticizing, and defending the accommodation obligation. This section examines the scholarly literature regarding the accommodation obligation before turning to the case law.

A *Conceptualizing and Defining the Accommodation Obligation*

As previously noted, unlike most anti-discrimination statutes that only prohibit employers from discriminating against people who are in particular protected classes, the ADA goes one step further and requires employers to provide reasonable accommodations to qualified employees with disabilities.[85] Although the term "reasonable accommodation" is not defined in the statute, the ADA does list some examples of accommodations, including: making facilities accessible, modifying job tasks, part-time or modified work schedules, reassignment to a vacant position,

[83] Porter 2019a, at 385.
[84] Porter 2019a, at 393–95.
[85] 42 U.S.C. § 12112(b)(5)(A).

acquisition or modification of equipment or devices, and the provision of qualified readers and interpreters.[86] This is a fairly broad list, and some of these things might be expensive, such as interpreters if they were needed full time, or perhaps some types of equipment. The only stopgap to the accommodation obligation is the undue hardship defense, which (as I will discuss more) is actually quite difficult for employers to meet.[87]

So why did Congress choose to go beyond simply prohibiting discrimination based on disability and add in an accommodation obligation? The reason is simple: In order to afford individuals with disabilities the same opportunities as non-disabled individuals, they sometimes must be treated differently; that different treatment is what constitutes reasonable accommodations.[88]

Consider this simple example: Picture someone who uses a wheelchair. If that person wants to apply for a job for which he is qualified in an office building, and that building is inaccessible for those who use wheelchairs, this employee will not be able to get his foot in the door (both literally and figuratively). Requiring this company to make their building accessible for people who use wheelchairs is necessary for this employee to be able to have the same opportunities as everyone else. Simply refraining from discriminating against him based on his disability is not enough to create an equal opportunity to apply and be considered for this job. He must be treated differently (making the building accessible for him or making other arrangements for his interview) in order to have the same opportunity as non-disabled applicants.[89]

Accordingly, most (albeit not all) accommodations can be seen as eliminating barriers that interfere with the ability of people with disabilities to perform their jobs in the workplace. In most cases, these barriers were not put in place because of animus against people with disabilities. Instead, they reflect a built environment and social structures (rules and policies) that were designed around an able-bodied norm unthinkingly, what is often called "benign neglect."[90] In fact, as universal design principles demonstrate, it usually does not cost more to make a building completely accessible and useable for all individuals, whether disabled or not. (Think about how ramps instead of stairs help parents pushing strollers and travelers pulling suitcases, in addition to helping those who use wheelchairs.)[91] The problem is that many businesses did not make buildings accessible from the start, so it seems (and sometime is) expensive to retrofit. But one should remember that, had those companies considered people with disabilities from the outset, the cost would have

86 42 U.S.C. § 12111(9).
87 Porter 2019d.
88 Stein 2004a, at 1184.
89 Burgdorf 1997, at 526.
90 Bagenstos 2000, at 425.
91 Bagenstos 207; Guevara 2021, at 281; O'Brien 2005; Satz 2008, at 560; Schur et al. 2013, at 13.

been negligible. Think about a time before women were in many workplaces and employers did not have restrooms for women, only for men. Once women began entering the workplace in significant numbers, the employers needed to add restrooms for women. This might have seemed like "special treatment" at the time, but it really was forcing employers to remedy the discriminatory barrier they had created by not having women's restrooms.[92]

Despite the reality that most accommodations remedy barriers imposed by employers and other institutions, some employers, courts, and scholars still characterize (and thus criticize) the ADA accommodation obligation as providing preferential treatment, like a social welfare law does. (An example of a social welfare law that applies to people with disabilities is Social Security Disability Insurance (SSDI) that provides financial benefits to people with disabilities who cannot work at all.)[93] Or some refer to the accommodation obligation as "affirmative action." Prominent scholars have debated the issue of whether the ADA accommodation obligation is an anti-discrimination provision or the equivalent of affirmative action. Although a full exploration of that debate is unnecessary, a brief summary should be helpful for understanding concepts later in the book.

Some scholars, such as Christine Jolls and Samuel Bagenstos, have argued that ADA accommodations are similar to other anti-discrimination provisions (and therefore dissimilar from affirmative action). For instance, Title VII prohibits "rational" discrimination, such as when an employer refuses to hire someone of a particular protected class because of customer preferences. This employer's business might suffer if it complies with the law, but it may not claim business loss or costs as a defense.[94] Moreover, Title VII prohibits disparate impact, requiring employers to change their hiring practices or other policies if they disproportionately affect a protected class.[95]

J. H. Verkerke's response to this is that disparate impact liability forces employers to hire based on merit and only imposes liability if the employer's practices cannot be justified by merit criteria or any other legitimate business reason, whereas an accommodation mandate requires employers to make costly exceptions to merit-based criteria.[96] Mark Kelman goes further, arguing that unlike a right to be free from discrimination, the accommodation norm is not a right but a claim for redistribution of resources.[97] He states "Accommodation claims are best conceived of as zero-sum, distributive claims to a finite pot of redistributed social resources."[98]

92 Stein 2003, at 135.
93 42 U.S.C. § 423(d)(2)(A).
94 Bagenstos 2003, at 866.
95 Jolls 2001, at 684.
96 Verkerke 2003, at 1390. As is discussed in Chapters 7 and 9, the argument that ADA accommodations are very costly does not reflect reality.
97 Kelman 2001, at 835, 837.
98 Kelman 2001, at 852.

He is not against providing accommodations but believes they should only be provided to those whose disabilities are stigmatized.[99]

Michael Stein challenges the empirical assumptions made in the aforementioned arguments—for example, that disabled employees are less productive and therefore accommodating them creates a net loss for employers. Instead, he demonstrates that many of the empirical bases for arguing that disabled workers are less efficient are flawed.[100] Moreover, Samuel Bagenstos argues that ADA accommodations are different from affirmative action because employers are not required to grant people with disabilities special treatment; employers remain free to provide the same types of accommodations to non-disabled workers.[101] (And as discussed in Chapter 6, as a practical matter, employers often do provide accommodations to non-disabled employees to avoid being perceived as giving people with disabilities preferential treatment.)

Scholars also make convincing arguments that reasonable accommodations are not preferential treatment but rather, remedial, "a necessary antidote to barriers and hindrances inherent in workplaces, facilities, practices, and procedures that were developed in ignorance or disregard of the possibility of participation by those having physical or mental impairments."[102] Employers create physical and social structures (workplace policies, practices, and norms) that are barriers to many people with disabilities.[103] As Bagenstos argues, employers' obligation to provide accommodations is based on the fact that employers participated in the construction and maintenance of a system that subordinates people with disabilities.[104] Conceptualized in this way, accommodation costs are nothing more than remedying what the employers should have done in the first place.[105]

Moreover, scholars point out the many concessions employers make in the workplace for typical, able-bodied workers—things like lunch breaks; adequate (and sometimes very expensive) lighting, even though blind people don't need or use that lighting; and heat, air conditioning, and office chairs (even though someone in a wheelchair brings their own chair).[106] As Robert Burgdorf points out, employers spend a great deal of money and energy accommodating their non-disabled employees without calling those things "accommodations" because most employers fail to see that they are viewing their workplaces through an able-bodied lens.[107] Finally, unlike affirmative action, which sometimes involves outright preferences for employees of a particular protected class, the ADA does not require employers to prefer people with disabilities at the hiring stage.

99 Kelman 2001.

100 Stein 2003; *see also* Harris, S. 2007.

101 Bagenstos 2000, at 459; *see also* Tucker 2001, at 346.

102 Burgdorf 2008, at 299; *see also* Anderson 2009, at 1300; Stein 2004c.

103 Burgdorf 1997.

104 Bagenstos 2003, at 866–67.

105 Bagenstos 2003, at 869; *see also* Burgdorf 2008.

106 Bagenstos 2003, at 867; Bagenstos 2017, at 431; Ball 2005; Cox 2012, at 479; Harris, S. 2007.

107 Burgdorf 1997, at 530–32; *see also* Waterstone & Stein 2008, at 1375.

Even if you agree with those of us who believe that the accommodation obligation falls closer to the line of an anti-discrimination mandate than an affirmative action mandate, we still need to define the boundaries of the accommodation obligation. In other words, how do we know which barriers employers are responsible for remedying or removing as part of their reasonable accommodation obligation and which they are not?

I addressed this issue in a 2013 article I wrote, *Martinizing Title I of the Americans with Disabilities Act*.[108] I proposed a test that both describes the confusing and seemingly inconsistent reasonable accommodation law and (if adopted) would help courts decide these difficult issues in the future. To start, I proposed that an accommodation is *unreasonable* if it "fundamentally alters the employer-employee relationship."[109] In order to apply this test, we first need to think about how we should define the employer–employee relationship. Specifically, what types of accommodations fall within the ambit of the employer–employee relationship?

The employer–employee relationship easily encompasses several types of accommodations. First, because the employer is responsible for the physical structure of its building, it is obligated to modify the physical structure of the building, including removing barriers to access for employees with disabilities. Second, an employer is responsible for the work environment, including providing the tools and equipment necessary for its workplace. Thus, if those tools or equipment are inaccessible or unusable for employees with disabilities, the employer would be responsible for modifying them or acquiring assistive devices to help the employee perform the functions of the job. Third, an employer is responsible for determining shifts and schedules, so if an employee with a disability is incapable of working a particular shift or schedule because of their disability, the employer is obligated to modify the shift or schedule, absent an undue hardship. This might include giving breaks for managing diabetes or moving the employee to the day shift if the disability prevents her from working the night shift.[110]

Finally, an employer is also responsible for remedying the more subtle barriers in the workplace caused by benign neglect. Lack of intent to harm employees with disabilities doesn't matter because the employer still *caused* the barrier. So if a deaf employee needs an occasional interpreter for meetings at work, an employer is obligated to provide one even though the employer did not intend to discriminate against the deaf employee by conducting its meetings verbally. This is one of many examples where we see workplaces structured around able-bodied employees. Accordingly, employers are responsible for remedying this structural bias by providing

108 Porter 2013.

109 Porter 2013, at 562. There is a second part to this test—an accommodation might also be unreasonable if it gives the employee with a disability an unfair advantage over non-disabled coworkers. Although I discuss this in Chapter 9, I won't be addressing it here.

110 Porter 2013, at 563–64.

accommodations, as long as they don't result in an undue hardship.[111] In sum, "as long as the accommodation remedies a socially or structurally imposed barrier, employers should provide it. These accommodations are required because they remove barriers that the employer itself caused or is responsible for perpetuating."[112]

To summarize the discussion, there are four types of accommodations that fall within the ambit of employer–employee relationship and therefore would be deemed reasonable and have to be provided (absent an undue hardship): (1) accommodations to make the physical building accessible; (2) accommodations to make the work environment accessible, including tools and equipment; (3) modifications to shifts and schedules; and (4) accommodations to remedy the subtle barriers in the workplace—the rules and structures built around the assumption of able-bodied employees.[113]

This might seem like a very broad test, and to be fair, it is. But that does not mean that *all* accommodations would have to be provided. Accommodations that fall outside the employer–employee relationship might include something like monitoring the employee's medications or health condition. This would not be required because it is not something we would normally expect employers to do for their employees.[114] Similarly, an employer does not have to provide its disabled employees with transportation to and from work. That is also beyond the scope of the employer–employee relationship. However, if the employee's disability makes it difficult for them to work a particular shift or if they need a parking spot provided to them, these modifications are part of the employer–employee relationship and should have to be provided, even though they could be framed as helping the employee commute to work.[115]

B *Accommodations under the ADA*

In the previous section I discussed the theoretical underpinnings of and justifications for reasonable accommodations. The discussion in this next section provides a brief snapshot of the current state of the law regarding reasonable accommodations under the ADA.

1 The Qualified Inquiry

The ADA requires employers to provide reasonable accommodations to individuals with disabilities who are *qualified* for the job.[116] Qualified is defined as someone

[111] Porter 2013, at 564.
[112] Bagenstos 2003; Porter 2013, at 565.
[113] Porter 2013, at 570.
[114] Porter 2013, at 565–66; Hogarth v. Thornburgh, 833 F.Supp. 1077, 1081–82 (S.D.N.Y. 1993).
[115] Porter 2013, at 567–68.
[116] 42 U.S.C. § 12112(b)(5)(A).

who is able to perform the essential functions of the job with or without reasonable accommodations.[117] The statute states that "consideration shall be given to the employer's judgment as to what functions of a job are essential, and if an employer has prepared a written description before advertising or interviewing applicants for the job, this description shall be considered evidence of the essential functions of the job."[118] This might seem that the employer's judgment is dispositive, or is the only thing courts should consider. And some courts do, in fact, give extraordinary deference to employers' statements of the essential functions.[119]

However, the EEOC's regulations provide other factors courts should consider when determining which functions are essential. Specifically, in addition to the employer's judgment and any job descriptions, courts should consider the amount of time spent performing the function; the consequences of not requiring performance of the function; the work experience of past incumbents of the position; and the current work experience of incumbents in similar jobs.[120]

Some courts get this analysis right, arguing that if courts completely deferred to employers' judgment about the essential functions, this would allow employers to circumvent their obligation to provide reasonable accommodations to employees with disabilities, simply by classifying a function the employee cannot perform as an essential function. Employers are never required to eliminate an essential function in order to accommodate disabled workers.[121] Especially when we apply this to the structural norms of the workplace (when and where work is performed), if an employer designates a workplace rule regarding when and where work is performed as an essential function, employers would never be obligated to provide an accommodation.[122]

2 The (Relatively) Easy Questions

The relatively easy accommodation questions all involve accommodations that do *not* have to be provided. There are several accommodations that courts, the EEOC, or both have said are always unreasonable. First, employers do not have to create a position for a disabled employee if there is otherwise no position for which the disabled employee is qualified.[123] Second, employers do not have to bump a non-disabled employee from their job in order to give it to a disabled employee.[124] Third,

[117] 42 U.S.C. § 12111(8).
[118] Id.
[119] *See, e.g.*, Knutson v. Schwan's Home Service, 711 F.3d 911 (8th Cir. 2013).
[120] 29 C.F.R. § 1630.2(n)(3).
[121] Holly v. Clairson Industries, LLC, 492 F.3d 1247 (11th Cir. 2007).
[122] Porter 2014b, at 70; Hill v. Walker, 737 F.3d 1209, 1217 (8th Cir. 2013).
[123] Porter 2013. *See, e.g.*, Turner v. Hershey Chocolate USA, 440 F.3d 604, 614 (3d Cir. 2006); Hoskins v. Oakland Cnty. Sheriffs Dep't, 227 F.3d 719, 729 (6th Cir. 2000); Fedro v. Reno, 21 F.3d 1391, 1396 (7th Cir. 1994).
[124] Porter 2013, at 531. *See, e.g.*, White v. York Int'l Corp., 45 F.3d 357, 362 (10th Cir. 1995).

employers do not have to promote disabled employees in order to keep them employed if they can no longer perform their current position.[125] Fourth, employers do not have to provide accommodations that are personal in nature such as medications or assistive devices that employees use in their personal life, for example, eyeglasses, hearing aids, wheelchairs, etc. Similarly, employers do not have to monitor an employee's health condition, including monitoring the employee's medications.[126]

Finally, although I disagree with this result,[127] the Supreme Court has held that employers are not required to reassign a disabled employee to a vacant position if there are other employees with more seniority according to a bona fide seniority system.[128] However, there is a possible exception to this rule if the plaintiff can demonstrate that the employer makes frequent exceptions to the seniority system, so that one more exception would not defeat the coworkers' vested interests in the position.[129]

3 Unanswered Questions

In part because of courts' fixation on the definition of disability, there are many reasonable accommodation issues that have not been decided by the courts.[130] The first deals with the reassignment issue just discussed with respect to the *Barnett* case. But instead of the competing employee having more seniority, the issue is whether the ADA requires the employer to reassign a disabled employee to a vacant position if there is a non-disabled employee who is more qualified for the position. There is a circuit split on this issue,[131] and although the Supreme Court was poised to resolve this debate in 2007, the case settled before the Supreme Court had a chance to decide it.[132]

Other unanswered accommodation issues include (1) whether employers have to provide leaves of absence either in the absence of FMLA coverage or once FMLA leave has expired; (2) whether employers have to provide parking or change shifts in order to help employees get to work; (3) whether employers must allow employees to work from home;[133] and (4) whether employers have to provide accommodations that place burdens on other employees, such as performing more

[125] Porter 2013, at 537; McBride v. BIC Consumer Prods. Mfg. Co., 583 F.3d 92, 98 n.4 (2d Cir. 2009).
[126] Porter 2013, at 547.
[127] Porter 2007.
[128] U.S. Airways, Inc. v. Barnett, 535 U.S. 391, 394 (2002).
[129] *Id.*, at 406.
[130] Anderson 2000, at 143–44.
[131] Porter 2013, at 540–41; Porter 2019c.
[132] Huber v. Wal-Mart Stores, Inc., 486 F.3d 480 (8th Cir.), *cert. granted*, 552 U.S. 1074 (2007), *cert. dismissed*, 552 U.S. 1136 (2008).
[133] This rapidly changing issue, courtesy of COVID-19, is discussed in detail in Chapter 5.

arduous duties or working different shifts.[134] (As discussed in Chapter 9, my answer to all of these questions is "yes" – employers are obligated to provide these accommodations.)

4 Undue Hardship Defense

The only statutory limit to the employer's duty to accommodate an individual with a disability is the undue hardship provision, which is defined as "an action requiring significant difficulty or expense, when considered in light of the factors set forth."[135] The factors to be considered are mostly concerned with the cost of the accommodation compared to the resources of the employer. Specifically, the factors include (1) the nature and cost of the accommodation; (2) the resources of the facility and how the accommodation would affect the expenses and resources of the facility; (3) overall financial resources of the covered entity (the parent company of the employer); and (4) type of operation of the covered entity, functions of the workforce of the entity, along with the relationship between the facility in question and the covered entity.[136]

Thus, the undue hardship provision is mostly concerned with financial burdens on employers. Although employers were concerned about the potential costs of providing accommodations when the ADA was first passed, that concern has turned out to be unwarranted. In fact, employers win very few cases based on high costs alone. In prior work, I examined cases that discussed the undue hardship provision. Although my initial search revealed hundreds of cases (1,997, to be exact), most of them merely cited to the statutory undue hardship language and did not discuss the issue in any depth. Of those 1,997 cases, only 120 of them discussed the issue in sufficient depth to be worthy of my analysis. Of those, only 16 actually discussed costs. (In the other cases, the issue was whether the accommodation was logistically difficult, an issue that arguably should have been decided under the analysis of whether the accommodation was reasonable.)[137]

Of those 16 cases, the defendants failed to meet their burden of proving undue hardship in most of them. In these cases, the employer failed to provide enough evidence of the actual costs or failed to provide evidence of its resources. Because the undue hardship provision compares costs with resources, the employer's resources are important to the analysis. Because these cases were decided at the motion for summary judgment stage, the plaintiffs did not necessarily "win" their lawsuits, but their cases did survive to litigate another day. Once an employer loses on its motion for summary judgment, settlement becomes much more likely.

[134] Porter 2013, at 547–52.
[135] 42 U.S.C. § 12111(10)
[136] 42 U.S.C. § 12111(10)(B).
[137] Porter 2019d.

There was only one case involving costs where the defendant won on the undue hardship defense.[138]

Defendants fared slightly better in cases where their undue hardship argument was based not on the costs of the accommodation but the logistical difficulty in providing the accommodation. And some of the cases where defendants prevailed on the undue hardship defense involved accommodations that would burden other employees.[139] This issue of whether a disabled employee should receive an accommodation when it would negatively affect non-disabled coworkers is discussed more in Chapter 6.

And apropos of the discussion in Chapter 5 of the entrenchment of structural norms, the cases where the employers were most successful in asserting an undue hardship defense were cases where the accommodation requested involved *when* and *where* work is performed rather than *what* work is performed or *how* it is performed. Many of the cases involved attendance issues, leaves of absence, requests to change schedules or shifts, and work-from-home accommodations.[140] Certainly, employers did not prevail on their undue hardship defense in all of these cases, but they did prevail much more often than in the cases involving the actual financial costs of accommodations.

Bottom line on the undue hardship defense: Although it is certainly possible for a defendant to prove undue hardship, it is not an easy burden for employers to meet, and cases where employers are successful are (relatively) rare.

C *The Special Case of Pregnancy Accommodations*

Pregnancy deserves special attention because it straddles the line between caregiving protections (under the Pregnancy Discrimination Act, which was an amendment to Title VII) and disability protections under the ADA. The reason the ADA is implicated is because sometimes a woman has complications with her pregnancy that (post-ADAAA) can be considered a disability under the broadened definition. And very often, pregnant women need accommodations in the workplace because of their pregnancies. Some accommodations are simple, such as time off for doctor's appointments or being able to drink water and take more frequent restroom breaks (which creates a vicious cycle with the extra water!). But some accommodations are more complicated, such as requiring periods of bed rest or being put on restrictions involving lifting or other arduous physical activities. In many of these cases, if the pregnant woman is not given the accommodation, she will either have to quit or she

[138] Porter 2019d, at 139–44; D'Eredita v. ITT Corp., 2015 WL 6801828, at *1 (W.D.N.Y. Nov. 5, 2015).

[139] Porter 2019d, at 148–49.

[140] Porter 2019d, at 149–56.

will be fired for not being able to perform the job's normal functions.[141] This section will briefly explore this developing area of law.

1 Pregnancy Discrimination Act

As discussed in Chapter 2, the Pregnancy Discrimination Act (PDA) was an amendment to Title VII that was enacted in response to a Supreme Court decision that had held that discrimination based on pregnancy was *not* sex discrimination.[142] Congress passed the PDA in 1978, which added a definitional section to Title VII that (for our purposes) does two main things. First, it makes clear that discrimination based on sex includes discrimination because of "pregnancy, childbirth, or related medical conditions."[143] So a refusal to hire a pregnant woman simply because she is pregnant would be considered sex discrimination and would violate Title VII. But the second clause does more: It provides that "women affected by pregnancy, childbirth, or related medical conditions shall be treated the same for all employment-related purposes, . . . as other persons not so affected but similar in their ability or inability to work."[144] It is this second clause that is relevant to an employer's obligation to provide accommodations to pregnant women.[145]

After the PDA was passed, courts struggled with how to interpret the PDA's second clause. Many courts held that employer policies that were "pregnancy blind," such as policies that reserved light-duty positions for employees with workplace injuries, did not violate the PDA. In other words, employees who had been given accommodations (often "light duty") because of some neutral policy were not appropriate comparators. This view allowed employers to favor accommodations needed because of workplace injuries, the ADA, or collective bargaining agreements. So even though other employees could receive accommodations, as long as those employees fell into one of these special circumstances, the courts held it was not pregnancy discrimination. If a pregnant woman had a workplace injury (as one example) and was denied a light-duty accommodation, she would have a claim under the PDA, but if her request for light duty was *because of* her pregnancy, most courts would hold that not granting her request did not violate the PDA.[146]

The legal landscape changed in 2015, when the Supreme Court decided *Young v. UPS*.[147] There, the plaintiff was a driver for UPS when she became pregnant after a history of miscarriages. Because of those miscarriages, her doctor placed her on restrictions—no lifting more than 20 pounds for the first 20 weeks of her pregnancy

[141] Bornstein 2020, at 304; Widiss 2021c.
[142] Gilbert v. General Electric Co., 429 U.S. 125 (1976).
[143] 42 U.S.C. § 2000e(k).
[144] Id.
[145] Porter 2020a.
[146] Bornstein 2020; Porter 2020a, at 76–77.
[147] 575 U.S. 206 (2015).

and no more than 10 pounds thereafter. Because UPS required drivers to be able to lift packages weighing up to 70 pounds, Young was not allowed to work with her restriction. Her request for an accommodation of "light duty" was denied and she was put on unpaid leave for the duration of her pregnancy, which eventually caused her to lose her health insurance.[148]

At the time, UPS allowed light-duty accommodations for three classes of employees: (1) those with workplace injuries; (2) those who had disabilities under the ADA; and (3) those who lost their Department of Transportation (DOT) certifications (even if that loss was caused by an accident or a drunk-driving incident). Because Young did not fall into one of those classes, her accommodation was denied. When she sued, she lost in the lower courts, which held that employers are not liable for failing to accommodate a pregnant woman if the accommodations that they do provide are "pregnancy neutral." The Supreme Court agreed to hear the case.[149]

The legal arguments and analysis in this case are complicated and are unnecessary for us to understand the bottom line of the Court's decision. After *Young*, the pregnant plaintiff must first show that the employer refused to grant her an accommodation but accommodated other employees who are similar in their inability to work (such as the same lifting restriction).[150] The employer then has to demonstrate that it had a legitimate non-discriminatory reason for not accommodating pregnancy, but (and this is key) the reason cannot simply be that it is more expensive or less convenient to accommodate pregnancy.[151] Then the burden shifts back to the plaintiff to establish that the "employer accommodates a large percentage of nonpregnant workers while failing to accommodate a large percentage of pregnant workers."[152]

Post-*Young*, courts are still struggling to apply the rules announced in the Court's opinion. Predictably, cases go both ways.[153] Often the claims fail because the Court isn't correctly applying the *Young* test. But they also fail because, unlike UPS, many smaller employers might not have policies for accommodating other employees. Of course, this ignores the fact that, even without a formal policy, employers would be *required* to accommodate an employee with a disability if that employee had a lifting restriction, for example.[154]

2 Pregnancy as a Disability

It might be strange to think of pregnancy as a disability. After all, pregnancy reflects something positive (and perhaps even miraculous) that many women's bodies do

[148] *Id.* at 211.
[149] *Id.* at 211–12, 217.
[150] *Id.* at 229.
[151] *Id.*
[152] *Id.* at 229–30; *see also* Grossman & Thomas 2020.
[153] Porter 2020a, at 94–107; *see also* Grossman & Thomas 2020.
[154] Porter 2020a, at 105–07.

quite naturally.[155] Prior to the ADA Amendments Act, courts followed this reasoning, and therefore, it was exceedingly rare for pregnancy to be considered a disability. Only if the pregnancy was accompanied by severe complications might it be considered a disability.[156]

But after the ADAAA dramatically expanded the definition of disability, the legal landscape has changed. Because pregnancy often leads to lifting restrictions, and "lifting" is considered a major life activity under the ADA, plaintiffs can often establish disability by claiming a substantial limitation on lifting. Alternatively, if restrictions are placed on a pregnant woman because of a history of miscarriages (such as Young), she should be able to claim a substantial limitation on the major bodily function of reproduction.[157]

Post-ADAAA, plaintiffs are sometimes succeeding in proving that their pregnancies constitute a disability under the ADA.[158] In cases I analyzed in 2019, pregnant plaintiffs succeeded more often than they failed on their ADA claims.[159] And some of the cases where they lost were because of poor lawyering or court errors, a problem I hope improves as we move forward. Also, many states are enacting legislation mandating employers to provide accommodations to pregnant employees.[160] I do not intend to paint the picture as too rosy. There are definitely many pregnant women struggling to receive the accommodations they need. When this happens, they are often forced to quit or are terminated, when (in many cases) accommodations would have been relatively easy to provide.[161] My proposals in Chapters 8 and 9 will significantly help pregnant women obtain the accommodations they need to remain employed during their pregnancies.

155 My favorite quote about pregnancy representing ability rather than inability is this quote by Christine Littleton: "[W]hat makes pregnancy a disability rather than, say, an additional ability, is the structure of work, not reproduction. Normal pregnancy may make a woman unable to 'work' for days, weeks, or months, but it also makes her able to reproduce. From whose viewpoint is the work that she cannot do 'work,' and the work that she is doing not work? Certain not from hers." Littleton 1987, at 1306.

156 Porter 2020a, at 78–79.

157 Porter 2020a, at 79–80.

158 *See, e.g.*, Mosby-Meachem v. Memphis Light, Gas & Water Division, 883 F.3d 595 (6th Cir. 2018).

159 Porter 2020a, at 84–90.

160 Bornstein 2020.

161 Bornstein 2020; Widiss 2021c.

4

Intersections

I INTRODUCTION

In Chapters 2 and 3, I described the challenges facing caregivers (mostly women) and people with disabilities, respectively, in the workplace. In doing so, I was inevitably painting with a broad brush. In this chapter, I delve into the many differences among these groups of employees, and often, the multiple layers of oppression and subordination they face.

This chapter is based on the theory of "intersectionality," which Kimberlé Crenshaw developed.[1] Crenshaw was critical of the feminist literature that assumed that all women shared the same experiences, which ignored the ways in which Black women's experiences are different from white women's experiences.[2] This is also referred to as essentialism, assuming that people can be defined by one identity or one characteristic. For many years, scholars have critiqued feminists for essentializing women and not recognizing differences based on race, sexual orientation, gender identity, age, and disability.[3] And the same can be said for disability.[4] Essentializing disability means assuming that all disabled individuals share the same experiences. Not only will disabled people's experiences vary based on their disability, but they might also vary based on their sex, race, sexual orientation, age, etc.[5]

What is intersectionality? Basically, it is the idea that discrimination operates independently of its components, so the experience of subordination cannot be described by any one classification, nor can the multiple grounds of subordination be simply added up.[6] Instead, intersectionality offers the "critical insight that race,

1 Crenshaw 1989.
2 Carbado & Harris, C. 2019.
3 Ball 2005, at 117.
4 Crossley 1999; Kanter 2011; Schur et al. 2013; Travis 2017; Wendell 1996.
5 Miller 1998; Moore 2019; Stein 2004c, at 627; Wendel 1996.
6 Harris, J 2021a, at 927.

class, gender, sexuality, ethnicity, national origin, ability, and age operate not as unitary, mutually exclusive entities, but as reciprocally constructing phenomena that in turn shape complex social inequalities."[7]

This chapter briefly explores how the following identities or characteristics—race, class, sexual orientation, gender identity, and age—intersect with sex and disability. Although it is common for there to be more complex intersectional identities—for example, someone could be a black, queer, disabled woman[8]—in the interest of space, I will not be exploring all possible multiple intersectional identities. However, I do explore how caregiving and disability intersect, in a section I call "Mothers with Disabilities,"[9] even though I recognize that not all caregivers are mothers.

II RACE

Volumes have been written about race discrimination in the workplace. Title VII of the Civil Rights Act of 1964 was passed primarily to end the employment discrimination against Black individuals, even though the statute also covers other protected classes—national origin, color, religion, and sex. At the time Title VII was passed, many employers either refused to hire Black and other minority workers at all, or if they were hired, they were segregated in the lowest-status positions, and often blocked from advancing.[10] Since Title VII was passed, most of this explicit discrimination has ended (i.e., you are highly unlikely to see a "Blacks need not apply" advertisement), but that does not mean that discrimination against minority workers is a thing of the past. Some discriminatory decisions are based on overt animus, but perhaps many more are based on implicit or subconscious bias. Black and other minority workers are also subject to harassment based on race and/or ethnicity.[11] With this brief history in mind, my focus here is primarily on how race intersects with a woman's role as a working mother, and how race intersects with disability.

A *Race and Gender*

Much has been written about discrimination against Black women. In fact, the experience of Black women was the subject of the first intersectional scholarship.[12] Most of this discrimination has nothing to do with caregiving status and instead is based on the subordination Black women face in the workplace in ways that are worse than Black men's experiences and worse than white women's experiences.

7 McGinley & Cooper 2020, at 302 (quoting Patricia Hill Collins).

8 For an excellent book written by a black, queer, disabled woman, see Piepzna-Samarasinha 2018; *see also* Karin et al. 2020, at 20 (we must attend to the "intersection of the intersections").

9 Porter 2018a.

10 Teamsters v. United States, 431 U.S. 324 (1977); Griggs v. Duke Power Co., 401 U.S. 424 (1971).

11 Onwuachi-Willig 2018.

12 Crenshaw 1989.

These claims are still hard to win.[13] In addition to discrimination against Black women, harassment of Black and other women of color is also a big problem.[14]

But my focus is on how race and sex intersect with respect to the caregiver conundrum discussed in Chapter 2. As Joan Williams has stated, women of every class and race hit the "maternal wall."[15] Employers' insistence on the ideal worker norm creates a disproportionate burden for low-wage workers because they often cannot afford high-quality care for their kids. Because these workers are disproportionately people of color, the racial inequality is exacerbated. Additionally, one study indicated that racial minorities are less likely to take leave, even when it is partially paid for under state law, in part because of real and perceived penalties for taking leave.[16]

On the home front, Black women, compared to white women, "are likely to have more children to support, to be never married, to be younger, [and] to not have another earner in the household."[17] Moreover, even when there are two adults in a minority family that are both working, their jobs are not always sufficient to make ends meet. In fact, the rate of poverty in Black families is constant regardless of whether the family is headed by just the mom or both parents.[18]

From a more positive perspective, there is also evidence that, when Black women are coupled with Black men (whether married or not), and they are both working, there is a more egalitarian division of the household labor than white couples experience.[19] Moreover, many Black women find their family lives to be rewarding and not oppressive like the workplace often is. Thus, depictions of wage work as always positive ignore the "harm, degradation and oppression of those less privileged women, especially women of color living in poverty."[20] Because one of the key expressions of white supremacy is the assault on the Black family, many Black women have seen the preservation of family life as an important political goal.[21] Caregiving work is often seen as a form of "powerful political resistance."[22] Many women of color also do not feel it necessary to order their priorities—work over family or family over work. Instead, they have historically worked both inside and outside the home, so the "practice of prioritizing and compartmentalizing relationships or identities is inconsistent with their life experience."[23]

[13] *See generally* Williams, JB 2022 (discussing the difficulty of bringing sex plus race intersectional claims).
[14] Onwuachi-Willig 2018.
[15] Williams, JC & Bornstein 2006, at 188.
[16] Albiston & O'Connor 2016, at 30, 38–39; Kaminer 2004, at 325.
[17] Dowd 1990, at 467; *see also* Bornstein 2020.
[18] Dowd 1990, at 464.
[19] Dowd 1990, at 468.
[20] Kessler 2001, at 382.
[21] Williams, JC 2001, at 180, 182.
[22] Kessler 2001, at 455.
[23] Crain 1991, at 1196; *see also* Hochschild & Munger 2012; Kessler 2001, at 390.

There are also different family models for Black families that are not always tied to marriage or even to the parent–child relationship. In other words, other family members might take care of young children for Black and other minority women.[24] This is important because, as the law currently stands, the FMLA only allows leave to care for an employee's own biological, adopted, or foster child.[25]

B *Race and Disability*

People of color and people with disabilities share similar experiences of oppression and subordination,[26] but there is very little scholarship on the intersection of people of color with disabilities.[27] Just as race intersects with gender in pernicious ways, it also intersects with disability, and of course, sometimes it intersects with both.[28] As intersectionality teaches us, it is important not to assume that all disabled people share the same experiences, just as it is important to recognize that it is not possible to simply add up the ways in which employees experience oppression based on race, gender, and disability. Disability interacts with race and ethnicity to create unique disadvantages for members of minority groups who are disabled.[29]

Despite the fact that there is not much scholarship on race and disability, I attempt here to summarize the scholarship that does exist. First, scholars have discussed the similarities between race and disability subordination. For instance, scholars have noted that race and disability are both social constructions.[30] And people with disabilities and racial minorities have faced similar discrimination, including "social practices that create a shared experience of discrimination and exclusion based on explicit and implicit bias, stereotyping, and structural inequality."[31] Of course, even if both people with disabilities and people of color experience stereotyping, the stereotypes surrounding disability might be different for people of color than for white people. For instance, some Black people who are admired for their strength might be unwilling to admit that they have a disability, because disability signifies weakness. For example, Chadwick Boseman was a Black actor who played Black Panther and disclaimed his disability, cancer. People of color who were his fans were upset if anyone referred to him as disabled.[32] And in one study, minority men who suffered spinal cord injuries by violence experienced stigma

24 Emens 2019; Dowd 1990, at 463; Widiss 2021b.
25 29 U.S.C. § 2612(a)(3).
26 Ribet 2010.
27 Ellis et al. 2019; Harris, J. 2021a, at 928.
28 Carey et al. 2020.
29 Schur et al. 2013.
30 McGinley & Cooper 2020, at 322–23; Nelson 2010, at 13; Wendell 1996.
31 Paul-Emile 2018, at 321; *see also* Ribet 2010, at 210.
32 Harris, J. 2021a, at 942–43. Boseman has since passed away.

because the "injury and resulting disability violated social understandings of what it means to be a man."[33]

The second major theme of this body of scholarship is the argument that race can often cause or contribute to disabilities. Institutional racism causes race-related stress that can negatively affect health, including the onset of illness and disease. In fact, Black people have a greater incidence of almost all diseases.[34] Jasmine Harris has noted that some people of color acquire disabilities because of structural inequities such as allocation of resources or poor housing that leads to exposure to environmental toxins.[35]

We saw this phenomenon during the pandemic, where people of color had increased exposure to COVID-19 because they are more likely to live in densely populated areas that made social distancing difficult. They were also more likely to be essential workers, who could not work from home. In many states, people of color had more difficulty accessing the vaccine. And because of a history of oppression by the government, many people of color were reluctant to trust the government and/or the medical establishment enough to get vaccinated.[36]

Third, and perhaps most controversially, some scholars have argued that Blackness itself can be a disability. In an article titled "Blackness as Disability?," Kimani Paul-Emile argues that under the social model of disability (discussed in Chapter 3), even though Blackness is not itself an impairment, when combined with inhospitable social or physical environments, it can create disability.[37] As she argues, the discomfort with seeing Blackness as a disability demonstrates a lack of understanding about disability—assuming that disability means a complete lack of functioning. But disability under the amended ADA is very broadly defined and can encompass a broad array of conditions, not all of which are stigmatizing.[38] As stated by Paul-Emile:

> When we stop thinking about disability in a pejorative, stigmatized way and acknowledge the reality and effect of structural race-based inequality, the relationship between blackness and disability becomes clear. Disability law allows us to do this. Once blackness is understood as disabling in many contexts and a marker of stigma around which virtually all social institutions were conceptualized and structured, we can see distinct legal solutions to the persistent and seemingly intractable problem of racial inequality.[39]

Some scholars are skeptical of this argument that Blackness should be seen as a disability. Doron Dorfman has argued that arguments such as these push the

[33] Schur et al. 2013, at 175.
[34] Paul-Emile 2018, at 347.
[35] Harris, J. 2021a, at 940; *see also* Piepzna-Samarasinha 2018; Ribet 2010, at 210.
[36] Guevara 2021; Kum 2020; Williams, JB 2022.
[37] Paul-Emile 2018, at 298.
[38] Paul-Emile 2018, at 299–300.
[39] Paul-Emile 2018, at 300.

boundaries of the social model of disability too far. Adopting a bio-psycho-social model of disability, Dorfman argues that using disability as a metaphor for disadvantage is troubling; it ignores the reality that many disabilities cause significant pain and also dilutes the lived experience of what it means to live with a disability. For Dorfman, there can be no disability without an impairment.[40]

On a more practical level, some scholars have studied the various employment rates of people with disabilities by race. In the United States, people with disabilities have lower employment rates than people without disabilities in all racial and ethnic categories. Among people with disabilities, the highest employment rate is for Asians (38%), and then Hispanics/Latinos (36%), whites (35%), and Native Americans (29%), with the lowest employment rate among African Americans who are disabled (26%). Stated another way, employment gaps between people with and without disabilities are highest among white non–Hispanics (76% compared with 35%) and African Americans (67% compared with 26%). Race and disability gaps combine to give racial minorities with disabilities the lowest employment rates. These employment disparities among racial minorities with disabilities also lead to higher poverty rates for Black people with disabilities and Native Americans with disabilities.[41]

Finally, some scholars discuss significant differences between how disabled people of color are treated in the workplace when compared to disabled white people. For instance, minority disabled workers might have a more difficult time getting the workplace accommodations they need because employers are more hostile to accommodation requests from workers of color.[42] A white person's accommodation is perceived as only being about that person's disability, whereas a person of color's accommodation request is often perceived as a scam or an attempt to cover a racial deficit.[43] One study suggests that Asian and white workers are given permission to vary their work hours more than workers who are Black and/or Hispanic.[44] "All of these combined dynamics create a context wherein People of Color with disabilities are disproportionately set up to fail, and … [the] models of disability success … are likely to be White."[45]

III CLASS

Although class and income are not protected classes, it is important to recognize how much class and income affect the experiences of workers with caregiving responsibilities and workers with disabilities.

40 Dorfman 2022.
41 Schur et al. 2013, at 182–83.
42 Lin 2021.
43 Ribet 2010, at 237.
44 McMenamin 2007 at 4.
45 Ribet 2010, at 239. *But see* Schartz et al. 2006a (stating that employers' willingness to accommodate was not related to any demographic variables).

A *Class and Motherhood*

Women are more likely than men to work in lower-paid jobs with few benefits.[46] And as I discussed in Chapter 2, although many high-income, professional women would prefer to work fewer hours, there is a significant portion of working mothers who need to work more hours.[47] Of course, this does not mean that they don't need flexibility. In fact, lower-income mothers are more likely to need flexibility because they often have less reliable childcare.[48] They need to be able to attend to a sick child without being punished. Studies show that high-wage workers are more likely than low-wage workers to be offered flextime, and almost twice as likely to receive paid sick leave or paid time off to take care of a sick child.[49] The problem is exacerbated by the fact that many low-income women are also single parents with no one to help at home.[50]

To make matters worse, gender norms put pressure on mothers with respect to balancing work and family that are often inconsistent with their desires. Upper-class women who do not have to work are pressured to stay at home with their children based on the argument that doing so is what is in the child's best interest. But lower-income mothers are supposed to work despite the lack of affordable quality day care options and even though many would prefer to stay home because their jobs might be monotonous and/or unpleasant.[51]

Another issue contributing to the difficulties experienced by working mothers is the increase in the number of workers employed in contingent, precarious jobs; these workers now constitute 40 percent of the workforce. These workers earn less, work irregular shifts, have fewer benefits, and enjoy less job security.[52]

Finally, as discussed more in Chapter 8, the FMLA's inadequacies are even more pronounced for lower-income workers. One-third of single parents and low-income workers have been employed for less than one year and are therefore not eligible for FMLA leave. They also are more likely to work for smaller employers (with fewer than 50 employees) who are not covered by the Act. Accordingly, the vast majority of lower-income employees are not entitled to FMLA leave.[53] And even if they are entitled to FMLA leave, it will most likely be *unpaid* leave. Many women who need maternity leave or leave to care for a sick child cannot afford to take it because they cannot afford to live without their income.[54]

46 Albiston & Fisk 2021; Bakst et al. 2020.
47 Selmi & Cahn 2006; Williams, JC 2001, at 112.
48 Schultz 2010; Williams, JC 2001, at 112.
49 Jones 2014, at 1286.
50 Albiston & Fisk 2021; Dowd 2004.
51 Selmi 2007; Williams, JC 2001, at 68, 188.
52 Albiston & O'Connor 2016, at 3; Albiston & Fisk 2021; Schultz 2010; Williams, JC 2001.
53 O'Leary 2007; Porter 2014d; Selmi & Cahn 2006.
54 Albiston & O'Connor 2016; Kessler 2007; O'Leary 2007; Selmi 2004.

In sum, for several reasons, the caregiver conundrum is much more pronounced for lower-income women with caregiving responsibilities.

B *Class and Disability*

Disability and class/income intersect in fairly predictable ways. People with disabilities have poverty rates much higher than non-disabled people in the United States.[55] Two reasons combine to produce this high poverty rate. First, their lower incomes contribute to the poverty rates, but also, most people with disabilities have increased costs related to their disabilities. To be clear, most of the lower income is attributed to lower levels of employment, and people with disabilities who are employed earn close to the same wages as working-age people without disabilities. For instance, in 2010, the average unemployment rate for people with disabilities was 14.8 percent, whereas the average unemployment rate of those without disabilities was 9.4 percent.[56] Another difficulty facing lower-income disabled workers is that they are less likely to be entitled to paid leave, and yet many disabled people need periodic leaves of absence.[57] Even though leave may be required under the ADA (although that is a heavily debated issue), it does not have to be paid leave.

IV LGBTQ+

How caregiving and LGBTQ+ status intersect is interesting in the sense that it is not *all* negative. On the positive side, there is ample evidence that same-sex parenting relationships are more egalitarian, because there are not built-in assumptions that the wife should be the primary caregiver and the husband the primary breadwinner.[58]

One major difference between gay families and heterosexual families is that individuals who identify as LGBTQ+ are less likely to live in traditional family relationships. For instance, LGBTQ+ baby boomers are more likely to be childless and rely on friends or "chosen family" to provide care if they are sick and/or disabled. LGBTQ+ youth of color are much more likely to be homeless and therefore may be more likely to rely on informal networks of chosen family. And members of the

55 Bagenstos 2000, at 422; Colker 2010; Kanter 2011; Schur et al. 2005; Schur et al. 2013, at 28–29; Stein & Stein 2006.

56 Schur et al. 2013, at 39. These numbers (especially the 14.8% *unemployment* rate for people with disabilities) might seem erroneous given that earlier I mentioned an *employment* rate for people with disabilities in the 30% range. The difference is attributable to the fact that unemployment rates measure people who are willing and able to work. There are many people with disabilities whose disabilities are too severe for them to work and who receive SSDI benefits. In reality, some (or maybe even many) of these people would be willing to attempt to work if the job market was accessible to them and if they didn't risk losing their SSDI benefits.

57 Shinall 2022.

58 Emens 2019, at 50; Hochschild & Munger 2012; Widiss 2012, at 777.

LGBTQ+ community are very likely to look to an unmarried partner or member of their extended family or chosen family for caregiving help.[59]

This alone is not problematic, or at least not more problematic than the animus surrounding LGBTQ+ relationships more generally. The problem arises because many caregiving leave policies and laws do not account for these non-traditional relationships. Remember that the FMLA only allows leave to care for a sick child, parent, or spouse. Although same-sex couples are legally allowed to marry after *Obergefell*,[60] many same-sex couples are not married. If they are married and have children, the spouse who does not have a biological connection with the children may not lawfully be considered the child's parent. Fortunately, the proliferation of state laws providing leave has improved this landscape because all of them have broader definitions of who is covered for purposes of family leave. However, the resentment employees experience when they are forced to cover for coworkers on leave is often exacerbated if the employee taking leave is doing so to care for non-traditional family members. Because LGBTQ+ and minority communities are more likely to rely on extended and chosen family, this resentment can become intertwined with racism and animus based on LGBTQ+ status. This is why Deborah Widiss argues that it is "crucially important" for leave laws and policies to be very flexible in defining when you are allowed to take leave to care for chosen family members.[61]

With respect to how disability intersects with LGBTQ+ status, the primary issues diverge significantly depending on which letters of "LGBTQ+" we are discussing. For instance, transgender individuals experience much more discrimination than individuals who identify as gay, lesbian, queer, or bisexual. Whether that discrimination is unlawful depends on the interpretation of Title VII and the ADA. Protection under Title VII was made simpler after the Supreme Court's 2020 decision in *Bostock v. Clayton County*, where the Court held that discrimination based on sexual orientation or transgender status is "sex" discrimination under Title VII.[62] If a transgender employee is discriminated against simply because of their transgender identity, they should be protected under Title VII.

However, some transgender individuals will need an accommodation either because they need time off for mental health treatment that is often required if an individual plans to obtain gender affirmation surgery, or they might need time off for the surgery itself. Title VII does not require employers to accommodate these medical needs. Accordingly, if a transgender employee needs an accommodation, they will have to depend on ADA protection. The law surrounding whether transgender status is considered a disability under the ADA is complicated, but a brief summary should suffice.

59 Widiss 2021b.
60 Obergefell v. Hodges, 576 U.S. 644 (2015).
61 Widiss 2021b.
62 Bostock v. Clayton Cty., Ga. 40 S. Ct. 1731 (2020).

The ADA specifically excludes from coverage "homosexuality and bisexuality" and "transvestism, transsexualism, . . . [and] gender identity disorders not resulting from physical impairments."[63] In recent years, there has been some debate about whether gender dysphoria should be considered a disability under the ADA. One district court held that gender dysphoria was a disability by interpreting the exclusionary phrase "gender identity disorders" narrowly to refer only to the condition of identifying with a different gender, and not to include the plaintiff's gender dysphoria, which "substantially limits her major life activities of interacting with others, reproducing, and social and occupational functioning."[64] Several scholars have argued in favor of including transgender as a disability, with varying opinions regarding whether such claims are likely to succeed.[65]

The other issue surrounding disability and LGBTQ+ status is that because of the oppression LGBTQ+ individuals experience, they are more likely to have a mental illness than the general population. In 2015, 39% of trans people admitted having a mental disability compared to 15–20% of the general population. In another study, 40% of bisexual men, 36% of lesbian women, and 36% of bisexual women reported having a mental disability. And the high rates of discrimination against LGBTQ+ individuals with disabilities often results in higher rates of poverty.[66]

V AGE

Age and gender/caregiving responsibilities intersect in interesting ways. Putting aside caregiving obligations for a moment, older women experience discrimination different from (and worse than) older men and younger women. Part of the reason for this is our society's emphasis on beauty (which is thought to diminish as women age) and on motherhood (the capacity for which most certainly *does* diminish as women age). But part of the reason for this disparity is because the divorce rate has increased, and divorce often leaves women poorer than men. This problem is exacerbated by the fact that women live longer than men, which means they will usually have more years of not earning a wage. And because retirement earnings are largely dependent on earnings during working years, and women earn less on average (courtesy of the pay gap), the poverty rate of older women greatly exceeds older men.[67]

As for how age interacts with workers who have caregiving responsibilities, perhaps one benefit of growing older is that children are usually older and therefore not in need of as much care. However, as the parent of a current 19-year-old and 21-year-old (in addition to a 28-year-old), I can confidently state that the mental stress

63 42 U.S.C. § 12211(a)–(b).
64 Blatt v. Cabela's Retail, Inc., 2017 WL 2178123, at *4 (E.D. Pa. May 18, 2017). But some recent cases have gone the other way. Rodriguez-Roldan 2020, at 435.
65 Cox 2019, at 321; Levi & Barry 2019, at 618–27.
66 Rodriguez-Roldan 2020, at 436, 438.
67 Bisom-Rapp & Sargeant 2016; Porter 2003.

of parenting obligations is certainly not over. As a friend of mine says—"little kids, little problems; big kids, big problems." She's right about that. On the other hand, I no longer have to make breakfasts or lunches; I don't do their laundry; I generally do not need to drive them anywhere (because they have their own cars, and I realize that is a privilege that many people do not have); and I am not responsible for any bathing or hygiene of my children During the early days of the pandemic, when hundreds of academic and professional moms I knew were struggling to keep their heads above water, trying to care for their children who could not attend school or day care, I was very productive. My children did not need much, and we weren't going anywhere, so it left a lot of time for me to write. In other words, my age and how it correlated with my children's ages, means that my work/life balance was better than most younger moms.

Having said that, I had my children young (very young (23) for the first and relatively young (33) for the last). These days, many women are waiting until later in life to marry and have children (assuming they wish to and can have children). This means that these women might be suffering from some of the stigma older women suffer from while still having the caregiving obligations that make work/life balance more difficult. And of course, women of many ages might have parents who are sick and/or disabled and in need of care. If these women also have children at home, they are part of a growing "sandwich generation" that is taking care of both their children and their parents.[68]

As for disability, age intersects with it in predictable ways. Part of the reason the number of people with disabilities is increasing is because the population is aging.[69] In fact, almost 70 percent of American adults with disabilities are over 55 years of age.[70] The incidence of several disabilities rises with age, including osteoarthritis, cancer, heart disease, dementia, high blood pressure, vision and hearing difficulties, and several structural impairments, such as with the knees, hips, and back.[71] Many of these impairments will affect the ability to work and therefore require accommodations if the person is to remain employed. In 2018, people with disabilities over the age of 55 had only a 13 percent labor force participation. In order to improve the workforce participation of older workers and therefore help lift these workers out of poverty, they will often need accommodations.[72] Older workers were raised during a time when there was greater segregation of and stigma surrounding people with disabilities, so they are less likely to advocate for their rights under the ADA.[73]

68 Clarke 2011, at 1267–68; Jacobs & Gerson 2004, at 998.
69 Schur et al. 2013, at 26.
70 Harris, S. 2020, at 204–05.
71 Harris, S. 2020, at 229; Stein et al. 2014.
72 Harris, S. 2020 at 210–11.
73 Schur et al. 2013, at 102.

VI MOTHERS WITH DISABILITIES

Most of this section discusses the unique (and uniquely subordinated) intersection of disabled women who also have caregiving responsibilities, usually for their own children but sometimes for other loved ones. Before we get there, however, it is important to point out that there are also intersectional effects of gender and disability, regardless of caregiving responsibilities. Although this scholarship is not as robust as the intersectional scholarship on gender and race, it is becoming more common for scholars to explore the unique intersection of gender and disability.[74]

In exploring this intersection, Michelle Travis notes that disability has become a "master status," the identity that trumps all other identities. The "degendering of disability is the process by which individuals with disabilities are perceived neither as men nor as women but solely as disabled."[75] Thus, those with multiple identities are often seen as atypical members of their respective identity groups. Because the image of a disabled person is usually a white, heterosexual man who uses a wheelchair, women with disabilities are considered atypical members of the disability community and therefore experience a sense of exclusion from the disability rights movement. Moreover, women with disabilities are also invisible within the feminist movement. As Travis explains: "Without a strong voice in either the disability rights movement or the feminist movement, women with disabilities have been unable to draw attention to their unique forms of multiple oppression: to what it means to be both female in a male-dominated society and disabled in a society designed for the able-bodied."[76]

On a more practical level, women with disabilities are less likely to be employed than either men with disabilities or non-disabled women, and they earn significantly less money than disabled men. They are also less likely to receive accommodations.[77] Overall, having a disability has a stronger negative impact on women's labor force participation than on men's.[78] And as Jennifer Shinall has discussed, there is evidence that the ADA has improved conditions for disabled men more than it has for disabled women. As she states "Sex discrimination, it appears, has a uniquely exacerbating effect on disability discrimination."[79] This means that there are discriminatory wage and employment effects for disabled women as compared to disabled men.

In a 2018 article, "Mothers with Disabilities," I explored the unique challenges facing disabled women who also have the caregiving responsibilities of children.

74 Porter 2018a, at 82.
75 Travis 2017, at 840.
76 Travis 2017, at 841–44.
77 Lin 2021.
78 Porter 2018a, at 83; *see also* Engel & Munger 2003 (disability and gender is doubly disabling).
79 Shinall 2017, at 1102–03.

A large part of that exploration involved challenges facing women with disabilities in the family realm, which is not relevant for this project.[80]

But more relevant to this book, I also explored the intersectional disadvantages facing women with disabilities and how this might affect their lives and their careers. In situations where a woman has a disability that does not preclude employment, and she has children, she is likely to be marginalized for both having a disability and having caregiving responsibilities. It is likely that both of these identities will at times require accommodation. She might need schedule changes or modified job duties to accommodate her disability. And because most women are the primary caregivers of their children even when they are married, she will likely need schedule changes or leaves of absence to care for her children. As discussed in Chapter 6, these needs for accommodations will likely cause special treatment stigma, which could have significant effects on her work life, such as lower pay, fewer advancement opportunities, and possibly even termination. Moreover, statistics demonstrate that disabled women are more likely to divorce, and being a single mother who is also living with a disability is likely to have a profound impact on her ability to manage her work life and home life, and ultimately might lead to job loss and poverty.[81]

I realize this is a gloomy picture, and certainly many women who are caregivers and have disabilities successfully manage both. But the challenges of these intersectional disadvantages should not be ignored or minimized. And at the risk of ending this chapter on an even more negative note, one intersection we have not yet discussed is women with disabilities who have children with disabilities. The challenges and advocacy efforts of parents of children with disabilities are explored in *Allies and Obstacles: Disability Activism and Parents of Children with Disabilities* but are beyond the scope of this project.[82]

[80] Porter 2018a, at 83–103.
[81] Porter 2018a, at 106–09.
[82] Carey et al. 2020.

5

The Entrenchment of Structural Norms

I INTRODUCTION

Prior chapters have explored the disadvantages suffered by employees who need accommodations or modifications in the workplace. This chapter is devoted to one type of accommodation that employees might seek—modifications to their employers' rules regarding when and where work is performed, such as policies regarding hours, schedules, shifts, attendance, work from home, and leaves of absence. Together, I call these the "structural norms" of the workplace.

There are two reasons these types of accommodations warrant their own chapter. First, accommodations to the structural norms are needed or desired by virtually all workers—those who have disabilities or caregiving obligations, those who might have a religious conflict with their hours or schedules, and frankly, everyone else. Modifications to the structural norms of the workplace are the most frequently requested accommodations by people with disabilities, and many employees without disabilities also request modifications to these structural norms.[1]

The second reason these norms play an outsized role in the lives of employees is that employers often perceive these norms as mandatory and inevitable.[2] They see the time and the place where work is done as being part of the actual job; therefore, they often refuse to allow any modifications to these policies. The experience with COVID-19 provides a good example. Before the pandemic, most employers did not allow employees to work from home; or if they did, only in rare (and often temporary) circumstances. If you asked employers at that time why they were unwilling to allow remote work, they would likely explain that it was impossible—that employees could not collaborate with other employees, clients, or customers if working from home, and that it would be impossible to supervise employees who are

1 Schur et al. 2014.
2 Finley 1986.

not at the central workplace. But COVID-19 taught us that working from home is not only possible but can be very successful.[3] Accordingly, COVID-19 has allowed us (to some extent) to dismantle the structural norm that all work must be performed at a central location.[4]

The goal of this chapter is to demonstrate how entrenched these norms are in most workplaces and to explain why this entrenchment exists. I first provide a history of many of the most common structural norms, including hours, shifts, attendance policies and leaves of absence policies, before demonstrating just how entrenched these norms are. Finally, this chapter briefly discusses the work-from-home experiment courtesy of COVID-19.

II HISTORY AND DESCRIPTION OF STRUCTURAL NORMS

So how did we get here? Why is the 40-hour workweek the norm? Why is 9:00–5:00 the traditional hours of most white-collar jobs? When and why did employers start using shift work (scheduling employees during non-traditional times)? This part discusses the history of these norms and describes where we are today.

A *Hours*

As discussed in Chapter 2, the advent of industrialization is what brought the separation of work and home. Before that time, husbands and wives (and their kids) generally worked together in their homes and on their farms, but despite doing different work at home and on the farm, both spouses' labor was considered valuable. However, with industrialization came jobs that could only be performed at a central location. (It is difficult to manufacture steel from home.) Women became associated with the private sphere and men with the public sphere. At the advent of the industrial revolution, employees' work was compensated based on tasks, often on a piecemeal basis, rather than based on time. A confluence of events, including the scarcity of land for agriculture and urbanization, made wage labor more important for family support. The family farm that used to provide all of the family's support went into sharp decline. Thus, the difference between wage labor and household labor became more clearly defined.[5]

Prior to the passage of the Fair Labor Standards Act in 1938, hours varied quite widely among employers, and many employers made their employees work very long hours. Before unionization became common, employees were at the mercy of their employers, and most of the time, of their foremen, who often wielded absolute

[3] Hickox & Liao 2020; Katsabian 2021; Porter 2021; Travis 2020.

[4] Hickox & Liao 2020; Katsabian 2021; Porter 2021; Travis 2020. *But see* Shu 2023.

[5] Albiston 2010.

power over their employees, including firing them for any reason or no reason. It's not surprising that employees during this time were not willing to push back against the hours they were required to work. Especially during depression eras, a job working too many hours was vastly preferable to no job at all. Modern expectations about management prerogatives, such as unilateral control over timing of work, are the result of the historical struggles between management and workers over how to define work. During this time, employers kept finding ways to obtain more and more control over workers' time and their productive process.[6]

Moreover, as discussed in Chapter 2, because of the separate spheres ideology that developed, men working during the industrial revolution had the ability to work as many hours as needed because they often had a wife who was at home and could handle the household and childcare responsibilities. And employers believed it was beneficial to promote a middle-class, wholesome family lifestyle because this was thought to minimize labor unrest.[7] By the time that women began entering the workforce in significant numbers, the full-time, year-round norms of work were already firmly established.[8]

In 1938, President Franklin D. Roosevelt signed the Fair Labor Standards Act (FLSA), which banned oppressive child labor, set a minimum wage (only 25 cents per hour back then!) and a maximum workweek. The main purpose of the Act was to minimize unemployment during the Depression.[9] This Act is often credited with giving us the 40-hour workweek, but when it was enacted, it only applied to about one-fifth of the labor force. Both before and after the enactment of the FLSA, unions were heavily involved in trying to get standardized schedules in order to take away some of the control of management.[10] So even though the 40-hour norm is so common, the history indicates that workweeks have been much longer at times, and also much shorter at times (during depressions).

Interestingly, even before we had the FLSA, employers sometimes voluntarily reduced employees' hours to minimize unemployment during times of depressed prosperity. As noted by historian Sanford Jacoby: "In order to reduce the number of layoffs, firms either shortened daily or weekly work hours or rotated shifts, thus maximizing the number of employed workers but reducing average earnings."[11] For instance, during the time period from 1929 to 1933, average weekly hours in manufacturing plants dropped from 44 to 38. Employers hoped that work sharing would lessen the likelihood of unemployment insurance and other public welfare measures that were ideologically repugnant to many employers and which could be

6 Albiston 2009; Albiston 2010; Jacoby 2004.
7 Jacoby 2004.
8 Albiston 2010.
9 29 U.S.C. §§ 201–219; Barzilay 2012, at 122.
10 Albiston 2010; Grossman, Jonathon 1978; Jacoby 2004.
11 Jacoby 2004, at 157.

costly. When the depression was at its worst in 1932, some unions were trying to get a six-hour day to avoid layoffs and unemployment.[12]

Some of the standardization we see with hours and schedules is the result of unionization, both actual unionization as well as the threat of unionization (for some employers). For instance, once unions had the legal protection of federal laws, management tried to standardize as many policies as possible as a way of avoiding unionization. Some of these policies were related to discipline and discharge. But some were related to standard hours. The idea was to take away some of the power that had previously been vested in foremen and to have decisions made at the company level rather than the department level.[13] Less discretion by supervisors leads to more consistent treatment, which is something unions care about.

So where are we now with respect to hours? Statistics vary, of course, but by many estimates, Americans put in more hours than any other industrialized nation.[14] From 1967 to 2000, the average number of hours worked in a year went up from 1,716 to 1,878. The average number of weeks worked in that same time period increased from 43.5 to 47. If you combine a married couple's hours (if they both work outside the home), the total increased from 3,331 in 1979 to 3,719 in 2000.[15]

Other studies indicate that the picture with respect to hours is not as clear as we once thought it was. As Jerry Jacobs and Kathleen Gerson discovered, although many Americans feel conflicted between work and family, not all of these people are working too many hours. There is a divide between those who work too many hours and those who work too few hours. Moreover, the reports of increased hours are more related to the fact that Americans take less vacation time rather than a per-week increase in hours worked. And to the extent study participants report more leisure time, this is likely the result of doing less work at home (either hiring it out or living with a dirty house) and not fewer hours at work. Nevertheless, even these researchers agree that for many Americans, long hours cause a real conflict with having enough time for their families.[16]

Several facts explain why employers have an incentive to force employees into working long hours. First, for employees who are salaried and therefore exempt from FLSA-mandated overtime, it is much cheaper for an employer to force those employees to work longer hours than it is to hire another employee. Moreover, the number of employees working in exempt positions has doubled since the FLSA was enacted in 1938. Second, even with non-exempt employees, who are entitled to time and a half for hours worked over 40, because of the costs of benefits, many employers still find it cheaper to pay for overtime rather than hiring additional employees. The cost of benefits has increased substantially—from 5.1 percent of

[12] Jacoby 2004.
[13] Jacoby 2004.
[14] Hochschild 1997.
[15] Befort 2004.
[16] Jacobs & Gerson 2004; Schultz & Hoffman 2006.

salaries in 1948 to 15.4 percent in 2000. Third, the desire to pay for overtime rather than hire additional employees is motivated in part because labor demands are unpredictable for many industries. Understandably, employers do not want to hire a bunch of new employees when labor demands are high, only to have to lay them off when the demand wanes.[17]

Although 2020 might not have been a normal year because of the COVID-19 pandemic, it is nevertheless useful to review relatively recent statistics regarding hours worked. Of all adults 20 years and older who were working, the average hours worked per week was 38.7, but this included people who usually work part time. The average hours worked for all adults who normally work full time was 41.6. Men's average was 42.5, whereas women's average was 40.3 hours per week. Interestingly, married men averaged 43 hours per week, whereas never married men averaged 41.2 hours per week. Married women averaged slightly more hours than never-married women (40.3 compared to 40.0) while widowed, divorced, or separated women averaged slightly more hours than both married women and never-married women (40.6 hours per week).[18] As we climb out of the pandemic, it remains to be seen what will happen with respect to hours worked.

B *Shifts*

What shifts we work is largely dependent on our jobs and industries. For instance, medical professionals tend to work long shifts, three 12-hour shifts per week rather than the traditional five 8-hour shifts.[19] For industries that require 24-hour operation (which includes but is not limited to the medical profession), employers must assign some employees to work the less desirable (usually night) shifts. But outside of the obvious businesses for which 24-hour operation is necessary—hospitals, hotels, police officers, and fire fighters—some businesses (especially in the manufacturing industries) make a conscious choice to operate 24/7. "Manufacturing companies realized decades ago that running an assembly line around the clock was cheaper and more efficient than shutting down production at night and starting it up again every morning."[20]

Not surprisingly, most people prefer not to work at night. (The one exception to this is a couple who decides to "tag team" parent so that someone is always home with the children.)[21] Assuming there are not enough employees who voluntarily choose to work the evening shifts, employers must come up with some method of assigning employees. For non-unionized companies, employers often had to pay

[17] Befort 2004; Schultz & Hoffman 2006.
[18] https://www.bls.gov/cps/cpsaat22.htm.
[19] Porter 2015, at 4.
[20] Bird & Mirtorabi 2006.
[21] Jacobs & Gerson 2004; Selmi 2007; Widiss 2021a, at 2199.

premium wages to entice employees to work at night.[22] But for companies where a union is present, seniority systems usually determine who must work at night. The most junior employees are assigned the unpopular shifts (often evening and/or weekend) until they have built up enough seniority to transfer to the day shift. Some employers who are non-unionized but who do not want to pay premium wages use rotating shifts, where employees work for some period of time on the day shift, and then rotate to the night shift for the same period of time (usually weeks or months but sometimes more often). When I was in private practice, some manufacturing plants operated with three shifts (7:00 a.m.–3:00 p.m., 3:00–11:00 p.m., and 11:00 p.m.–7:00 a.m.) but rotated employees through all three shifts weekly—one week on day shift, one week on afternoon/evening shift, and one week on the "graveyard" shift. I can't even imagine how difficult it must be to change working hours (and therefore sleeping hours) so frequently.

There are significant costs of shift work, both for workers and employers. As stated by two commentators: "What practice contributes to the world's most devastating industrial accidents, costs employers $206 billion annually, promotes fatigue, depression, flu, infertility, obesity and heart disease, yet receives negligible judicial recognition and attracts little attention from legal scholars? The answer is deceptively mundane: shiftwork."[23] About 13 percent of the American workforce works non-standard shifts. These employees suffer all kinds of health consequences, and their employers "pay" for non-standards shifts in terms of the high costs of workplace accidents. All of these costs are exacerbated when employers use rotating shifts (rather than a straight night shift).[24]

C *Attendance Policies*

As noted, during the early days of industrialization, foremen had virtually complete control over every aspect of their employees' jobs and this included attendance policies.[25] Even today, many employers continue to have very strict attendance policies. When I was in-house counsel, several of the manufacturing plants had very stringent, "no-fault" attendance policies. Under these policies, employees would incur a "point" or "occurrence" for every absence, regardless of the reason (unless it was protected under the FMLA, which is discussed more in Chapter 8). They were only allowed seven such absences over an entire year. After seven, they would be terminated. Think about how fast an employee could incur those seven absences—car trouble, employee is sick (but not sick enough to qualify for FMLA leave), child is sick, child's school has a snow day, child's

22 Bird & Mirtorabi 2006; McMenamin 2007.

23 Bird & Miratorabi 2006, at 384.

24 Bird & Miratorabi 2006.

25 Jacoby 2004.

in-home day care is closed or the nanny or babysitter is sick. I left my in-house job in 2004, and honestly, I thought these no-fault policies were an anomaly. Not so, according to a recent article.

The organization A *Better Balance* published an article in June 2020 discussing the attendance policies of 66 of the nation's largest employers who together cover 18 million workers. The basic message of the study and article is that many employers have policies that do not comply with federal and state laws. But for our purposes, the import of this article is that many large employers continue to use "no fault" attendance policies, where employees incur points for all absences, regardless of the reason. In reality, it is unlawful for an employer to penalize an employee for taking FMLA leave, and some employees would be entitled to miss work because of a disability under the ADA, but many of these employers' policies did not notify employees of their right to leave under FMLA or ADA and sometimes provided misleading information about the employees' rights to use those laws.[26]

Overly stringent attendance policies sometimes lead to employees having to make impossible choices between their own health (or the health and well-being of their loved ones) and their jobs. A single mother incurred a point when her eight-month-old had pneumonia. Another worker received a point after visiting the emergency room because she was vomiting blood. Some of the policies called for discipline after only two occurrences (points), and some probationary employees could be terminated with only one absence.[27]

The fact that troubled me most was that many of these policies encourage employees to come to work if they are sick so that they do not incur a point that could lead to discipline, including termination. Coming to work sick has always been a problem, but it has taken on new significance during the COVID-19 pandemic, especially given that many of the employers studied were in the meatpacking or manufacturing industries, where employees work close together. One meatpacking employer offered $500 bonuses to any worker who did not miss a shift for any reason between April 1 and May 1, 2020. The employer would excuse absences related to COVID-19 only if the employer ordered them to stay home or they had a doctor's note. But as many readers know, getting a doctor's note during the early days of the pandemic was close to impossible.[28]

To be clear, it's not all bad news. As noted in an article by Deborah Widiss, many full-time employees have access to a week or two of paid sick days each year. This is helpful for people with disabilities and other health conditions. However, most employers do not allow employees to use sick days to care for family members.[29] Moreover, sick days cannot be used for all of the other things that might make an

26 Bakst et al. 2020; *see also* Williams, JC 2010.

27 Bakst et al. 2020.

28 Bakst et al. 2020; *see also* Smith 2001; Williams, JC 2010.

29 Widiss 2021b.

employee miss work (despite her best efforts), such as day care or school being closed or a babysitter being sick.

D *Leaves of Absence*

Before the passage of the FMLA, employees had no federally protected right to leave if needed for their own health conditions or disabilities, or because they needed to care for a family member. The United States was the only industrialized nation that did not have national parenting leave (and is still the only country that has no right to *paid* leave). Even though the Pregnancy Discrimination Act (PDA) was passed in 1978, it did not require employers to provide job-protected leave to pregnant woman who give birth, unless the employer offered leave to other employees in similar circumstances. Many employers refused to provide maternity leave at all. In fact, before the PDA, it was common for employers to fire employees once they were close to their due date (if not earlier—some employers would fire pregnant women when their pregnancies began to show). Moreover, even when employers offered leave, they would not always reinstate the employee once she returned from leave.[30]

As will be discussed more in Chapter 8, only 60 percent of the population has access to the federally guaranteed right to 12 weeks of unpaid leave via the FMLA. But the situation is actually slightly better than that statistic would reveal because many employers provide leave even when not required to. But this leave is not always (or even often) paid,[31] and many low-wage workers cannot afford to take lengthy leaves of absence unpaid. In recent years, several states have adopted leave statutes that provide partial pay and require employers to provide the leave for an employee's own health needs or for employees to care for family members with medical needs.[32]

However, despite the advent of FMLA leave, state leave laws, and employers who voluntarily provide leave even without a legal mandate, taking leave is still stigmatized. All of these leave laws have not changed the default entrenched norm of year-round employment with perfect attendance.[33] This norm favors able-bodied, married men who have spouses who don't work.

III ENTRENCHMENT OF STRUCTURAL NORMS

With an understanding of the history of structural norms and a snapshot of where we are today, we now move to a discussion of just how *entrenched* (or sticky) these

30 Porter 2014d.

31 One statistic reveals that only 12% of the workforce has access to employer-provided paid family leave, and lower-paid workers are less likely to have access to paid family leave. Albiston & O'Connor 2016, at 5.

32 Widiss 2021b.

33 Albiston 2010.

workplace norms are. This part discusses how employees themselves see these norms as entrenched and unavoidable, before turning to the perceptions of employers and courts. As stated succinctly by Catherine Albiston, workplace practices are so taken for granted that it is hard for courts, employers, and employees, to imagine work being organized in any other way. These policies seem so natural, normal, and inevitable that they appear to be an unchangeable reality rather than workplace conventions.[34] Michael Selmi agrees that one of the mysteries is just how uniform employment practices remain and how rigid the labor market has proven to be.[35]

A *Employees' Perceptions of Default Time Norms*

In order to conceptualize this issue, picture you have just been offered a new job. One of the first things you will want to know (perhaps after the pay) is the hours you will be expected to work. For some jobs, where employees punch time clocks, you will want to know about how many hours you will be working and which shifts you will be assigned to work. (And for many people, this information might determine whether they accept the offer.)[36]

But even if you're being offered a professional (salaried) job rather than an hourly job, you will still want to know the hour and schedule culture at this particular workplace. At a law firm, you might want to know the billable hour quota or expectations. But you might also want to know whether the culture of the workplace involves a certain amount of "face time," and if so, how much face time. Although this varies quite a bit and has undoubtedly changed because of COVID-19 (discussed more shortly), most law firms (and undoubtedly many other professional jobs) require a certain amount of face time. So even lawyers who bill a lot of hours and take work home nightly might still be denigrated if they are not in the office enough (although how many hours is *enough* is often amorphous).

A couple stories from my own experience might help to illustrate these issues. When I was an associate at a law firm, the partner who worked next door to me would walk around the office a little after 5:00, and if you weren't in your office at the time, he would turn off your light. Of course, I wouldn't have known this if I had left the building for the night. But I often would be in a colleague's office and would come back to see my light turned off. Although this could have been his attempt to save on electric bills, it appeared to me to be a passive aggressive way of the partner saying: "It's 5:15, and I am [erroneously] recognizing that you have already left for the day."

After my law firm job, I took a job as in-house counsel for a manufacturing company. "In-house counsel" are lawyers who are employed by the company, and

34 Albiston 2010.

35 Selmi 2007.

36 Conaghan 2006, at 104 (discussing the importance of hours in how we define a job).

that company is their only "client." In this role, I no longer had to bill hours (yay!), but there was a strong face-time norm. The legal department was located within the corporate headquarters of this company. And even though the headquarters generally operated on an expected 8:30–5:00 workday, the legal department had an unofficial norm of working 8:30–5:30. I was expected to keep these hours even though I rarely worked directly with any other employees located in my building. Most of my interactions were with the human resources professionals in manufacturing plants (and time zones) across the country. I either addressed their legal needs through phone and email, or I frequently traveled to plants to meet with the management team in person, which involved very long hours. I also had a company-provided cell phone where I could and did receive work-related phone calls during evenings and weekends. None of this mattered for the face-time requirements in the legal department. I was still expected to be there until 5:30 every day. Of course, 5:30 is not very late (and especially not for an attorney), but the day care we had chosen for my three-year-old daughter was a home-based day care that closed at 5:30. (This was after a very difficult experience at a commercial day care.) The home-based day care was located about 20 minutes from my office with no traffic but could easily take 45 minutes or longer in traffic. My (now ex) husband is visually impaired and therefore cannot drive. So, in order to make this day care arrangement work, I needed to leave no later than 5:00 and I preferred to leave earlier to give myself a little more cushion so that I would never be late.

The 5:30 time norm was so strong, and the office was set up in such a way, that leaving early without saying something was not possible. I was very anxious about leaving early, which is ridiculous when I think about how many excess hours I regularly worked at night and on the weekends and especially when traveling. So I asked my boss (the general counsel for the company) if I could take a 10 percent pay cut in order to leave at 4:45 every day (45 minutes before the expected end time). He was worried about the precedent that would set so instead asked me to sneak out when I had to but to try and stay late as often as I could to make up for the times I left early to pick up my daughter. I think back to that now and realize just how entrenched that time norm was. And the reason for it was never very clear—except perhaps that, as lawyers, we made good money and we were supposed to work harder and longer than anyone else. Perhaps more importantly, we needed everyone else in the company to see how hard we were working. Hopefully COVID-19 has somewhat disrupted this connection between face time and working hard, but my guess is that the connection still remains in the minds of many.

These performative long hours are common in many industries. Bragging about long hours (even pulling all-nighters) is also very common. Blue-collar workers who get paid overtime will brag about their long hours and how much extra money they are bringing home (likely to fulfill their gender-normed obligation to be the breadwinners for their families). And professionals will brag about their long hours (even though they don't get paid for extra hours directly) because they believe those extra hours will pay off in terms of raises and advancement.[37]

Put simply, our lives revolve around when and where we work. When jobs deviate from the standard 40-hour, five day-a-week schedule, we reference the deviations—part-time work, flextime, shift work, etc. Although work can be organized in many ways, most desirable and better-paying jobs incorporate the dominant time norms around full-time uninterrupted labor.[38] And asking for a change to one's hours is usually a very big deal, causing the employee a great deal of anxiety.

Long hours are not the only structural norm that is entrenched. Shifts are, too. As noted, most employees do not want to work night shifts or rotating shifts. But many workers are not given a choice. And yet, despite the fact that most employees would prefer to have more control over their shifts, we accept these norms as natural and unavoidable.[39] Certainly, for some industries, they are. We understand why hospitals need to staff nurses and doctors 24/7, and their reason for scheduling 12-hour shifts—continuity of patient care—makes sense. But many of the structural norms that employees must abide by have no justification other than tradition and employers wanting to maintain control.

In a recent study, researchers polled workers regarding how they describe "good" employees. Sure enough, most of their answers revolved around the ideal worker norm. Specifically, respondents reported that hours worked and consistent attendance were central to their employer's idea of a good worker, even more so than good performance. Respondents also reported that employers "especially valued workers who put work before other obligations, sacrificed for the employer, and were willing to put in extra time on the job."[40] Some other responses included "[A]lways coming to work and never [asking for time off]"; "at work every day on time, stays when overtime is needed"; and "being there all the time."[41]

Frustratingly, employers expect these "ideal workers" long after they have stopped providing the types of jobs that would allow employees to be ideal workers—jobs with sufficient wages to support a family on one income with benefits and job security. In other words, employers expect even low-wage workers who have insecure hours to still live up to this norm. Some have referred to this as a "one-way honor system." And employees themselves accept without question that employers have the right to demand the ideal worker ethic even though the employers are giving little in exchange.[42]

These norms are so expected and inevitable for employees that they often do not take advantage of their employers' flexibility even when it's offered. There are several

[37] Hochschild 1997.
[38] Albiston 2009, at 1104; Albiston 2010.
[39] Albiston 2010.
[40] Albiston & O'Connor 2016, at 33–34.
[41] Albiston & O'Connor 2016, at 35.
[42] Albiston & O'Connor 2016, at 36.

possible reasons why employees do not take advantage of some flexibility options. First, employees are worried about the stigma that accompanies these options. (I address this "special treatment stigma" in the next chapter.) Second, many employees who take advantage of the flexibility offered by their employers find that their schedule is not honored, or they experience career disadvantages from having taken advantage of the flexibility. In fact, some studies reveal that even requesting time off might lead to career disadvantages.[43]

One example is attorneys who want to reduce their hours. A common arrangement in law firms is the 80/80 plan, where the lawyer (usually women with children) gets 80 percent of their regular pay in exchange for a billable hour quota that is 80 percent of the normal full-time quota.[44] For many of these attorneys, one or more of the following things happen after transitioning to such a schedule. First, it might not get honored. Many attorneys find that their hours begin to slowly (or not so slowly) creep up after the change in schedule. They might be called in on a scheduled day off or simply given more work than they can possibly do during their arranged reduced-hours schedule. Second, many attorneys find that the quality of the work given to them diminishes. This might be because their supervising attorneys perceive them to be less committed to their jobs. Or more innocently, partners might not give work to the reduced-hours employee because they think the attorney is too busy or because the attorney is not in the office when the partner is looking for someone to get involved on a new case or project. And third, the attorney who works a reduced-hours arrangement might suffer from diminished advancement opportunities. For instance, when it comes time for raises or bonuses, the reduced-hours attorney might notice that their raise or bonus is less than it was when they were full time and less than other similarly situated attorneys. And to be clear, I am not referring to a raise or bonus that is proportionately less. We would expect that attorneys on the 80/80 plan would get 80 percent of a normal raise or bonus. But often, they are given much less. Similarly, associate attorneys on an 80/80 arrangement should still be able to advance to partner, even it if takes 20 percent longer to do so. But many attorneys find that when they go on a reduced-hours schedule, they are taken off the partnership track completely and put on the "mommy track." Because of this reality, many employees avoid flexibility options even when available.[45]

One interesting example of this is the study of a fortune 500 company in Arlie Hochschild's popular book, *The Time Bind: When Work Becomes Home and Home Becomes Work*. Although this book was written more than 25 years ago, it still resonates with me, and there is still plenty of evidence that the problems identified still exist.

[43] Albiston & O'Connor 2016, at 37–38; Williams, JC 2001; Williams, JC & Segal 2003.

[44] Porter 2006.

[45] Porter 2006; Williams, JC & Segal 2003.

As discussed in Chapter 2, this book was detailing Hochschild's several-year study of a real corporation fictionally named "Amerco" that was purported to be a national leader in work/life balance. Yet of all employees with children under 13, only 3 percent worked part time, 1 percent job-shared, 1 percent used work-from-home options, and only one father had officially taken paternity leave. This company is not alone. A 1990 study of 188 Fortune 500 manufacturing companies found that although 88 percent of the companies offered part-time work, only 3 to 5 percent of their employees made use of it.[46]

Amerco's changes were born out of the fact that it was losing female employees faster than male employees. Each time it lost an employee, it cost the company a ton of money to recruit and train a replacement. Thus, it announced its mission to help workers balance their work lives with their home lives. The first types of programs it put in place were actually very successful, because they were programs designed to allow employees to work *more*. These were things like company-sponsored, high-quality childcare, childcare for sick children, emergency backup childcare, before- and after-school programs, and referral services for elder care. It was the second set of programs that never got off the ground. These included policies that allowed parents to work more flexible or shorter workdays, part-time work, job sharing, flexible hours, and working from home. The fact that this company had a strong culture, good intentions, and a rising number of two-job families who needed more time at home should have made it a very promising place for family friendly reforms. And yet, even though the company offered flexible working options, almost no one took advantage of them. The programs that allowed employees to work undistracted by their family obligations were endlessly in demand, but the policies offering shorter hours or more flexibility went unused.[47]

Hochschild considered and dismissed several possible explanations: (1) workers could not afford to work fewer hours (those who made the most were least likely to take advantage of options to work less); (2) workers were afraid of being laid off (no layoffs to speak of); (3) employees were not aware of the policies (yes they were); (4) the policies were just for show and would not actually be honored (the CEO actually was committed to making these policies work to attract and retain the most talented workforce); and (5) middle management were not supporting the policies. This last one appeared to have a kernel of truth to it. Some middle managers complained that the flexible policies caused headaches. However, even the disgruntled middle managers could not entirely explain the gap between the desire for family friendly policies and the actual use of such policies. Accordingly, Hochschild's study was an attempt to figure out what was happening.[48]

[46] Hochschild 1997.
[47] Hochschild 1997.
[48] Hochschild 1997.

One answer, it appears, is that many of these employees enjoyed work more than they enjoyed the "work" they had to do at home. Hochschild details how several employees found more joy at work than at home, especially women who found themselves being overburdened with housework and childcare when they were at home. But the bigger answer seemed to be that these workers defined their value by their hours, as did their supervisors. Some managers believed that those who got ahead were not the smartest but the hardest working. Another manager refused to accept the meritocratic principle of judging the work, not the face time. He lived by the principle that the time an employee works is as important as the results accomplished within that time. "Time is a symbol of commitment."[49] When one manager was asked to define commitment, he stated: "I don't think we can get commitment with less than fifty or sixty hours a week. That's what other corporations are doing. To be competitive, that's what we need to do. In my gut, I can't believe we can do it any differently."[50] The corporate culture viewed ambition and shorter hours as mutually exclusive. Even those managers who were fine allowing their subordinates to work fewer hours refused to do so themselves. One woman executive felt that to be credible as an executive, she had to work inflexible, long hours. The twelve top managers Hochschild interviewed all worked between 50 and 70 hours per week. Even though the company was not imposing those long hours on the managers, the type of employee who is ambitious enough to make it to the management level is the type who will always put in long hours.[51]

All of this is to emphasize just how sticky these time norms are; how often employees have internalized the view that long hours are necessary and that employers do and should have complete control over when and where their employees work. As stated by Catherine Albiston, institutional norms surrounding when and where we work are so taken for granted that we rarely see them as choices and instead see them as "natural and inevitable background features of our everyday lives."[52]

B *Employers' Control over Structural Norms*

Although workplaces provide more flexibility to their employees today than ever before, there are still many, many employers who insist on rigid start/end times, refuse anything other than full-time work, have strict attendance policies, and are stingy with leaves of absence. And empirical research indicates that employers often deny modifications to these structural norms even when the law requires such modifications, and even when their official policies allow such modifications.[53]

[49] Hochschild 1997, at 92.
[50] Hochschild 1997, at 94.
[51] Hochschild 1997.
[52] Albiston 2010, at 23.
[53] Albiston 2010.

Michelle Travis calls this the "full-time, face-time" norm, and as she notes, this norm has become quite entrenched and has shown "remarkable resilience" to attempts to change it and to legal challenges. The full-time, face-time norm includes full-time work with long hours, unlimited overtime, rigid work schedules, uninterrupted work lives, and performance of the work at a central location (as opposed to working from home). As she states, this not just a descriptive norm; it is also normative, describing how workplaces *should* or *must* be designed.[54]

What is surprising is that these norms have continued despite evidence that they have negative consequences. As stated by Travis, providing more flexibility to employees not only improves recruiting but also reduces absenteeism and turnover, and can increase productivity.[55] Accordingly, the big question is why? Why are employers so wedded to their default organizational norms?

One reason the long-hours norm has been so entrenched is because employers have a hard time assessing workplace output, so hours logged serve as a proxy for effort and productivity.[56]

Michelle Travis identifies a second reason why these norms are so sticky. Most successful managers are able to meet these norms (they perform as ideal workers), so they expect everyone else to. In fact, studies show that supervisors who are married to homemakers provide less flexibility than supervisors who have employed spouses.[57]

A third reason for this entrenchment is that employers want to avoid giving too much discretion to individual supervisors and managers. This actually is not a bad idea; many employment lawyers would advise their employer clients to try to avoid giving too much discretion to low-level supervisors and managers because there is a fear that the discretion will be exercised in discriminatory ways (or in ways that can be perceived as discriminatory). So for instance, imagine a supervisor routinely allows one employee to leave work an hour early but then refuses another employee's similar request. If the worker who leaves early is white and the worker who is refused is Black (or the leaving-early worker is a man and the refused worker is a woman), the refused worker might perceive that the decision was discriminatory. It might or might not be (it could just be favoritism, which is wrong but not illegal) but that discretion often causes a perception of discrimination, so employers have an incentive to take away as much discretion from supervisors as possible.[58]

Finally, scholars have blamed the cognitive processes of supervisors and managers, including fundamental attribution error, which overestimates the role of a person's internal characteristics and underestimates the power that the external situation has in controlling the other person's conduct. This theory predicts that

54 Travis 2005.

55 Travis 2005; *see also* Jacobs & Gerson 2004; Shinall 2020; Williams, JC 2010; Williams, JC & Segal 2003.

56 Albiston & O'Connor 2016, at 51.

57 Hochschild & Munger 2012; Travis 2005.

58 Albiston 2009; Harris, J. 2021b; Jacoby 172.

decision makers will attribute any failures of their employees to internal characteristics of the workers rather than to the situational constraints of a workplace that is organized around the full-time face-time norm. So when a supervisor tries to decide why women or individuals with disabilities are not succeeding in the workplace, they blame the employee's personal circumstances and "the workplace itself simply fades into the background."[59]

C *Courts Perpetuate This Entrenchment*

Thus far, this chapter has demonstrated how time, schedule, and shifts norms are entrenched in the minds of both employees and employers. This section turns to exploring the evidence that courts perpetuate this entrenchment. As noted by Catherine Albiston, courts often rely on established cultural meanings of work and time, rather than on statutory mandates, to resist enforcing changes to institutionalized time norms.[60]

In my prior work in the ADA context, I have demonstrated that courts are more reluctant to require employers to provide accommodations when those accommodations involve the structural norms of the workplace than when the accommodations requested involve the physical functions of the job. I explored this issue when discussing the effects of the ADAAA on the case law and then again when exploring the undue hardship defense.[61] In both articles, my research confirmed my suspicion that courts are less likely to require employers to provide accommodations when those accommodations involve when and where work is performed.

Catherine Albiston's research demonstrates the same phenomenon—that despite accommodation mandates under the ADA, plaintiffs have little success obtaining changes to the schedule of work, even though schedule adjustments are usually far less expensive than changes to the physical structures of work. Accommodations such as schedule changes are the most likely to be denied, whereas accommodations to the physical environment are the least likely to be denied. Courts are skeptical of proposed accommodations that change time standards. They reject as unreasonable any accommodation that modifies the employer's time schedules without looking at whether these changes can be accomplished easily. This is true for accommodations regarding attendance policies, leaves of absence, reduced-hour schedules, etc.[62]

There are many cases where employers refused to allow a variation of the rules and norms regarding when and where work is performed, and when those employees sued, they lost. The way most courts analyze these cases under the ADA is to state that the structural norm (the employer's rule regarding when or where work is

[59] Travis 2005, at 18.
[60] Albiston 2010.
[61] Porter 2014b; Porter 2019d; *see also* Arnow-Richman 2003.
[62] Albiston 2010; *see also* Arnow-Richman 2003, at 362–64; Cox 2022.

performed) is an *essential function* of the job.[63] Once something is deemed an essential function under the ADA, the employer is not required to eliminate that function. For instance, if strict punctuality is deemed an essential function, allowing an employee to be late to work because of a disability would not be a reasonable accommodation, because it would eliminate the essential function—strict punctuality.[64]

Michelle Travis has discussed this in both the context of ADA claims and disparate impact challenges under Title VII (when workplace structural norms have a disparate impact on women). As she states "[J]udges have assumed that jobs are defined at least in part by the default organizational structures that make up the full-time face-time norm, thereby placing those structures beyond the reach of antidiscrimination law and undermining the law's transformative potential."[65] The only thing the employer must do is present *some* evidence that it considered the structural norm to be an essential function of the job. Employers meet this quite easily by writing job descriptions stating that working full time, overtime, strict punctuality, reliable attendance, etc. are essential functions of the job. Or employers might implement policies addressing these structural norms. Once they've done so, it is a rare case for the court to challenge the employer's judgment.[66]

Moreover, plaintiffs' claims are usually defeated before the court even considers the employers' affirmative defenses. In the ADA context, that means that courts rarely address the issue of whether a modification to the structural norms would cause an undue hardship. In disparate impact claims under Title VII (under the theory that mandatory overtime or rigid attendance policies have a disparate impact on women because of their caregiving responsibilities), courts often dismiss these claims at the plaintiff's prima facie stage by holding that the structural norm is not a "particular practice" that is subject to disparate impact review. Courts consider these norms to be part of the work itself, rather than a choice by the employer. In this way, employers are never required to defend their structural norms as being job related and consistent with business necessity.[67]

D *How This Entrenchment Harms Workers*

Although Chapters 2 and 3 explored the problems people with disabilities and workers with caregiving responsibilities face, it is worth reiterating why these entrenched structural norms are harmful. For all (or certainly most) employees, the lack of flexibility in many workplaces is problematic. One way these policies hurt

[63] Arnow-Richman 2010; Travis 2005.
[64] *See, e.g.*, Holly v. Clairson Industries, LLC, 492 F.3d 1247 (11th Cir. 2007); Albiston 2010.
[65] Travis 2005, at 6.
[66] Travis 2005.
[67] Travis 2005.

workers is by straining the marriages of couples who have two working spouses.[68] But for some employees, the long hours and strict schedules are not just undesired, unfortunate, and inconvenient—they are dangerous to their health or to the safety and well-being of their children (or both). Many employees with disabilities have difficulty working overtime, or sometimes even full time if they are recovering from an illness or surgery. Some of the disabilities that have led employees to request more reasonable hours include multiple sclerosis, hepatitis C, some mental illnesses, diabetes, and cancer.[69] And of course, long hours and stringent attendance policies are difficult for parents who are the primary caregivers of their children, especially when they are single parents.[70] As discussed in Chapter 2 and earlier in this chapter, stringent attendance policies sometimes lead parents to have to make the impossible choice between their jobs and taking care of their children. And of course, even when parents choose caring for their children (and therefore lose their jobs), the lack of income makes continuing to care for their children more difficult.

IV COVID-19 AND WORKING FROM HOME

Prior to the COVID-19 pandemic, this chapter would have discussed work-from-home accommodations along with the other structural norms, because structural norms refer to both when and *where* work is performed. But given the outsized importance of work-from-home during (and likely after) the pandemic, this topic deserved special emphasis.

Remote work is often coveted by working parents because it saves time on commuting and allows parents to be home when children are not attending their normal school/day care arrangement.[71] Working from home is also desirable or required (intermittently or permanently) for many people with disabilities. Some disabilities that might require a work-from-home accommodation include bowel or bladder issues (where constant and close access to a bathroom is necessary), obsessive compulsive disorder (or other mental illnesses), complications from pregnancy that require an employee to be on bed rest, pressure ulcers as the result of paraplegia and sitting in a wheelchair, and flare-ups of diseases like rheumatoid arthritis or multiple sclerosis.[72]

Pre-pandemic, although many employers allowed some employees to work from home, most employers did not. Many employers refused such requests to work from home because they could not imagine how it could work. How could employees be

68 Hochschild 1997.
69 Cox 2022; Schur et al. 2013.
70 Selmi & Cahn 2006; Widiss 2021a.
71 Travis 2003.
72 Kanter 2022; Porter 2021; Schur et al. 2013.

supervised, meet with clients, and interact and brainstorm with colleagues if they were working from home?[73]

When employees with disabilities sued because their work-from-home accommodations were denied, most of the time they lost. Employers approach this accommodation request in various ways. Obviously, working from home is not possible for millions of jobs, including most jobs in the manufacturing, hospitality, service, and health care sectors. It is impossible to manufacture a car, clean a hotel room, cut someone's hair, or take care of patients in a hospital from home. But even when it is possible to do a job from home, the general rule for decades has been that working from home is not a reasonable accommodation in most cases. Several courts have held that in-person presence is an essential function of the job. Although some courts have been willing to truly scrutinize the plaintiff's job to see if it can be performed at home, most courts defer to the employer's judgment in this regard.[74]

And then came COVID-19, which forced the country to shut down, causing many American workers to have no choice but to work from home. Employees continued to perform their job duties from home, relying on existing technology such as Zoom and other online platforms that allow video conferencing. These platforms have made both teamwork and remote supervision possible. Even things like court hearings and trials, which we never previously imagined could be performed at home, were being performed successfully.[75]

More importantly, there is plenty of evidence that work-from-home arrangements have been very successful. Many employees have been more productive working from home. Some employees have increased their workday by three or more hours per day and have suffered less absenteeism. Other benefits to employers from allowing work-from-home arrangements include decreased attrition and increased loyalty. Employees who can telecommute also report higher morale. In one survey, half of all workers who were working from home during the pandemic stated they would like for it to continue after the pandemic is over.[76]

Moving forward, there is plenty of evidence that employers might voluntarily extend these work-from-home arrangements, having seen the benefits firsthand. Several large employers have already indicated plans to allow most (or all) eligible employees to continue to work from home part or all of the time.[77] For those employers who are more skeptical of working from home (and there are several), it remains to be seen whether courts will change course from the pre-pandemic general rule that working from home is not a reasonable accommodation. In my

[73] Hickox & Liao 2020; Porter 2021; Travis 2020.
[74] Kanter 2022; Albiston 2010; Porter 2021.
[75] Porter 2021; Travis 2020.
[76] Kanter 2022; Porter 2021; Travis 2020.
[77] Hickox & Liao 2020; Porter 2021.

opinion, it seems likely that our experience with working from home during the pandemic will move the needle on the legal issue, at least in part.[78]

Therefore, one of the few benefits that might come out of this global pandemic will be that employers will have been forced to reimagine their workplaces—to realize that *where* employees do their work is not nearly as important as *how much* or *how well* the employees work. And if we can reimagine the workplace with respect to this structural norm (in-person presence), can we also reimagine modifying or eliminating other workplace structural norms? Chapters 8 and 9 provide a blueprint for such a reimagining.

[78] Porter 2021.

6

Special Treatment Stigma

I INTRODUCTION

When we think of the stigma and bias that people with disabilities experience, most people think of discomfort, pity, disgust, and sometimes fear. Many people with disabilities also live with stereotypical assumptions being made about them and their capabilities. To be sure, these biases and stereotypes are leveled at many people with visible disabilities, such as people who use wheelchairs, who are intellectually or developmentally disabled, who are missing a limb, and maybe those who are blind and deaf.[1] But given the broadened definition of disability after the ADA Amendments Act (ADAAA) discussed in Chapter 3, a great many people will be considered disabled under the amended ADA, even if they have what we might consider relatively minor impairments such as high blood pressure, asthma, knee or back injuries, irritable bowel syndrome, and many others. These individuals are unlikely to experience the type of stigma just discussed. In other words, the person with high blood pressure is not likely to have people viewing him with discomfort, disgust, or fear. But that does not mean that people with more minor disabilities don't suffer from stigma at all. Instead, they suffer from what I call "special treatment stigma."[2]

What do I mean by special treatment stigma? I am referring to both the workplace consequences of requiring special treatment in the workplace and the resentment of coworkers when accommodations are given to some employees. This is most common in the disability context because, as I described in Chapter 3, employers have a legal obligation to accommodate people with disabilities. But pregnant women and caregivers might also experience this stigma. Even though employers do not have a legal obligation to accommodate caregivers, they sometimes do

[1] Anderson 2000; Porter 2022; Waterstone 2015a.

[2] Porter 2016a, at 215–16.

through "family friendly" workplace policies. And as discussed in Chapter 3, pregnant women are sometimes accommodated, pursuant to the ADA, the PDA, or both. Moreover, FMLA leave (and other types of leave mandated by state law or voluntarily provided by employers) is also seen as a type of accommodation mandate that benefits people with disabilities and employees (mostly women) who have caregiving responsibilities.[3]

Accordingly, because both groups of employees experience this special treatment stigma, and because I believe this stigma is a significant obstacle to ending the subordination of both people with disabilities and employees with caregiving responsibilities, I devote a chapter to this concept. First, I present the evidence that employers are reluctant to accommodate workers regardless of whether the accommodation is needed because of a disability, pregnancy, or caregiving responsibilities. Second, I describe what happens when employers *do* accommodate workers—both in terms of what workplace consequences flow from those accommodations, and how those accommodations affect the accommodated employees' relationships with their coworkers.

II EMPLOYERS' RELUCTANCE OR REFUSAL TO ACCOMMODATE

The primary consequence of special treatment stigma is that employers are less likely to hire people who need accommodations.[4]

Some examples: Imagine someone who uses a wheelchair has an excellent phone interview (or maybe a Zoom interview in our post-COVID-19 world), but when he shows up in person for a second round of interviews, the manager who first interviewed him is noticeably surprised to see the wheelchair, and the applicant finds the rest of the interview being very stilted and uncomfortable. Or (and this is a true story of someone I know) a woman who is visually impaired is interviewing for a position for which she is well qualified, but the interviewer asks several questions about what types of accommodations she would need and how expensive they are. She doesn't get the job and surmises (probably correctly) that it was her disability and the perceived cost of accommodations that led to that result.[5]

Or imagine a pregnant woman who is not yet showing. She might be experiencing a great interview until she reveals that she is pregnant, after which the employer makes up a half-hearted excuse for why they are not considering her further. Or, if you ask around, many younger women will report interviews where they were asked pointed questions about their marital status and whether they have children (and if so, how many) or if not, when they plan to. Many of these women do not get the job. Although we don't always know the reason why, the questions asked during the interview are suspicious.

[3] Albiston 2010.
[4] Lin 2021.
[5] Kanter 2022.

Of course, this is only anecdotal evidence of this problem. What evidence do we have that this problem actually exists? First, when the ADA was passed, it not only failed to increase the employment rate of people with disabilities, but there is some evidence that the employment rate of individuals with disabilities *decreased*.[6] Most scholars attribute this to the accommodation mandate in the ADA and employers' fears about the costs of those accommodations.[7] In fact, many employers were opposed to the ADA in part because they feared the perceived costs of providing accommodations.[8] Similarly, statistics demonstrate that employers are less likely to hire pregnant women and women with caregiving responsibilities (especially those who have young children).[9]

Second, there are plenty of situations where employers are willing to provide informal accommodations to an employee until and unless the employee requests an accommodation that signals a possible legal obligation.[10] For instance, in one case, the pregnant plaintiff alleged that, before she became pregnant, other employees assisted her in performing her more strenuous job duties, but after she became pregnant and asked for the same assistance due to her doctor's recommended restrictions, the employer refused. The court sided with the employer, stating that there was a difference between coworkers voluntarily helping an employee and being forced to because of a legally mandated accommodation.[11]

More importantly, when employees do request accommodations (often because they cannot perform their jobs without the accommodations), employers often refuse.[12] Sometimes they refuse to accommodate even if they are (or should be) required to accommodate under the ADA or the PDA (for pregnancy accommodations). Their reasons often are related to the expense (believing it's too expensive to provide a particular accommodation)[13] or a concern about treating an employee more favorably than other employees ("we can't allow you to sit on a stool while you ring up customers' groceries because then everyone will want the same accommodation").[14]

The consequences of this failure to accommodate are quite dire. In the disability context, this often means the employee either has to risk their health by performing their jobs without an accommodation, or (more likely) they will quit or be fired for

6 Bagenstos 2004; Harris, S. 2007; Leonard 2005; Waterstone 2005.

7 Anderson 2009; Bagenstos 2009; Emens 2008; Satz 2008.

8 Leonard 2005, at 56; Porter 2019d.

9 Porter 2010a; Shinall 2018, at 752.

10 Arnow-Richman 2010; Schur et al. 2014, at 595.

11 Serednyj v. Beverly Healthcare, LLC, 656 F.3d 540, 549 (7th Cir. 2011).

12 Miller v. Illinois Dept. of Transp., 643 F.3d 190 (7th Cir. 2011) (supervisor responded to an accommodation request by stating: "I'll tell you right now, we don't grant requests."). *But see* Hoffman 2011, at 1543 (pointing to how often employers *do* accommodate people with disabilities).

13 Harris, J. 2021b, at 1732; O'Brien 2005, at 140; Shinall 2020.

14 Lee v. Harrah's New Orleans, 2013 WL 3899895 (E.D. La. July 29, 2013); *see also* Porter 2016a, at 249–51.

not meeting the employer's expectations.[15] In the pregnancy context, if a pregnant woman cannot do her job without an accommodation, she might be forced to take a leave of absence. Even if she is eligible for FMLA leave, she is only entitled to 12 weeks (of unpaid leave), so depending on when in her pregnancy she is placed on the restriction, she might have very little (or no) leave left once her baby is born. This is what happened to the plaintiff in the *Young* case (discussed in Chapter 3), and she even lost her health insurance.[16] Alternatively, a pregnant woman might risk the health of her pregnancy by performing her job without the accommodation. In one case, the plaintiff was a juvenile detention officer who was scheduled to complete a 1.5-mile run as part of a periodic physical fitness test. She tried to schedule the run early in her pregnancy but her supervisor refused. She attempted and failed the run, leading to a hospitalization with a placental bleed. When she returned to work, her run was rescheduled. Based on her doctor's orders, she sought an accommodation to be excused from the run. Her supervisor refused to excuse her, so she completed it and ended up hospitalized again.[17]

Finally, in the caregiving context, although there is no legal right to an accommodation, employees who are primary caregivers might need a variation of stringent attendance policies, and if they cannot get one, they might have to neglect their caregiving responsibilities, which can sometimes lead to disastrous consequences (such as children dying when left alone), or they might lose their jobs. Caregivers are likely to experience stress, depression, and guilt over not being able to properly care for their loved ones.[18]

III CONSEQUENCES OF SPECIAL TREATMENT STIGMA

Now imagine that employers *do* accommodate their employees—either because they are legally required to or because they don't want the negative reputational consequences that might flow from failing to provide accommodations. At first glance, it would seem like the problem is solved—employees are being accommodated. But these accommodated employees might also experience special treatment stigma, either because their employers treat them worse or their coworkers resent them (or both).

A *Workplace Consequences*

Some employees with disabilities who receive accommodations are treated worse by their employers. Supervisors might be irritated and annoyed that the employee

[15] Porter 2016a, at 251–52; Miller v. Illinois Dept. of Transp., 643 F.3d 190 (7th Cir. 2011).
[16] Young v. United Parcel Service, Inc., 575 U.S. 206 (2015).
[17] Thomas v. Florida Parishes Juvenile Justice Commission, No. 18-2921, 2019 WL 118011 (E.D. La. Jan. 7, 2019).
[18] Albiston & O'Connor 2016, at 50; Porter 2010a.

requested accommodations, and this might lead them not to consider the employee for promotions or other workplace benefits. A supervisor might also begin perceiving the employee as less competent because they could not do the job without special treatment. This perception, despite likely being erroneous, will also affect how the supervisor treats the employee with respect to evaluations, raises, and advancement.[19]

In the case of accommodations for caregivers, such as reduced hours, working from home, part-time hours, or simply flexibility in the hours worked, employers might perceive these workers as less committed to the workplace, and therefore might treat them worse because of it. These women might have their careers sidelined and be permanently placed on the "mommy track."[20] As one female attorney said when she returned from maternity leave and was given assignments better suited for a paralegal—"I had a baby, not a lobotomy."[21] One study demonstrated that when employers provided paid caregiving leave (under state law; it's not required under federal law), those employers would find a way to penalize those workers, most often by changing their schedules or drastically cutting their hours. Employees who reported this fully understood that it was in retaliation for taking the leave.[22]

B *Resentment of Coworkers*

As stated at the outset of this chapter, coworkers are often resentful when employers allow individuals with disabilities or workers with caregiving responsibilities to deviate from the normal workplace rules or to have their job tasks modified in any way.[23] One reason for this resentment is that workplace rules are often so entrenched that any deviation is perceived as unfair special treatment. Coworkers resent that others get a benefit that they do not. These coworkers might also resent the fact that employers sometimes require them to pick up the slack of the worker who was given an accommodation.[24]

Taking this latter reason first, in the disability context, several accommodations are perceived as having a negative effect on other workers. Recall from Chapter 3 that accommodations can include job restructuring, part-time or modified work schedules, leaves of absence, and reassignment to a vacant position.[25] Job restructuring might require other employees to perform tasks that a disabled employee cannot perform because of his disability; some of those tasks might be more arduous or

19 Porter 2016a; Williams, JC & Segal 2003.

20 Cox 2022; Hampson 2017, at 5; Schultz 2010, at 1216; Schultz & Hoffman 2006, at 137; Williams, JC 2001, at 88.

21 Williams, JC 2001, at 69.

22 Albiston & O'Connor 2016.

23 Schur et al. 2005.

24 Arnow-Richman 2003, at 392; Porter 2014e, at 1111–12; Travis 2009b. This can also happen with religious accommodations. Flake 2015, at 179.

25 42 U.S.C. § 12111(9).

unpleasant. Part-time or modified work schedules and leaves of absence could require other workers to work longer or different hours to make up for the absences of the disabled employee. And of course, reassigning employees with disabilities to other positions can cause conflicts with non-disabled coworkers who might also be interested in those positions.[26]

In many cases, this resentment is explicit. For instance, in one case, the plaintiff had type II diabetes, which necessitated regular breaks to eat and manage her condition properly. Because of these breaks, she was the "subject of derogatory comments and complaints from coworkers who contended that they were required to do more" because of the plaintiff's diabetes.[27] Another employee with a disability reported being harassed when they were on leave for a brain tumor.[28] Even the employees who are being accommodated are worried about this resentment, which might lead them to avoid requesting necessary accommodations in the first place.[29]

As noted earlier, employers are sensitive about this resentment, which often leads them to deny accommodations.[30] For instance, one employer refused to provide an accommodation that would allow an employee with a disability to avoid the heavy lifting of the job because this would have required other employees to do more heavy lifting.[31] And courts often side with these employers, holding that accommodations that cause other workers to work longer or harder are not required.[32]

One example from my practice days when I was in-house counsel for a large manufacturing company should help to illustrate this issue. One of the plants at the company where I worked had a shipping and receiving department that operated 24/7 and had three shifts to cover those hours: a day shift (7 a.m. to 3 p.m.), an afternoon shift (3 p.m. to 11 p.m.), and a night shift (11 p.m. to 7 a.m.). All employees in the department were required to rotate through one week on each shift—one week on the day shift, one week on the afternoon shift, and one week on the night shift. One of the employees in the department had kidney failure and had to go on kidney dialysis while he waited for a kidney transplant that was necessary to save his life. Because of his kidney dialysis schedule and the resulting fatigue after the treatment, he asked for an accommodation to work only the day shift. The plant management allowed this for a couple of months but in doing so, they kept the other employees' rotation schedules the same, which caused the department to be overstaffed on the day shift (to allow the employee with a disability to always work the day shift) and understaffed on either the afternoon or night shift. I asked the plant

[26] Porter 2007; Porter 2014e, at 1112; Schur et al. 2009.
[27] Porter 2016a, at 241–42.
[28] Albiston 2010.
[29] Engel & Munger 2003; Heyer 2007.
[30] Hamspon 2017, at 70; Schur et al. 2020; Shinall 2020.
[31] Porter 2016a, at 240–41.
[32] *See, e.g.*, Kallail v. Alliant Energy Corporate Services, Inc., 691 F.3d 925 (8th Cir. 2013); Rehrs v. Iams Co., 486 F.3d 353 (8th Cir. 2007); Turco v. Hoechst Celanese Corp., 101 F.3d 1090 (5th Cir. 1996); Milton v. Scrivner, Inc., 53 F.3d 1118 (10th Cir. 1995); *see also* Cox 2022.

management why they did not just start a rotation schedule where the other employees would rotate through the two non-day shifts more often so the company would not be overstaffed or understaffed. Their response was that they did not want to harm the other employees by making them rotate through the more undesirable shifts more often, and they believed the other employees would be resentful of the disabled employee.[33] It is unclear to me whether the employees would actually be resentful, given that the employee in question was enduring a fairly terrifying time in his life where he faced being on dialysis forever unless and until he could get a kidney transplant. But regardless of whether the employer's perceptions were correct, their decision to deny the accommodation based on the anticipated resentment is what matters here. (As an aside: This story has a happy ending. Although they did not allow the employee to continue to work a straight day shift long term, he was fortunate enough to have long-term disability insurance, which allowed him to take a leave of absence with two-thirds pay until he received the kidney transplant. After recovering from his transplant, he came back to work and continued to be a productive member of the team.)

Accommodations made to caregivers are also likely to cause resentment. The most common accommodations requested by caregivers are reduced hours and leaves of absence. In both cases, coworkers might be called upon to pick up the slack for the employee on leave or working reduced hours.[34]

Even if accommodations do not cause non-accommodated employees to work harder or longer, those workers might still be resentful because they might covet the same accommodation, and therefore, will be upset because of what they see as unfair preferential treatment being given to the accommodated employee. Examples of these types of accommodations include light duty, permission to sit rather than stand, schedule modifications, and reassignment to a vacant position that other employees want.[35]

This resentment is even more acute in the caregiving context because, other than FMLA leave (which is not available to almost 40 percent of all workers), accommodating caregiving is not legally mandated, so coworkers might resent the fact that the employer is giving preferential treatment (usually a change in schedule or shift) to caregiving employees. Trina Jones is one of the scholars who has discussed this issue. Jones argues that providing family friendly benefits only to parents involves "implicit assumptions about the personal activities of [child-free workers] and risk[s] perpetuating the notion that the people and activities in a [child-free worker's] life are not as important as the people and activities in the lives of married couples or parents."[36] Even though Jones recognizes the societal value of caregiving, she counters that

33 Porter 2016a, at 244–45.

34 Albiston 2010, at 173; Arnow-Richman 2003, at 392; Hampson 2017, at 120; Jones 2014; Williams, JC 2001, at 113.

35 Kelman 2001, at 879; Lester 2005, at 44; Porter 2016a, at 249–51; Travis 2009b.

36 Jones 2014, at 1301.

other employees engage in socially valuable activities such as assisting a sibling who has lost a job, doing volunteer work for a community center, and furthering one's education.[37]

Arlie Hochschild told a story of this type of coworker resentment in her book. A female secretary, Connie, wanted to leave work early once a week to take her son for his asthma shots. Although Connie tried to sneak out, her coworker told Connie's boss so that the coworker could get credit for covering for Connie. The manager was furious and told Connie to make other arrangements. When this manager was interviewed, his reasoning for refusing the request was: "If I let Connie take Wednesday afternoons, I'll have Laura asking me for time off next. She's got three-year-old twins. Rena has the desk on the other side of Connie, and her dad had a stroke. We have a business to run."[38]

To be fair, not all coworkers are resentful; some workplaces are infused with a cooperative spirit. In the disability context, the case of *Miller v. Illinois Department of Transportation* is a good example. In this case, the plaintiff was assigned to a bridge crew as a highway maintainer, along with four other highway maintainers and a bridge technician. Miller had a phobia regarding working from heights, especially when he was unsecured. Because of this fear, he was unable to perform some of the work, such as walking a "bridge beam." But despite his disability, he was able to work at heights if he was enclosed, and he estimated his fear kept him from performing only 3 percent of his job duties. Miller's supervisor informally accommodated him by allowing other employees to handle the tasks that Miller could not perform, and in turn, Miller helped his coworkers with tasks those employees could not or did not want to perform. After the employer refused to allow this arrangement to continue and terminated Miller, he sued. When denying the employer's motion to dismiss the case, the court focused on the willingness of Miller's coworkers to help each other, stating: "In short, … the team worked effectively as a team, taking advantage of each member's abilities and accommodating each member's limitations."[39]

The plaintiff was not so lucky in a case discussed earlier, *Serendnyj v. Beverly Healthcare, LLC*. As previously noted, the plaintiff's duties as activity director in a nursing home included some physically strenuous tasks, such as rearranging dining room tables and pushing patients in wheelchairs. Before she became pregnant, other employees voluntarily helped the plaintiff with these more strenuous functions. Shortly after the plaintiff became pregnant, she began having complications, and in order to avoid a miscarriage, her doctor ordered her to avoid all strenuous activities. Accordingly, she asked for an accommodation—to allow other employees to continue to help her with some of her more strenuous job tasks. Even though her

[37] Jones 2014, at 1304, 1308; *see also* Arnow-Richman 2003; Smith 2001.
[38] Arnow-Richman 2010; Hochschild 1997, at 140.
[39] 643 F.3d 190, 192–93 (7th Cir. 2011).

coworkers were willing to continue assisting the plaintiff, the employer refused to allow the informal arrangement to continue and fired her. But unlike the *Miller* case, in this one, the court sided with the employer.[40] These cases demonstrate that, even when coworkers are *not* resentful of accommodations provided to their disabled or pregnant coworkers, their employers might still refuse to grant the accommodation.

C *Stigmatic Effect of Identifying as Belonging to a Protected Class*

The final stigma flowing from receiving special treatment in the workplace is the stigma of belonging to a protected class. In order to be legally entitled to receive accommodations (or at least possibly entitled to accommodations), an employee either needs to have a sincere religious belief that conflicts with work, be pregnant, or be disabled, as defined by the ADA.[41]

Although establishing one's religion is not difficult, an employee might consider it private and prefer not to share it. This is especially true if the employee belongs to a minority religion and/or one that is not well known. Those who belong to religious minorities are often stigmatized in (and outside of) the workplace.[42] Moreover, if the employee's religion is not a well-known religion, the employer might insist on proof that the employee's religious belief is sincere.[43] (From a liability perspective, this is a bad idea, but it still happens.)

As for pregnancy, there is some evidence that stigma still exists for pregnancy.[44] Moreover, a pregnant woman might need an accommodation before she is ready to disclose her pregnancy. Most women wait until they are "showing" or until their second trimester before disclosing their pregnancy. This is partly because if a woman is going to have a miscarriage, it is much more likely to occur in the first trimester of the pregnancy. And if a woman has a history of miscarriages, she might especially want to keep the pregnancy hidden until she is out of the danger period, but her history of miscarriages makes it even more likely that her doctor will place her on workplace restrictions. If she is forced to disclose her pregnancy in order to get an accommodation because of the doctor-imposed restrictions, and then she miscarries, she will have no choice but to disclose the miscarriage, which would be even more traumatic.[45]

Finally, having to identify as disabled in order to receive the protection of the ADA and the right to request accommodations is likely to be stigma-inducing for

40 656 F.3d 540, 545–46 (7th Cir. 2011).
41 Porter 2016b, at 123.
42 Trans World Airlines, Inc. v. Hardison, 432 U.S. 63 (1977) (Marshall, J. dissenting).
43 Macfarlane 2021.
44 Shinall 2018.
45 *When Is the Best Time to Announce Your Pregnancy?*, HEALTHLINE (Dec. 26, 2018), https://www.healthline.com/health/pregnancy/when-to-announce-your-pregnancy#takeaway.

many people. As I've explored elsewhere, many people who would be considered disabled under the expanded definition of disability after the ADA Amendments Act do not identify as disabled and will often affirmatively "disclaim" their disabilities (or refuse to "claim" their disabilities). In many cases, this will cause them to lose the protection of the ADA even if their impairments would qualify as disabilities. Although some of this disclaiming problem is caused by a lack of understanding of the broad coverage of the ADA, a great deal of it is caused by the stigma of admitting you have a disability. Despite the passage of the ADA in 1990, and despite the substantial efforts of the disability rights movement, disability is still very stigmatized.[46]

Accordingly, as discussed more in Chapter 9, one of the many benefits of accommodating everyone is avoiding the stigma of identifying as being in one of the protected classes that receive special treatment.

[46] Porter 2022.

7

Theoretical and Practical Justifications for the Reimagined Workplace

I INTRODUCTION

At first glance, this chapter might seem a little chaotic. It starts with the theoretical and practical justifications for protecting the two groups of marginalized employees I've been studying—people with disabilities and workers with caregiving responsibilities. I hope to convince you that, as a society, we *should* want to help these groups of employees become employed, remain employed, have rewarding jobs or careers, and successfully balance work and home.

But because I am a realist, I am not sure I can convince you (or more importantly, employers, coworkers, and society) to care about protecting these groups of employees. Or more specifically, I'm not sure I can get people to care about these groups of employees to the extent such caring creates any burden on everyone else. We are, after all, a country that is highly focused on individual rights and liberty. The fight over wearing masks and getting vaccinated during COVID-19 are perfect examples of that focus on individual rights to the exclusion of what's best for society. Accordingly, the second section of this chapter explains and justifies why I am proposing two reforms that will protect *everyone*.

II JUSTIFYING ACCOMMODATIONS FOR CAREGIVERS AND EMPLOYEES WITH DISABILITIES

A *The Theoretical Justification*

Legal scholars and other theorists have been debating theories of equality for decades. This section first provides a brief description of various theories that have been discussed and debated over the years, recognizing that a fuller exploration of these theories is beyond the scope of this book. I then turn to the theory that most resonates with me as a justification for providing accommodations to people with disabilities and workers with caregiving responsibilities—communitarian theory.

1 Other Theories

Other theories have not made much progress in achieving equality in the workplace. Traditional liberal theory is focused on "formal equality," which is also referred to as "equal treatment." Formal equality is the easiest to understand. It is the simple premise of treating likes alike and treating those who are differently situated differently.[1] It's understandable why this theory is so ingrained in our society. After all, who can quarrel with the idea that similarly situated people should be treated the same?

It is the theory upon which most of our anti-discrimination law is based.[2] For instance, Title VII of the Civil Rights Act of 1964 makes it unlawful to take an adverse employment action against an employee because of that employee's protected class—race, color, religion, national origin, and sex.[3] For a simple example of equal treatment, consider this: two employees (one white and one Black employee) engage in the same kind of misconduct at work—they both steal something from their employer. The Black employee is fired, and the white employee is merely given a warning. Without knowing more, are you suspicious that the employees' race might have played a part in that decision? You should be. As described, the employees were alike (both engaged in the same misconduct) and yet were treated differently. If there are not any additional facts to suggest that they really were not similarly situated, we would likely infer discrimination in this case. But if additional facts revealed that the item the Black employee stole was significantly more expensive than the item the white employee stole, then these two employees might not be seen as "similarly situated," so treating them differently would likely not violate the law.[4]

The allure of equal treatment should be obvious. Most people see the world as a meritocracy, where they believe that most employment decisions are (and should be) made based on seniority, merit, or some combination of the two.[5] Even feminists were initially in favor of equal treatment (the late Justice Ginsburg was a huge fan). Feminists argued that in order to achieve equality in the workplace, women must demonstrate that they are just like men, for all practical purposes.[6] Of course, pregnancy caused some difficulty for the equal treatment proponents, because it is the one major way in which women are really truly different from men.[7] The work

1 Ball 2005, at 111–12; Fineman 2013.
2 Issacharoff & Nelson 2001, at 314.
3 42 U.S.C. § 2000e-2(a).
4 *See, e.g.*, McDonnell Douglas Corp. v. Green, 411 U.S. 792 (1973).
5 Arnow-Richman 2003, at 392; Kessler 2007, at 330; Leonard 2005, at 31.
6 Chamallas 1999, at 23–25; Porter 2010a, at 392.
7 Bornstein 2020; Finley 1986, at 1145.

around, however, was adopted by Congress when it passed the Pregnancy Discrimination Act (PDA). The PDA only requires employers to treat pregnant women the same as it treats other employees who are similar in their ability or inability to work.[8] So if an employer would provide six weeks of leave for an employee who breaks a leg or is recovering from surgery, the employer must give six weeks of leave to the mother recovering from childbirth.[9] By structuring the PDA in this way, equal treatment proponents hoped to get employers (and society) to ignore the differences between the sexes caused by the biological fact that only women can get pregnant.

Under formal equality, the outcome is worse for women with caregiving responsibilities. Formal equality is unable to account for differences that are culturally based (rather than biologically based), which includes most of women's caregiving roles. Given that women are still responsible for the majority of caregiving work, men and women are not similarly situated, and therefore, the formal equality principle allows employers to treat them differently.[10]

Beginning in the 1980s, some feminists began criticizing formal equality. "Special treatment" feminists generally believe that women need to be given modifications of normal workplace rules and policies to make up for the disadvantages caused by pregnancy, childbirth, and caregiving responsibilities. Special treatment has also been called "substantive" equality as opposed to "formal" equality. Substantive equality advocates note that even if we treat people alike, this might not lead to equal results. To make people equal, we often need to provide varying amounts of substantive entitlements.[11]

As discussed in Chapter 3, accommodations for people with disabilities also violate this equal treatment or formal equality norm, because the person with a disability is being treated differently—often being allowed to violate a neutral rule that others must follow or being given a "benefit" in the form of accommodations. Thus, the ADA requires employers to violate the equal treatment norm. This is why those theorists who believe in formal equality are troubled by the ADA's reasonable accommodation provision.[12]

Formal equality is similar to anti-classification theory. Under this theory, an employment decision based on any identity characteristic should be unlawful. Theorists who favor formal equality or anti-classification theories generally prefer "symmetrical" laws over "asymmetrical" laws. Title VII is a symmetrical law—it protects everyone against race or sex discrimination, even those who are in the

[8] 42 U.S.C. § 2000e(k).
[9] Porter 2010a, at 376.
[10] Finley 1986, at 1153–54; Porter 2010a, at 391.
[11] Arnow-Richman 2003, at 350; Ball 2005; Finley 1986, at 1146–47; Kessler 2001, at 439; Littleton 1987.
[12] Kelman 2001, at 837; Verkerke 2003.

majority (e.g., white men).[13] And as discussed in Chapter 3, the ADA is asymmetrical and only protects those employees who can prove that they have a disability.[14]

Naomi Schoenbaum argues that symmetrical laws are preferable because they are better at combatting stereotypes and can minimize employers' incentive to not hire individuals who are deemed more expensive to employ. In other words, if everyone is entitled to the same benefits in the workplace, employers will not make hiring decisions based on protected identities. Important to my project here, symmetrical laws are believed to avoid special treatment stigma.[15] To be clear, however, even those who agree that symmetrical laws might eliminate special treatment stigma do not necessarily support universal benefits for all.[16] And although I am proposing employer mandates in Chapters 8 and 9 that would benefit *all* employees, I am not in favor of symmetrical laws (or, more accurately, I do not oppose asymmetrical laws). For instance, I do not believe an employee without a disability should be able to sue an employer using the argument that they were discriminated against in favor of a disabled employee.

Just as anti-classification is related to formal equality, anti-subordination theory is related to substantive equality. Anti-subordination theorists recognize that not everyone who is treated differently because of a protected class is subordinated by that different treatment.[17] As a white person, I might not get a job if it is given to a person of color pursuant to a valid affirmative action program, but I am not oppressed or subordinated based on my race so under an anti-subordination theory, I should not have a claim.[18] Anti-subordination theory is also concerned with eliminating barriers that harm historically oppressed groups regardless of the fault of the decision maker.[19]

Anti-subordination theory supports the ADA's accommodation mandate, because even if employers were not intentionally discriminating against people with disabilities when they structured their workplaces (both the physical environment as well as social structures, such as workplace policies), these structural barriers harm people with disabilities, who have suffered a history of discrimination.[20] Anti-subordination theory also explains why the ADA does not allow "reverse" discrimination claims. Because people who do not have disabilities have not been historically oppressed based on their lack of disability, under the ADA, they cannot sue an employer if that employer gives some employment benefits to a disabled person.[21] The most

[13] Areheart 2017, at 1092. Bradley Areheart argues that symmetry is different from anti-classification because symmetry does not aspire to be blind to all classifications; rather, it protects all individuals regardless of those classifications. Areheart 2017, at 1102.

[14] Schoenbaum 2017a, at 83.

[15] Areheart 2017; Schoenbaum 2017a.

[16] Clarke 2011.

[17] Schoenbaum 2017a, at 83.

[18] Moore 2019, at 256.

[19] Clarke 2017, at 155.

[20] Colker 2007.

[21] Paul-Emile 2018, at 297.

significant criticism of the anti-subordination theory is that providing benefits to certain classes of people creates special treatment stigma, which I discussed in Chapter 6 and am trying to avoid.

The problem with anti-subordination theory segues nicely into my discussion of vulnerability theory. Vulnerability theory began with Martha Fineman.[22] Fineman's focus is to eliminate the negative connotations associated with dependency. As she states, dependency is "inevitable and universal ... All of us were dependent as children, and many of us will be dependent as we age, become ill, or suffer disabilities."[23] Because dependency is universal and inevitable, it should not be condemned and instead should be supported. Fineman's work focusing on supporting caregivers is based on the argument that the work performed by caregivers is necessary for our society's survival. But her theory can be equally applied to people with disabilities[24] because those with disabilities are criticized for needing care, just as caregivers are criticized for needing workplace accommodations to allow them to care for others. The basic premise of the vulnerability theory is helpful for my project. In other words, because everyone is vulnerable to dependency, needing care (people with disabilities) and giving care (workers with caregiving responsibilities) should not be stigmatized.[25]

However, one critique of Fineman's theory is that it is fairly abstract. In other words, the theory itself tells us little about *how* the government should support caregiving and nothing about what role employers should have in supporting caregiving or helping people with disabilities who sometimes need care.[26] It also does not address issues regarding how we should respond when workplace accommodations affect other workers.

To sum up where we are so far, formal equality (a/k/a equal treatment or anti-classification) cannot account for the differences both people with disabilities and workers with caregiving responsibilities face in the workplace. Substantive equality (a/k/a special treatment or anti-subordination) would allow workplaces to treat certain workers differently because of their different circumstances but would create the stigma that accompanies special treatment. Vulnerability theory tries to address that stigma by getting us to recognize that, because we all are vulnerable to dependency, vulnerability should not be stigmatized. But vulnerability theory is mostly focused on the state and how the state should support the caregiving needs of all vulnerable members of society.

In prior work, I struggled to find a theory to support the broad reform I was proposing, which argued in favor of providing accommodations to both workers with

22 Martha Fineman has written volumes regarding her vulnerability theory. Much of what I say here is derived from Fineman 2000.

23 Fineman 2000, at 18.

24 *See generally* Satz 2008.

25 Kohn 2014, at 9–10.

26 Kohn 2014, at 12–14.

disabilities and those with caregiving responsibilities. What theory would address special treatment stigma—that is, how can we justify accommodations and other assistance given to particular groups of employees in a way that eliminates the resentment felt by both employers and coworkers? And with respect to caregiving, the theory needed to address the concepts of autonomy and choice. Why should caregivers who have made seemingly autonomous decisions regarding having children and how they arrange their family lives be entitled to any special assistance in the workplace? I believe communitarian theory responds to these concerns.[27]

2 Communitarian Theory

Communitarianism rests on the idea that we have a mutual responsibility to each other as citizens and that a stable community depends on this shared responsibility. Communitarians criticize the idea that we are fully independent beings with no obligation to each other except to "avoid the active infliction of harm."[28] The contemporary communitarian movement began in 1990 when a group of ethicists, social philosophers, and social scientists met to discuss the issues that harm our society.[29] One such issue was Americans' tendency to demand "rights" with no regard for responsibilities toward each other.[30] Although communitarians believe rights are important, they believe that those rights are secondary to our responsibilities to others.[31] They believe that focusing on the communities to which we belong can help overcome some of the problems in America.[32] As leading communitarian Amitai Etzioni states "We adopted the name Communitarian to emphasize that the time has come to attend to our responsibilities to the conditions and elements we all share, to the community."[33]

Nowhere was this debate between rights and responsibility to others more prominent than during the pandemic. Anyone who was not living under a rock during the pandemic is well aware of the debates over wearing masks and the COVID-19 vaccine. In both cases, the "rights" demanders insisted that wearing a mask or getting a vaccine was (or should be) a purely independent choice that they get to make for themselves. On the other side of the debate (and frankly, the right side of the debate) were those Americans who recognized that wearing a mask and getting a vaccine was not only about their own health and safety but was necessary to protect others in their community. Although the "rights" demanders were very vocal, it is

[27] Porter 2010a; Porter 2014e.

[28] Porter 2014e (quoting David Abraham, *Are Rights the Right Thing? Individual Rights, Communitarian Purposes and America's Problems*, 25 Conn. L. Rev. 947, 956 (1993)).

[29] Etzioni 1993, at 14–15.

[30] Etzioni 1993.

[31] Kessler 2001, at 430.

[32] Ball 2005.

[33] Etzioni 1993, at 15; *see also* Dowd 1990.

perhaps reassuring to know that about 80 percent of the population supported wearing masks to protect others during the pre-vaccine period of COVID-19.[34] And around 60 percent of the population supports vaccine mandates, although vaccines (more than masks) also protect oneself.[35] Perhaps this is a positive sign that we are ready to move away from an over fixation on rights and embrace a communitarian perspective.[36]

The communitarian theory supports accommodating people with disabilities and caregivers. The resentment non-disabled coworkers feel toward individuals who receive some type of special benefits in the workplace is evidence of an overemphasis on individual rights. If we instead viewed the workplace as a community and understood our responsibilities toward others in our community, we should support rather than resent our coworkers who need accommodations in order to perform their jobs.[37]

Consider this example. Imagine that you work as a cargo handler for a major airline. You have worked in this job (which is often physically arduous) for 20 years. Every so often, a position opens up in the mailroom, which is a much less physically arduous position (but same pay and status). Every time you apply for this lateral position (for which you are qualified), another employee who has more seniority also bids on the position. Based on the airline's seniority system, the airline must give the position to the most senior employee. When the position opens once again, you realize you will be the most senior person to bid on it. You are excited to finally be in a job where your knees won't ache. But before it's given to you, you find out that the airline is considering whether it must give the position to an employee with a disability who has also applied for the same position. This coworker can no longer perform the duties of his cargo handler position because of his disability. Because the airline is protecting the employee's privacy (and because this is a very large employer), you don't know who the other worker is. All you know is that the coworker is junior to you on the seniority list and that he will be terminated if he is not given the mailroom position. Also assume that no one else has bid on the position, so it's between you and the disabled coworker. What is your reaction to this? Do you think you should be given the position? Or should the employer give it to the disabled employee so that he remains employed?

This hypothetical is loosely based on the facts of a real case, *US Airways v. Barnett*.[38] Every year when I teach this case, I ask my students the same questions posed here. They often want to know more about the disabled employee. Do they

34 Fearnow 2021.
35 Jones, J. 2021.
36 Jacoby 2020, at 519.
37 Porter 2014e.
38 U.S. Airways, Inc. v. Barnett, 535 U.S. 391 (2007).

know him? Is he a friend? Is he a nice person or kind of a jerk?[39] When I take all of those variables off the table, their responses are mixed (as I imagine yours will be).

Although I do not know this to be empirically true, I suspect that many of you reading this (and maybe even the majority of you, although I hope not the *vast* majority) will think that you should get the position over the disabled employee. You've worked really hard and have been a very loyal employee for many years. This mailroom position is one of the benefits of your loyalty and you should get it over someone who hasn't been employed as long. If the employer gives it to the disabled employee, many of you would be resentful and maybe even angry.[40]

But some of you will feel differently. Some of you would be disappointed not to get the position but would recognize the fact that your disabled coworker will *lose his job* if he is not given the mailroom position. Maybe he has a family to support. Maybe he's older. Even if he's not older, you recognize that his disability might preclude him from easily getting another job. You determine that keeping your coworker employed is more important than the airline giving the job to you. Plus, you know a similar position will likely become available again in the future and you will still be at the top of the seniority list and will probably get it. If this was your response, you now understand and embrace communitarian theory. Or at the very least—your response is consistent with communitarianism.[41]

B *The Practical Justification*

Although I believe employees *should* care about the well-being of their coworkers (especially if those coworkers might be terminated if not accommodated), I recognize that many workers will nevertheless resent what they see as "special treatment" given to coworkers.[42] Accordingly, this section explains why everyone benefits when workers with disabilities and coworkers with caregiving responsibilities are accommodated. In other words, if you're not on board with communitarian theory, I hope to convince you that you should still support accommodating caregivers and people with disabilities.

[39] *See* Schur et al. 2020 (whether coworkers support accommodations for disabled employees often turns on how well-liked the disabled employee is).

[40] One other variable worth mentioning—the employer in my hypothetical is under no *legal* obligation to follow its seniority system. This is quite unusual because most employers who use seniority systems are unionized so the seniority system is part of the collective bargaining agreement (CBA) between the employer and the union. In such a situation, if the more senior employee is passed over for the transfer in favor of the less senior disabled worker, the union arguably has a grievance against the employer for violating the CBA. In the actual case, the employer was not unionized; its seniority system was unilaterally imposed; and therefore, no one had a valid cause of action if the employer violated it. U.S. Airways, Inc. v. Barnett, 535 U.S. 391 (2007).

[41] Porter 2007.

[42] Travis 2009b; *see also* Engel & Munger 2003 (stating that "forced empathy" is not the answer).

1 Benefits of Accommodating People with Disabilities

The ADA provides many benefits to non-disabled employees. Perhaps most importantly, non-disabled employees should feel a stake in the ADA's future because anyone might become disabled and fall into the ADA's protected class at any time. This is the one minority group you might join at any time.[43] This is especially true after the ADAAA made it much easier to meet the definition of disability. But even if a person never becomes disabled, there are still tangible benefits the ADA provides to non-disabled employees.

First, the ADA has increased the privacy protections for medical information in the workplace. The ADA has very specific provisions regarding when employers can ask medical-related questions, how they can ask them, and what they can do with the information. After the ADA was enacted, most employers ended their routine practice of asking invasive medical questions.[44]

Another benefit the ADA provides to non-disabled employees is what Michelle Travis calls "remedy spillover," where the employer changes the workplace to meet an accommodation demand or remedy an ADA claim, and that change or remedy benefits others in the workplace. Examples include installing a ramp or elevator that makes getting around the office easier for everyone; ergonomic redesigns to offices or purchases of equipment that other employees can use to make lifting or other tasks easier; higher cubicle dividers for an employee with a mental disability but that also help eliminate distractions for all workers; a new air filtration system for an employee with severe asthma that improves the air quality for everyone; and other accommodations that might be experimental but that, if effective, will be useful for many non-disabled employees.[45]

Finally, the ADA's interactive process has led many employers to engage in discussions about accommodations with non-disabled employees as a way of avoiding litigation and potential liability. Stephen Befort calls the ADA's interactive process a "procedural revolution." Employers often accommodate non-disabled employees to avoid having to make the determination of whether the employee is disabled or not (and therefore entitled to accommodations). The reason employers do this is because, if they are wrong about their conclusion that an employee is *not* disabled and they refused to accommodate her, they could be liable for that failure. Thus, risk-averse employers will try to accommodate employees even if they do not know (or cannot easily determine) whether the accommodation would be required by the ADA.[46]

43 Anderson 2000, at 150; Hickox 2016, at 196; Kanter 2011; O'Brien 2005; Waterstone 2015b.

44 Travis 2009b.

45 Emens 2008; Engel & Munger 2003; Fishkin 2014; Harris, S. 2007; Hickox 2016; Hickox & Case 2020; Schur et al. 2013; Travis 2009b.

46 Befort 2004; Travis 2009b.

In addition to the benefits to employees (and employers, discussed shortly), accommodating people with disabilities also benefits society. Specifically, accommodating disabled workers will allow them to remain employed and therefore decrease the cost to society of dependence.[47]

2 Benefits of Accommodating Caregivers

Just as accommodating disabled employees benefits non-disabled employees, accommodating caregivers benefits non-caregivers for several reasons. First, just as everyone could become disabled at any time, everyone could be forced into a caregiving role at any time. Even those who choose not to have children might unexpectedly find themselves caring for a sick or disabled spouse, partner, parent, or other loved one.[48] As noted by Martha Fineman, dependency is inevitable. We all begin life dependent on others, most of us will give care to others who depend on us, and almost all of us will end life dependent on others.[49] Therefore, all employees stand to benefit from a law that requires employers to provide flexibility to workers with caregiving responsibilities, either because we might be caregivers or because we might need care, and will therefore reap the benefits of having institutional structures in place that will allow our loved ones to care for us without having to sacrifice their jobs.[50]

Second, we all benefit from parents' choices to procreate because society needs procreation to continue and employers rely on procreation to continue to staff their workplaces.[51] As noted by Fineman, all of society is dependent upon caretaking labor in order to reproduce itself.[52] More importantly, everyone lives with the consequences of children who are not brought up well and who then harm communities through misconduct and crime. Giving parents the tools necessary to responsibly balance work and family ultimately benefits everyone. There are many studies about the harms of too little parental supervision.[53] Moreover, marginalizing women in the workplace contributes to the poverty of children.[54] Finally, there are also benefits to allowing disabled or elderly adults to be cared for by loved ones. Not only do adults have better health and happiness outcomes when cared for by loved ones, but also, society needs the 33 million unpaid family caregivers to

47 Bagenstos 2000, at 463; Burgdorf 1991; Coker 2005; Rothstein 2019; Stein 2003; Stein et al. 2014.

48 Arnow-Richman 2003; Porter 2010a; Porter 2014e; Porter 2016b.

49 Fineman 2000; Fineman 2013, at 17; *see also* Eichner 1998; Widiss 2021b.

50 Porter 2016b; *see also* Albiston & Fisk 2021; Lester 2005; Williams, JC 2001.

51 Kaminer 2004, at 319; Kessler 2001, at 453; Roush 2009. *But see* Jones 2014, at 1301 (no social utility in reproduction because the planet is already overcrowded).

52 Fineman 2000.

53 Eichner 1998; Dowd 2004; Kainer 2004, at 316–17; Lester 2005; Williams, JC 2010.

54 Jacobs & Gerson 2004; Kessler 2001, at 388.

continue giving that care—the long-term care system would collapse without the unpaid labor of family caregivers.[55]

3 The Business Case for Accommodations

I just explained how accommodating people with disabilities and workers with caregiving responsibilities benefits coworkers (and society). This subsection discusses how providing these accommodations benefits employers. The literature on the "business case" for flexible workplaces is voluminous. Several scholars have studied the social science literature that demonstrates that employers benefit when they provide more flexibility in their workplaces. These benefits include decreased attrition (with all of its attendant costs of recruiting, hiring, and training new employees); increased productivity; decreased absenteeism, and improved loyalty and morale.[56] Moreover, workplace flexibility can improve consumer and workplace safety, as distracted workers are more likely to make costly mistakes or become injured. Reduced stress might also lower employers' health insurance and related costs.[57]

Attrition costs alone are no joke. Joan Williams has cited costs of replacing an hourly worker as ranging from 40 to 75 percent of the worker's annual salary. Williams also tells the story of a case where a bus driver was fired for missing work because of a family conflict. In a subsequent dispute over the termination, an arbitrator questioned the wisdom of the employer's decision to terminate given that the demographic composition of that workforce indicates that the terminated employee's replacement is also likely to experience work–family conflicts.[58]

Some scholars are skeptical about the argument that employers benefit from providing workplace flexibility policies. For example, Michael Selmi makes a law and economics argument that if there was significant evidence that these benefits existed, employers would voluntarily choose to provide flexible workplace options to their employees.[59] I do not find this argument persuasive, for several reasons.

First, there is very little reason to believe that employers (or more specifically, supervisors and managers) know about these studies, as most of this work is in academic journals and academic press books.[60] Second, because providing employees *more* benefits seems counterintuitive to the common goal of keeping labor costs down, it is possible that managers and human resources personnel would discount these studies even if they were aware of them. When you think about the fact that

55 Porter 2016b.

56 Anderson 2000, at 123; Arnow-Richman 2003, at 382; Case 2020; Flake 2020, at 1722; Harris, J. 2021b; Harris, S. 2007; Hickox & Kaminer 2004; Jacobs & Gerson 2004, at 1887; Kanter 2022; Schur et al. 2014; Smith 2001, at 1478; Williams, JC 2010, at 77; Williams, JC & Segal 2003.

57 Flake 2015, at 175; Schartz et al. 2006a; Williams, JC 2010.

58 Williams, JC 2010, at 81–82.

59 Selmi 2007, at 582–85.

60 Arnow-Richman 2010, at 1107.

most upper-level managers who have decision-making authority are (even today) men who have stay-at-home spouses, it's no wonder that they do not see any real need to help their employees better balance work and family. And finally, as I have argued before, the effectiveness of providing flexibility benefits is unpredictable. Regardless of the research that indicates it is financially feasible and even beneficial in the long run for employers to provide family friendly workplace policies, employers cannot predict the future. In other words, even if we know (and believe) that, on average, providing workers with a more flexible and humane work life will lead to increased productivity and loyalty of those employees, it is impossible to know in any given case whether that benefit will accrue. When employers are asked to respond to individual accommodation requests, they are often having to guess as to whether the particular employee who is making the request is going to be one of the more loyal employees who stays and becomes more productive or whether they will (for all kinds of reasons) take advantage of the flexibility or leave the workplace altogether. This uncertainty makes employers more reluctant to take a gamble on providing some of these benefits.[61]

Accordingly, despite the skepticism expressed by some, the business case for providing workplace flexibility is strong. But even though I have (hopefully) demonstrated the benefits of accommodating people with disabilities and caregivers, my proposals in Chapters 8 and 9 are universal in nature, protecting *all* employees. How can I justify that universal coverage? I turn to the benefits of protecting *everyone* next.

III JUSTIFICATIONS FOR PROTECTING EVERYONE

In this section I will discuss five primary benefits of protecting all workers, rather than having a targeted mandate that only benefits specific groups of employees: (1) eliminating special treatment stigma; (2) avoiding the necessity (and difficulty) of claiming a particular identity; (3) providing work/life balance to everyone; (4) dismantling employers' structural norms; and (5) in addition to the argument that workplace flexibility is efficient (just discussed), employers will also benefit from the simplicity of administering mandates that require very little recordkeeping.

A *Eliminating Special Treatment Stigma*

As should be obvious from what you've read so far, one of my main goals is to eliminate (or at least minimize) special treatment stigma. Accordingly, the most important justification for these universal mandates is that they should eliminate special treatment stigma. Why? Because if all employees were entitled to the

[61] Porter 2010b; *see also* Arnow-Richman 2003, at 384; Arnow-Richman 2010; Jacobs & Gerson 2004.

workplace benefits I propose in Chapters 8 and 9, no one would be receiving special treatment, so special treatment stigma would disappear.

Similar arguments have been made by other scholars about universal mandates.[62] For instance, a group of scholars argued that accommodating every *body* (distinct from accommodating *everyone*) will remove the perception that accommodations are stigmatizing.[63] Several other scholars have argued for a broad definition of disability in order to minimize the stigma that accompanies receiving accommodations in the workplace.[64]

Similarly, in the caregiving context, several scholars have argued that providing workplace flexibility to all employees will eliminate the stigma of only providing family friendly benefits to caregivers.[65] In sum, because providing accommodations only to some employees is so stigmatizing, eliminating that stigma through universal solutions is the primary goal of and justification for this book's proposals.

B *Avoiding Problems with Proving Protected Class*

Another benefit of this proposal is that universal benefits will mostly avoid the stigma of classification. In order to be protected under current law, an employee has to fall into a particular protected class. Primarily, this includes people with disabilities, but it also includes those who need accommodations for religious practices or because of pregnancy.[66] Moreover, Chapter 8's proposal regarding absences from work is also universal in nature. This proposal would avoid the necessity of claiming the very narrow protection of the FMLA.

In addition to the discussion in Chapter 6, that proving membership in a protected class is stigmatizing, it also might be difficult. The definition of disability, although broadened after the ADAAA, remains complicated and many litigants lose on this threshold question.[67] Sometimes they lose because they don't understand the breadth of the definition of disability. Sometimes they make statements during their deposition that tend to downplay or disclaim their disabilities, and then courts use this testimony to negate the existence of their disability, which causes them to lose their case.[68] Under my proposal in Chapter 9, employees would need to report that they have a physical limitation that necessitates an accommodation to perform the job's essential functions, but it does not matter if that limitation is caused by old age, pregnancy, disability, or simply small stature.

62 Schur et al. 2014; Selmi 2007.
63 Stein et al. 2014.
64 Burgdorf 1997; O'Brien 2005, at 5, 21; Porter 2022; Porter 2014a, at 326; Travis 2009b; Satz 2008.
65 Albiston 2010; Arnow-Richman 2003; Jones 2014; Williams, JC 2001.
66 Porter 2016b, at 123–24.
67 Porter 2019a; Stein et al. 2014.
68 Porter 2022.

Although leave under the FMLA does not involve claiming a protected class, proving FMLA coverage can be difficult. The primary reason employees apply for FMLA leave is for their own serious health conditions, and to a lesser extent, because of the serious health condition of a child, spouse, or parent who needs care. The regulations that implement the FMLA's definition of a serious health condition are very complicated. Accordingly, many employees who apply for FMLA leave are denied.[69] The proposals discussed in Chapter 8 relating to leaves of absence protect all employees, so workers will avoid the difficulty of proving FMLA coverage.

C *Providing Balance to Everyone*

Especially after COVID-19, where many of us were (and still are) available for work via our cell phones and computers at all hours of the day, creating some balance between our work lives and personal lives is even more urgent. But even before the pandemic, scholars had renewed their efforts to get employers, courts, and policy makers to understand that it is not just parents who need balance; everyone is happier and healthier when they have a good balance between their work lives and personal lives.[70]

Trina Jones has argued that providing flexibility benefits only to parents involves "implicit assumptions about the personal activities of [childfree workers] and risk[s] perpetuating the notion that the people and activities in a [childfree worker's] life are not as important as the people and activities in the lives of married couples or parents."[71] First of all, child-free employees might have caregiving responsibilities for other people in their lives, whether they are related by blood or not. Second, employees might engage in many other activities that are beneficial to the community, such as volunteering with a homeless shelter or other community organizations. Third, it is not healthy for *anyone* to work extremely long hours; these employees are likely to experience burnout, which could affect their physical or mental health and lead to lower productivity at work.[72]

Vicki Schultz and Allison Hoffman argued that work/life balance is so important for all workers that they proposed a reduced-hour workweek for all employees.[73] As I discuss in Chapter 8, I do not agree with their proposal, but I do agree with its rationale.

D *Dismantling Structural Norms*

The proposal discussed in Chapter 8, with respect to leaves of absence and other short-term absences will have the effect of dismantling two structural norms: (1) the

69 *See infra* Chapter 8.

70 Befort 2004; Clarke 2011, at 1236–38; Heyer 2007, at 289; Jacobs & Gerson 2004; Jones 2014; Kaminer 2004; Schultz & Hoffman 2006; Smith 2001; Williams, JC 2001.

71 Jones 2014, at 1301; *see also* Jacobs & Gerson 2004.

72 Jones 2014, at 1304, 1308.

73 Schultz & Hoffman 2006, at 131, 135.

norm that demands an uninterrupted career with no time off for caregiving and/or illness or disabilities; and (2) the norm that requires perfect attendance unless an absence falls into very specific (and often very narrow) exceptions. But Chapter 9 proposes an individual accommodation mandate. It might seem odd to think that an individual accommodation mandate could work to dismantle the structural norms regarding hours, schedules, shifts, or where work is performed. In fact, one well-known quote states "You can't solve an institutional problem with an individual accommodation."[74] Respectfully, I disagree.

Although I discuss this in much more detail in Chapter 8 when I explore alternative solutions, the basic idea is this. Individual accommodations have the potential to encourage employers to see the benefits of making broader structural changes to their workplaces.[75] For instance, if several employees in one workplace seek an accommodation of flextime hours (starting and stopping work at different times of the day), the employer might realize that allowing flextime is not only relatively simple, but also that it would be more efficient for the employer to set up a system whereby all employees can work flextime hours rather than making individual modifications for those employees who seek this accommodation. Similarly, several requests for the same modification of one of the physical functions of the job might cause the employer to realize that there is a better way of performing a particular function or that there are assistive devices that could help all employees perform that function.[76] For instance, there are many employees who have lifting restrictions—because of disabilities (back or other impairments), because of advanced age, because of pregnancy, or even because of small stature. If these employees all seek a modification of the heavy lifting functions of a job, the employer might find a way to restructure the job to avoid (or at least minimize) the heavy lifting required.[77]

Disability scholars who proposed a similar universal accommodation mandate also tout the possibility of a universal accommodation mandate causing employers to change their workplace structures. As they state, their proposal should lead "employers who value efficiency and innovation to prophylactically implement changes in policy so as to make the workplace more accessible for everyone."[78] In some ways, this proposal is similar to proposals in favor of "universal design," which is an architectural principle in which environments are designed to be useable by

[74] Williams, JC & Segal 2003, at 71; *see also* Schultz 2010.

[75] Porter 2016b, at 124; Travis 2009b, at 352–53.

[76] Stein et al. 2014.

[77] Emens 2008; O'Brien 2005; Porter 2016b, at 124–25.

[78] Stein et al. 2014, at 751. To be clear, their proposal is different than my universal accommodation mandate that I first proposed in 2016 and elaborate on in Chapter 9. Their proposal is focused only on modifications needed if an employee cannot perform the physical functions of the job. It would not cover employees who seek accommodations for caregiving obligations or any other reason. *See generally* Stein et al. 2014; *see also* Porter, 2016b, at 111.

everyone to the maximum extent possible.[79] As noted by Michael Stein and his coauthors, if "employers anticipate having to make more accommodation-related changes to the workplace environment, they may be more apt to invest time and effort on the earlier 'design' end to avoid subsequent needs to retrofit."[80]

The experience with work from home during the COVID-19 pandemic is a perfect example of this. As discussed in Chapter 5, for many years before the pandemic, employers often refused to let employees work from home. This was true if an employee wanted to work from home for caregiving reasons (e.g., to be home when kids get home from school, etc.). And it was also true even if employees *needed* a work-from-home accommodation because of a disability. Employers would routinely argue that in-person presence is an essential function of the job and courts most often sided with the employers. Working from home for many jobs was simply unimaginable.[81] But the pandemic changed all of that. Remote work became feasible and often very successful. Moving forward, many employers will voluntarily allow employees to work from home.[82]

Although it took a pandemic to dismantle the structural norm of in-person presence, one way to mimic the experience of the pandemic with other structural norms is to have many employees seeking similar accommodations. As discussed, many employees seeking the same accommodation should cause employers to realize that it would be more efficient to restructure the workplace than to consider dozens of individual accommodation requests. This would not (and cannot) happen if only people with disabilities have the right to seek accommodations. Even with the broadened definition of disability, there simply are not enough disabled employees seeking the same accommodation that would make an employer realize that restructuring the workplace is more efficient than considering and granting individual accommodation requests.

E *Benefits to Employers*

Although my proposals are primarily motivated at ending the subordination of workers who cannot meet the ideal worker norm, I know that for any proposal to obtain the support of employers, it needs to benefit employers (or at the very least, not harm employers). I believe this proposal does.

First, the business benefits of providing "family friendly" benefits to caregiving employees (discussed previously) apply equally to accommodating all workers, not just caregiving workers. Employers will benefit by keeping valuable employees employed rather than having to undergo the significant costs of attrition, which

[79] Porter 2016b, at 125; Satz 2008, at 560; Stein et al. 2014, at 751.
[80] Stein et al. 2014, at 751.
[81] Porter 2021.
[82] Porter 2021.

include recruiting and hiring costs, as well as training costs. Moreover, evidence suggests that employees who are accommodated are more productive, have less absenteeism, and are happier and more loyal.[83] A related benefit that might accrue to employers is a reduction in the number of employees getting injured on the job, which could reduce the employers' workers compensation costs.[84] Health insurance costs might decrease if employees have better health outcomes from having a flexible workplace.[85]

Second, providing benefits to everyone (both the leave benefits discussed in Chapter 8, and the open-ended universal accommodation mandate discussed in Chapter 9) will avoid the significant administrative expenses of determining whether employees meet the requirements of various statutory protections. This is a corollary to the argument just made regarding the benefits to workers of not having to claim a particular protected class. As I discuss more in Chapter 8, human resources professionals and managers dedicate thousands of hours to determining whether employees are entitled to leave or whether their absences should be excused. And because determining whether someone has a disability under the ADA has become more complex since the Amendments, employers often must engage legal services to determine whether an employee has a disability. These costs are significant and would be avoided with my proposed universal solutions.[86]

IV CONCLUSION

I hope I have accomplished two things with this chapter. First, I hope I have convinced you that the workplace community benefits when people with disabilities and workers with caregiving responsibilities are allowed to successfully combine their jobs with their health needs and/or the needs of their families. But even if I haven't, I hope I have convinced you that universal solutions are the best way to eliminate the subordination experienced by people with disabilities and workers with caregiving responsibilities, and the best way to allow *all* workers the ability to successfully combine their work lives and their personal lives. In the next two chapters, I turn to the logistics of this workplace reimagined.

83 Galinsky et al. 2008; Porter 2016b at 126; Schur et al., at 607, 612–13.
84 Galinsky et al. 2008; Porter 2016b, at 125.
85 Albiston & O'Connor 2016; Galinsky et al. 2008.
86 Clarke 2011; Travis 2009b, at 360.

8

The Workplace Reimagined, Part I

Tackling Time Off

I INTRODUCTION: EXPLORING THE ALTERNATIVES

In Chapter 1, I explained what a reimagined workplace looks like. First, it recognizes that bodies and brains come in all shapes, sizes, abilities, and different ways of performing various tasks. Second, it recognizes that virtually all workers will sometimes need modifications to one or more of the following workplace norms: 40+ hours, mandatory overtime, 9–5 schedule, few or no absences, and work that must be always performed at a central location. Accordingly, a reimagined workplace allows *all* employees to benefit from the ability to perform job tasks in a different way and to have access to some measures of workplace flexibility.

In this chapter, I begin a two-chapter discussion of how we get there. But before I get to the specifics of the first part of my proposal, it's important to survey the literature proposing other reforms in order to explain why my proposals are different.

I believe it's accurate to divide up all major proposals (directed at employers[1]) into four categories: (1) litigation using current laws; (2) collective action; (3) legislation that would mandate changes to workplace rules and policies directly; and (4) individual accommodations.

Two other proposals have been made that I will not be addressing in depth. First, scholars have proposed amending our anti-discrimination laws to specifically include "parental status" (or more broadly, "caregiver status") as a protected class. This is not at all directed at people with disabilities and, as explained by Peggie Smith, would not effectuate large-scale reform of the magnitude I am proposing

[1] To be clear, there are certainly good reasons to argue that the government should take some responsibility for helping both people with disabilities and workers with caregiving responsibilities. Samuel Bagenstos and Martha Fineman (respectively) have made these arguments (Bagenstos 2004; Fineman 2000). But my focus is on employers and the employment relationship.

here.[2] Second, in part borrowing from the United Kingdom's experience, several scholars have discussed the benefits of a "process law" that would allow employees to ask for accommodations without fear of retaliation and would force employers to consider those accommodations and provide a reason if the employer rejects the request.[3] This idea has gained some traction; the Flexibility for Working Families Act has been proposed in Congress as a way of allowing employees to request accommodations without penalty, but the employer is under no obligation to grant the request.[4] Although I believe there is a significant benefit in simply being allowed to ask for an accommodation, asking alone is not enough.

A *Litigation*

Some scholars argue that our laws already provide all of the necessary tools to achieve workplace equality for both workers with disabilities and employees with caregiving responsibilities.[5] With respect to disabled workers, I agree that the ADA could be (and should be) interpreted to require employers to grant all kinds of accommodations, but the success rate for failure-to-accommodate claims is low, even after the ADA Amendments Act.[6] And as discussed in Chapter 5, when workers with disabilities request modifications to the structural norms of the workplace, employers and courts are even more reluctant to allow those accommodations.

With respect to providing flexibility for caregiving employees, as I discussed in Chapter 2, our current laws have not meaningfully provided the workplace flexibility needed to successfully balance work and family. Joan Williams is probably the most prominent scholar to argue otherwise. To be sure, there has been a dramatic increase in the number of "family responsibilities discrimination" suits brought and won (or settled for large amounts of money).[7] But these successful cases are not cases where a caregiving employee requested a workplace accommodation, was denied, and sued.

Williams has frequently argued that the accommodation model cannot work for caregiving and that it is not the best solution. With respect to the accommodation model for religious practices (under Title VII) and disabilities (ADA), she argues that in both of those situations, employees have a wide variety of needs; thus, only an individual accommodation mandate can work. She then states

2 Smith 2002.
3 Arnow-Richman 2010; Schoenbaum 2017b; Travis 2005.
4 Flexibility for Working Families Act, S. 777, 114th Cong. (2015); Albiston & O'Connor 2016, at 56.
5 Travis 2005; Williams, JC & Segal 2003.
6 Befort 2013; Colker 2010; Eyer 2021; Lin 2021.
7 Williams, JC & Bornstein 2006.

> In the work-family arena, there is not a dazzling array [of needed accommodations] but a dyad. The question is whether workplaces will continue to be designed around the bodies and life patterns of men, with "accommodations" offered to women, or whether workplace norms will be redesigned to take into account the reproductive biology and social roles of women and family caregivers, as well … What women need, in other words, is not accommodation but equality.[8]

What confuses me about this statement is that it is unclear to me whether Williams is advocating for forcing employers (presumably through legislation) to modify structural norms or suggesting that successful lawsuits can be brought arguing that workplace norms designed around men's lives are discriminatory. The latter suggestion would presumably be accomplished through disparate impact claims under Title VII, which assert that a workplace norm (e.g., mandatory overtime) has a disproportionate effect on women. Michelle Travis and others have written about how disparate impact lawsuits could (and should) work to transform the workplace, but these lawsuits have yet to gain much traction.[9] And Joan Williams devotes very little time to discussing disparate impact claims. But she also does not seem to be suggesting that we enact legislation that would change the structural norms directly. She states that it is unlawful to structure the workplace around male's lives, but then virtually all of the lawsuits she discusses are individual intentional disc. claims arguing that the employers made adverse decisions based on bias or stereotypes.[10]

Williams has been critical of scholars who discuss the limitations of using litigation to effectuate significant progress, stating: "While scholarship and free inquiry should flourish, having feminists devote their energies to the excavation of case law that will be used to defeat women's claims in court seems an odd role for feminist jurisprudence."[11] Lucky for me, I don't have the time or space to delve into particular cases that have been unsuccessful, so I can't be accused of being a bad feminist. And I am not suggesting that litigation has no value. In fact, in this area, the litigation and advocacy efforts of the Worklife Law Center[12] that Williams runs has done some really great work bringing these cases and theories to the attention of plaintiffs' lawyers, employers, and courts. And there is evidence that *some* employers have changed *some* of their workplace policies to recognize the work/family conflicts their employees are experiencing.[13] But litigation has not caused (and short of a significantly revitalized disparate impact claim, *cannot* cause) all employers to modify their policies regarding the structural norms of the workplace.

8 Williams, JC & Segal 2003, at 84–85.
9 Albiston 2010; Grossman & Thomas 2020; Travis 2005; Williams, JC 2001.
10 Williams, JC 2001; Williams, JC & Segal 2003.
11 Williams, JC & Segal 2003, at 112.
12 https://worklifelaw.org.
13 Williams, JC & Bornstein 2006.

B Collective Action

For decades, scholars have advocated for collective action to change the entrenched norms of the workplace and to make the workplace better for all workers.[14] Back in 1997, Arlie Hochschild, advocated for redefining time norms by using collective action. As she states "The more daunting but ultimately more promising approach to unknotting the time bind requires collective—rather than individual—action: workers must directly challenge the organization" of American workplaces.[15] Hochschild notes that it is not just women with children who are eager to break the time binds; men also want to work less (either to have a better work/life balance themselves or to give hours back to a laid-off colleague). She believes that employees should ban together to advocate for working fewer hours and to change the workplace culture that judges merit based on the number of hours logged rather than the amount of work that is completed or the quality of that work. As one inspiring example of the collective coming together, Hochschild points to the experience of one company:

> When a demand for a product is down, normally a company fires some people and makes the rest work twice as hard. So we put it to a vote of everyone in the plant. We asked them what they wanted to do: layoffs for some workers or thirty-two-hour workweeks for everyone. They thought about it and decided they'd rather hold the team together. So we went to a thirty-two-hour a week schedule for everyone during a down time. We took everybody's hours and salary down—executives, too.[16]

Other scholars have similarly argued about the merits of collective action. For instance, although sometimes critical of how disabled employees are treated in unionized settings (more on that shortly), Stacy Hickox argues in favor of the "greater role of collective bargaining in providing accommodations for the benefit of the employer, union, and employees with disabilities."[17] She argues in favor of a provision in collective bargaining agreements that would spell out a procedure for the parties to consider accommodation requests. She opines that bargaining over accommodations should lead to several benefits to employers (such as avoiding discrimination claims and contractual claims under the CBA) and should lead to more and better accommodations for employees with disabilities. If these accommodations are negotiated with the union, this can lead to better results not only for the employee with a disability but also for coworkers. Because accommodations might benefit non-disabled coworkers, harm those workers, or be neutral with regard

[14] Dominguez 1991 at 285; Smith 2001; Williams, JC 2001.

[15] Hochschild 1997, at 230.

[16] Hochschild 1997, at 138.

[17] Hickox 2016, at 151–52.

to the effects on coworkers, the union could be careful to structure accommodations in a way that would minimize the burden on other employees.[18]

On the other hand, some have argued that unions have not traditionally been supportive of the needs of women or people with disabilities.[19] Hickox points to studies indicating that the coverage of a CBA negatively affected the possibility that a person with a disability would be accommodated. Collective bargaining agreements are usually against flexibility, but flexibility is what is needed for most accommodations.[20] Marion Crain has argued that historically, unions cared more about men's role as breadwinners and therefore did not prioritize issues that primarily benefit women, such as equal pay, maternity leave, or other flexible policies.[21]

More importantly, even if unions began taking seriously the workplace flexibility needs of all their workers, the union density is simply too low to accomplish any significant change.[22] I am all in favor of higher levels of unionization; however, achieving that goal is beyond the scope of this book.

C *Legislation to Change Structural Norms Directly*

Given that most employers continue to have very rigid norms regarding when and where work is performed, one possible solution is legislation that would force employers to change those norms.[23] The passage of the Fair Labor Standards Act (FLSA) that gave us the 40-hour workweek is an example of such legislation. Although the FLSA was somewhat successful in ending the practice of requiring very long hours without overtime pay, the breadth of its exceptions makes it ineffective in giving workers the flexibility many of them need.[24] And in fact, it has had the effect of entrenching the 40-hour workweek, so employers, courts, and even employees assume that 40 hours is somehow a magic number that cannot be changed.

Not surprisingly, one of the proposals that has been made over the years is to mandate reduced hours for everyone. Vicki Schultz and Allison Hoffman proposed this reform in 2006, arguing that mandating reduced hours for all employees would better improve women's equality in the workplace. They argued that the excessive hours norm makes it difficult for women to successfully balance work and family, and that it also harms men by compromising their health and relationships with their children. Moreover, many employees are underworked, not working enough hours to make ends meet. Schultz and Hoffman claim that a society in which some

[18] Hickox 2016; *see also* O'Brien 2005.
[19] Lin 2021; Williams, JC 2010.
[20] Hickox 2016, at 150; Schur et al. 2005.
[21] Crain 1991; *see also* Barzilay 2012, at 133; Lester 2005, at 11.
[22] Harris, S. 2020, at 215 (only 6.3% of the private sector is unionized).
[23] Albiston 2010, at 101.
[24] Albiston 2009, at 1114.

people are forced to work long hours at the expense of their families and others are limited to too few hours, is an unequal and unjust society. Even apart from the extreme hours on either end, the traditional 40-hour workweek is burdensome for many people, including dual-earner couples and single-parent households. The authors also argue that reduced hours is preferable to other reforms because it doesn't suffer from the stigma that occurs when women ask for variations of the traditional time/schedule norms.[25]

Therefore, they propose reducing working hours from 40 to 35 hours per week for all employees, mandating pro-rata benefits for all employees tied to the number of hours they work, and eliminating the FLSA exemptions from overtime for professional/managerial employees. They argue that reducing the workweek for everyone would reduce the stress levels of all workers and would hopefully create greater equality between spouses. It would also minimize the stigma facing caregivers who are often seen as not committed.[26]

Other commentators have made similar arguments.[27] Arlie Hochschild is also in favor of reduced hours for everyone. Although she does not specifically propose legislation to accomplish this (but rather, collective action, as discussed), her reason for reducing the hours for all workers is similar to the reason Schultz and Hoffman urged—to improve work/family balance for all workers.[28]

Other than mandating reduced hours for everyone, the other major proposal for legislation that would attempt to directly dismantle structural norms is mandatory time off/leaves of absence. Several scholars have made this argument and it is the primary subject of the first part of my proposal, so I discuss it more shortly.

But in addition to reduced hours and leaves of absence, we could imagine legislation that would attack other structural norms directly. Employers could be forced to provide parity (in terms of pay and benefits) for part-time positions.[29] We could enact legislation that would mandate schedule flexibility (flexible start/end times), although doing so seems incredibly complicated. We could enact legislation that would prohibit employers from using rotating shifts and require premium pay for all shifts outside the normal Monday–Friday day shift. We could adopt a 4-day workweek, giving employees one day of the week to attend to caregiving needs or their own health-related needs.[30]

But here is the problem with these suggested proposals: Other than more lenient attendance and leaves of absence policies, which benefit *all* workers, the other proposals would only help *some* workers, because the scheduling needs of workers with caregiving responsibilities and workers with disabilities vary dramatically.

[25] Schultz & Hoffman 2006.
[26] Schultz & Hoffman 2006.
[27] O'Brien 2005.
[28] Hochschild 1997.
[29] Cox 2022; Williams, JC 2001.
[30] This latter one has been suggested by other scholars. *See, e.g.*, Arnow-Richman 2010.

In other words, each proposal would benefit some workers but would be unnecessary or even harmful for other workers.

First considering workers with caregiving responsibilities, some might want to work reduced hours (for reduced pay), but low-income and/or single parents might need to work more hours to make ends meet.[31] Mothers with young children might prefer the 4-day workweek if they have good childcare to cover the four long days each week but enjoy having an extra day home with their child(ren). Mothers with school-aged children might prefer to work five days but get home earlier in the day to be with their children after school. Single moms likely would have difficulty working non-traditional shifts (because there are few if any day care options available during the evenings and weekends). But married couples might deliberately choose to tag-team parent.

Regarding workers with disabilities, some might need more lenient attendance policies. Other workers need to avoid overtime or work part time. However, because of the correlation between disability and poverty, many people with disabilities need to work full time. Some might benefit from a 4-day (but full time) workweek so they can schedule necessary medical appointments on their day off. But other people with disabilities could not work four 10-hour days. Bottom line: There is no one-size-fits-all solution.[32]

One good example of this phenomenon is the COVID-19 experience with remote work. For years, scholars have been advocating for the benefits of working from home (or "telecommuting," as it used to be called).[33] The benefits to caregivers include avoiding the extra hours it takes to commute and being home if the kids occasionally are home from school at odd hours. For workers with disabilities, remote work might be needed or preferred because of difficulties getting to work (transportation problems), inaccessible workplaces, or disability-related needs for easy access to bathrooms and periods of rest.[34] And employees who do not (currently) fall into either category might still enjoy more time for exercise or leisure from the lack of commute, as well as money saved by not commuting.

In some ways, the COVID-19 experience with remote work, where millions of employers were forced to close their doors and millions of employees began working from home, has been the equivalent of legislation mandating that all employers allow all eligible employees to work from home. Because so many employees were working from home at the same time, employers quickly learned that the imagined problems with remote work—inability for teamwork and collaboration, and inadequate supervision—were not the insurmountable barriers that employers once thought they were.[35]

[31] Jacobs & Gerson 2004.

[32] Arnow-Richman 2007, at 45; Arnow-Richman 2010; Jacobs & Gerson 2004; Kaminer 2004.

[33] Travis 2003, at 295.

[34] Porter 2021.

[35] Porter 2021.

But as we also learned from the pandemic, not everyone benefits from remote work. Caregivers who were stuck trying to work with young children at home who needed care and/or help with remote school did not find remote work to be particularly beneficial. (Although, in many cases, the ability to work from home was preferable to the experience of some parents who had to quit their jobs or were fired because their jobs could not be performed at home and they had no one to watch their kids.) And many employees did not have the space, quiet, or technology needed to successfully work from home. Accordingly, as I've argued elsewhere, mandating work from home for all employees would be ill-advised.[36]

Although employees' needs regarding when and where work is performed vary widely, the one exception is regarding attendance policies and leaves of absence. As will be discussed more, *all* workers can benefit from paid days off and more lenient attendance policies. Employees sometimes miss work for all kinds of reasons—illness, a sick child, routine or non-routine medical care, car trouble or other transportation problems, flare-ups caused by a disability, children's school closures, etc. But other than this need for paid time off without penalty, legislation that would directly attack any single structural norm would be ineffective because of the varied and individual needs of employees.

D *Individual Accommodation Mandate*

Having dispensed with the prior options as insufficient *on their own* to minimize the marginalization experienced by people with disabilities and workers with caregiving responsibilities, we are left with the fourth option—an individual accommodation mandate. Mandating accommodations has been proposed over the years to ameliorate the disadvantages of working caregivers[37] and of course, as discussed in Chapter 3, the ADA already contains an accommodation mandate designed to help people with disabilities navigate workplace structures that were designed around an able-bodied norm.

Peggie Smith has made a convincing argument in favor of an individual accommodation mandate in order to ameliorate disadvantages experienced by working caregivers.[38] As discussed in Chapter 7, my proposal is broader, allowing *all* employees to seek accommodations, regardless of the reason. The details of Smith's accommodation proposal are discussed in Chapter 9. At this juncture, I will briefly explain why an individual accommodation mandate is superior to the reform options just discussed.[39]

36 Porter 2021; *see also* Hickox & Liao 2020; Katsabian 2021.

37 Kaminer 2004; Kessler 2001.

38 Smith 2001.

39 Clarke 2011.

An accommodation mandate is necessary because workplace needs vary so much. Because everyone recognizes that the needs of people with disabilities vary quite a bit, this discussion will focus on the needs of employees with caregiving responsibilities. As mentioned earlier, Joan Williams has stated that, in the work-family arena, there is not a dazzling array of accommodations needed, but rather, a dyad.[40] I honestly do not understand this argument. Caregivers have very different needs and those needs will require modifications of various structural norms.[41] Here are a few examples, organized around each structural norm:

Hours (full time, part time, overtime)

- A single mom needs to work full time but cannot work much overtime because she has no day care available for the extended hours.
- A mother of four loves her job but wants to work slightly fewer hours so she can be with her children when they return home from school.
- A worker asks for reduced hours for a several-month period because she is helping her mother recuperate from major surgery.
- A mother needs a leave of absence while she is caring for a child who is recuperating from an illness or accident.

Shifts/Schedules

- A single mom needs to avoid the night shift because she would have no one to watch her children overnight.
- A mother of school-aged children wants to work from 7–3 instead of 9–5 so that she can be home in the afternoon to drive her kids to their after-school activities.
- A married couple asks each of their employers to keep them on a consistent shift so that they can tag-team parent (one works days and the other works nights, so one of them is always home with their children).
- An employee caring for a disabled family member asks to come in late every morning (and work later in the evening to make up the hours) because the family member has medical needs that can only be attended to in the morning.

Because caregivers' needs vary as much as the needs of people with disabilities, only individual accommodations can allow each caregiver or employee with a disability to successfully combine work and the rest of their lives.[42]

[40] Williams, JC & Segal 2003.

[41] Arnow-Richman 2010, at 1085.

[42] Lester 2005, at 4.

E *The Perfect Solution: A Combination of Two Solutions*

As is true in most cases, the perfect solution is actually a combination of solutions. As stated, a reimagined workplace means different things for different people. Most of the previous discussion was focused on the structural norms of the workplace—when and where we work. But workers often need modifications to the actual job tasks in addition to (or instead of) modifications to the structural norms. Certainly employees with disabilities will sometimes need modifications to the physical tasks of the job, but they are not alone in requiring such accommodations. Pregnant workers sometimes need workplace modifications to the physical tasks of the job. So do older workers. Although it is true that both pregnancy and impairments caused by advanced age might be disabilities under the expanded definition of disability in the ADAAA, there are benefits to both employees and employers in not having to prove that a particular limitation is in fact a disability. These are all reasons why the individual accommodation mandate discussed in Chapter 9 is so important.

However, even though I concluded in Subsection C that legislating changes to structural norms (such as reduced hours) is not a good idea, there is one structural norm that is universally needed—occasional time off.[43] Accordingly, my two-part proposal consists of: (1) a paid time off mandate; and (2) a universal accommodation mandate. The rest of this chapter focuses on paid leave, and Chapter 9 focuses on the universal accommodation mandate.

II IMPORTANCE OF LEAVE FOR PEOPLE WITH DISABILITIES, CAREGIVERS, AND EVERYONE ELSE

Although "leaves of absence" are sometimes thought to encompass single days off work as well as longer leaves of absence, I think it is important to distinguish between the two. In this section I discuss the importance of long-term leave and shorter-term absences for people with disabilities, employees with caregiving responsibilities, and frankly, everyone else.

A *Long-Term Leave*

Many employees will at some point in their careers need a long-term leave of absence. (For definitional purposes, I'm (somewhat arbitrarily) defining long-term as more than two weeks.) Both employees with disabilities and workers with caregiving responsibilities might need leaves of absence. The most common reasons caregiving employees need long-term leave are for the birth (or adoption) of a baby and for situations where the employee has a child, spouse, or other family member who is in need of long-term care due to disability or injury.

[43] Lester 2005, at 5.

Some workers do not have a legal right to leave at all. As mentioned earlier, almost 40 percent of all workers are not covered by the FMLA. For these employees, they might have to outsource care of sick family members in ways that are detrimental to the health and well-being of the family members who need care. Moreover, the stress from being unable to take care of those loved ones can cause negative health outcomes for the employee, such as anxiety and depression.[44]

Some workers have access to leave but cannot afford to take it because it's unpaid. As mentioned, the FMLA's mandated leave does not require *paid* leave, and 80 percent of the population does not have access to paid leave.[45] And some workers who have access to paid leave do not take it because they surmise (often correctly) that there will be negative career consequences from taking that leave.[46]

Similarly, employees with disabilities might need leaves of absence for many reasons, including flare-ups of disabilities (such as multiple sclerosis), cancer treatment, heart surgery, severe depression or other mental illness, recovering from injuries due to a car accident or other traumatic incident, or recovering from back or knee surgery, to name just a few. Under the expanded definition of disability after the ADAAA, all of these examples should be considered disabilities.

Without a right to a leave of absence, pregnant women, workers with caregiving responsibilities, and workers with disabilities risk being fired when they need leave. Accordingly, leaves of absence are vitally important for ensuring that these marginalized employees can achieve equality in the workplace.

B *Short-Term Leave*

Although most (but not all) workers will need a longer leave of absence at some point during their careers, the need for occasional days off is universal.[47] Consider the examples mentioned earlier: illness, a sick child, routine or non-routine medical care, car trouble or other transportation problems, children's school closures, etc. No one is immune from getting the sniffles or needing to go to the dentist. And although there used to be a kind of heroism in going into work while sick,[48] I sincerely hope COVID-19 has put an end to that ill-advised practice.

Those who have professional jobs (and perhaps especially academics) might assume that it's no big deal to take time off for a cold or doctor's appointments. But there are millions of employees that do not have this right and that live with the constant fear of discipline or termination for attending to the most basic (and unavoidable) needs. In a recent study of 66 large employers, impacting 18 million workers, most of these employers used no-fault attendance policies where every

[44] Albiston & O'Connor 2016, at 49.
[45] Widiss 2021a, at 2183.
[46] Albiston & O'Connor 2016.
[47] Selmi 2007.
[48] Bakst et al. 2020.

absence for any reason (unless for a qualifying FMLA reason) would accrue points, and those points lead to discipline and discharge.[49] Some employers allow only seven absences (points) in an entire year; the eighth one leads to termination. Most of the employees subject to these draconian attendance policies are the most vulnerable among us, working low-income jobs with no job security. Their lower income contributes to many of the reasons they might miss work. Lower-income people tend to be less healthy (and this was especially a problem during COVID-19); they tend to have less reliable day care; and they are more likely to have transportation problems. Many of these employees are also single parents, or if coupled, have a partner/spouse who also needs to work full time.[50] There is also a correlation between disability and poverty.[51] So, even though people with disabilities do not generally have worse attendance records than other employees, if they do need to miss work related to their disabilities, they often do not have the right to do so.[52]

The good news is that the law and employer practices are improving with respect to providing paid (and excused) days off. As of 2021, 16 states and DC guarantee paid sick days for an average of about one week.[53]

Bottom line: All employees occasionally need time off. But (some) caregivers and (some) people with disabilities are more likely to be harmed by the lack of job-protected time off. And of course, lower-income workers are more likely to suffer if time off is not paid. Unfortunately, as we will see in the next section, the FMLA's coverage is inadequate both with respect to *who* it covers and *what* it covers.

III THE CURRENT STATE OF THE FMLA

This section will provide a brief background of the FMLA, including its history and primary provisions before turning to the pros and cons of the FMLA, which is the only federal statute regarding leaves of absence (both short term and long term).

A *Background of the FMLA*

Congress passed the FMLA in 1993, and President Clinton signed it. The bill had gone through eight years of lobbying and two vetoes by President George H. W. Bush, but it ultimately passed by a wide margin in both the House and the Senate. The FMLA provides employees up to 12 weeks of job-protected leave for parental leave, for the care of family members, and for the worker's own illness. The stated purposes of the Act are "to balance the demands of the workplace with the needs of families, to promote the stability and economic security of families, and to promote

49 Bakst et al. 2020.

50 Albiston & Fisk 2021; Travis 2009a, at 408.

51 Rothstein 2019, at 299; Schur et al. 2013, at 28–32; Travis 2017, at 845–46.

52 Albiston & Fisk 2021.

53 Widiss 2021b.

national interest in preserving family integrity."[54] This language's focus on families is interesting given that the FMLA also covers leave for an employee's own serious health condition. There is some evidence that the self-care provisions were added in an effort to encourage men to take leave. Even though the FMLA is gender-neutral so both men and women can take leave after the birth of a baby or when a family member needs care, advocates and legislators were concerned that if the statute focused too much on family leave, women would continue to take most of the leave, and this would perpetuate the stigma women suffer in the workplace. The perception that women are most of the leave-takers creates a disincentive for employers to hire women, especially women who are of child-bearing age. Accordingly, the self-care provisions were included in the statute to incentivize men to take leave, which would minimize (although not eliminate) bias against women based on the perceived costs of hiring them.[55]

The FMLA provides up to twelve weeks of unpaid leave per year in the following circumstances:

(a) Because of the birth of a son or daughter of the employee and in order to care for such son or daughter.
(b) Because of the placement of a son or daughter with the employee for adoption or foster care.
(c) In order to care for the spouse, son, daughter, or parent of the employee, if such spouse, son, daughter, or parent has a serious health condition.
(d) Because of a serious health condition that makes the employee unable to perform the functions of the position of such employee.[56]

To qualify for FMLA leave, an employee has to work for a covered employer, which is an employer who employs at least 50 employees within a 75-mile radius of the employee's worksite, and the employee must have worked for at least one year, and for at least 1,250 hours in the past 12-month period.[57]

Importantly, the FMLA only requires unpaid leave, not paid leave. However, if an employer has a policy that provides for income replacement, the employee can request or the employer can require that the paid leave allowed by the employer's policies accrues concurrently with the FMLA leave. This allows for some income replacement for some employees, but it does not allow the employee to stack the two types of leave on top of each other. In other words, a woman who just gave birth cannot take six weeks of short-term disability leave,

[54] 29 U.S.C. § 2601(b)(1).
[55] Porter 2014d.
[56] 29 U.S.C. § 2612(a)(1)(A)–(D). In 2008, the FMLA was amended to address leave for workers in the military and their family members. 29 U.S.C. § 2612(a)(1)(E). These amendments are beyond the scope of this project.
[57] 29 U.S.C. § 2611(2)(A)–(B)(ii)

which might be paid at two-thirds of her normal pay, and then take an *additional* 12 weeks of unpaid FMLA leave.[58]

An employee's primary obligation with respect to FMLA leave is to provide notice to the employer at least 30 days before the leave is to begin or as soon as is practicable.[59] Not surprisingly, in cases where the leave is unanticipated, parties frequently dispute whether the notice requirement was met. An employee is also required to provide the employer with medical certification, substantiating the need for the leave when such leave is for the employee's or a family member's serious health condition.[60]

An employer's obligations include maintaining the employee's health insurance (if applicable) while on leave; and reinstating an employee after her leave to the position she left or "to an equivalent position with equivalent benefits, pay, and other terms and conditions of employment."[61]

B *Advantages of the FMLA*

Most of what I have to say about the FMLA is negative. So let's start with the positive. Before the FMLA, American workers had *no* federal legal right to job-protected leave. As discussed in Chapter 2, women who were pregnant were often expected to quit their jobs once their baby was born (and sometimes well before the baby was born). Although the ADA was passed in 1990, the definition of disability was interpreted so narrowly that, before the FMLA was passed, employees who needed time off work to recover from accidents, have knee surgery, or get treatment for cancer had no federally protected right to take a leave of absence. Accordingly, the FMLA is an improvement over what we had.

And although the FMLA has not led to a *federal* right to paid leave, it is perhaps partially responsible for spawning a whole slew of *state* laws that do provide job-protected paid leave. As discussed by Deborah Widiss, as of 2021, 16 states and DC provide paid sick days. As for longer leave, 9 states and DC provide some wage-replacement for longer leaves of absence.[62]

Moreover, Catherine Albiston has made a convincing argument that because the FMLA "challenges implicit fundamental assumptions about the nature of work . . . and takes away some of employers' unilateral control over the schedule of work" it has the potential to change cultural expectations about work and leave.[63] As the first legislation to focus on the features of work itself (uninterrupted attendance) rather than on the identity of the workers it protects, Albiston argues that the FMLA is

58 Porter 2014d.
59 29 U.S.C. § 2612(e)(2)(B).
60 29 U.S.C. § 2613(a).
61 29 U.S.C. § 2614(a)(1)(A)–(B).
62 Widiss 2021b.
63 Albiston 2010, at 24.

better suited to end "institutional inequality."[64] The FMLA recognizes the value of caring for others and the need for time off for illnesses and injuries. Because leave is an entitlement rather than a discretionary benefit, employers cannot defend against liability by asserting a business reason for denying leave or undue hardship. By taking away management prerogative to penalize employees who take time off, the FMLA directly challenges time norms and the implicit model of an ideal worker.[65] It also avoids special treatment stigma. Although Albiston recognizes many of the limitations of the FMLA (which I will discuss in the next section), she states that the FMLA has the potential to dismantle structural norms of the workplace without reifying gender and disability as naturalized social categories.[66]

C *Disadvantages of the FMLA*

Having addressed some of the benefits of the FMLA, next I discuss some of the problems with the FMLA from both the perspective of employees and employers.

1 Problems for Employees

First and foremost, the FMLA leaves many workers unprotected. Specifically, three limitations combine to create the reality that almost 40 percent of all workers are not entitled to FMLA leave. This means that if they are not in a state that requires job-protected leave, they can be fired for having a baby or being treated for cancer. The first limitation is employer coverage; employers must have 50 or more employees to be covered by the Act, so all employees who work for smaller employers are not covered. Second, the FMLA only protects employees who have worked for their employer for more than one year. And third, the employee must have worked 1,250 hours in the past 12 months, which excludes many part-time employees. These three limitations cause almost 40 percent of workers to be unprotected, and most of these employees are women. Moreover, these eligibility criteria have negative class and race implications as well.[67]

Second, the most frequent criticism of the FMLA is that it does not require any paid leave. Thus, there are many employees who are entitled to leave but cannot afford to take it.[68] Although an increasing number of employers offer paid leave for recovering from childbirth or other physical illnesses and disabilities, it remains rare to have paid leave to care for family members.[69] Moreover, the employers that tend to offer any type of paid leave are often employing middle- and upper-class

64 Albiston 2010, at 29, 36.
65 Albiston 2009, at 1158.
66 Albiston 2010, at 222.
67 Porter 2014d, at 339.
68 Grossman, Joanna 2004; Kessler 2007, at 326; Selmi 2004.
69 Widiss 2021b.

employees, with working-class employees left out of most paid leave.[70] Moreover, scholars have also documented the problem that, even when workers are entitled to take leave, their employers often "punish" them by dramatically reducing their hours or finding other ways to force them to quit.[71]

Third, the FMLA does very little to ameliorate the work/family conflict. This is because there are many absences caused by routine caregiving obligations that are not covered by the FMLA, including a sick babysitter; a sick child (with a routine illness); routine doctor, dentist, and orthodontist appointments for children; school closures due to weather, COVID-19, or a myriad of other reasons; and parent/teacher conferences or other school events that require a parent's presence. Thus, most scholars have agreed that the FMLA is a pretty useless tool for alleviating the burden of work/family conflict.[72]

Fourth, the FMLA has not improved gender equality in the workplace or at home. It was hoped that because the FMLA was gender neutral, and because it included coverage for an employee's *own* serious health condition, that the statute would do two things. First, that it would eliminate the situation where mostly women were taking leave. And second, that more men would start taking family leave and thereafter become more involved parents.[73] Unfortunately, neither of these things have happened. The FMLA has not led to an appreciable increase in the number of men taking leave, except for their own serious health conditions.[74] Part of the reason men are not taking significantly more FMLA leave is because it is unpaid, and men tend to be the higher earners, so families are worse off economically if the dad takes unpaid leave than if the mom does.[75]

2 Problems for Employers

Surprisingly, despite the business community being opposed to the FMLA and worried about the burdens of long-term leave (such as 12 weeks after a woman gives birth), most of the evidence indicates that anticipated leaves (such as for the birth of a baby) have not been very burdensome at all. Most employers found little or no effect of the FMLA on profitability or productivity, and most employers found the FMLA easy to administer.[76]

Instead, the problems with the FMLA from the employer's perspective mostly arise with respect to short-term, unplanned, and intermittent absences. Employers'

70 Befort 2004, at 621–22; Porter 2014d, at 339–40; Widiss 2021a, at 2183; Widiss 2021b.

71 Albiston & O'Connor 2016, at 17.

72 Grossman, Joanna 2004; Kaminer 2004; Lester 2005; Porter 2014d, at 340–41; Selmi 2000; Selmi 2004; Smith 2001.

73 Grossman, Joanna 2004.

74 Selmi 2004.

75 Malin 1994; Porter 2014d; Selmi 2000.

76 Albiston 2010, at 122; Selmi 2000.

objections fall into two main categories: (1) employee abuse of the right to FMLA leave; and (2) FMLA compliance is onerous and complicated.

First, when employees take leave for illness (their own or a family member's), rather than longer leaves after the birth of a baby, it creates the potential for abuse (or the suspicion of abuse). These abuses fall into two different categories: (1) taking longer leave than necessary to fall under the definition of "serious health condition," and (2) abuses of the intermittent leave provisions.[77]

The first abuse is where employees stay out of work longer than necessary to make an otherwise unexcused absence qualify as FMLA leave. This is often the result of two factors—the definition of serious health condition and employers' stringent attendance policies that will not excuse a "sick" day unless it is for an FMLA-approved reason. Under the regulations implementing the FMLA, a serious health condition is defined (among other things) as an illness requiring three days of being unable to work (or unable to attend day care or school for children) and the continuing treatment of a health care provider.[78] Take the common example of a child's ear infection. Most ear infections will clear up within a day or so with antibiotics. But because of the definition of serious health condition, if an employee's child has an ear infection (and the applicable employer uses a no-fault attendance policy, where only FMLA-related absences are excused), the employee now has the incentive (and maybe even the *need*) to keep the child home from school/ day care for three days and take the child in for a follow-up appointment to the doctor (which is not always requested by the doctor). This allows the absences to be eligible for FMLA coverage and therefore not subject to discipline.

The second abuse is regarding intermittent leave. If an employee has a chronic serious health condition, the FMLA allows that employee to be certified by her doctor as entitled to intermittent leave.[79] This allows the employee to take FMLA-protected leave in very small increments of time based on the need for continuing medical treatment or the inability to work due to the chronic serious health condition. So if an employee suffers from migraine headaches and gets certified for intermittent leave for those headaches, she can simply call off work on a day she has a migraine headache without having to provide additional documentation. (After all, who goes to the doctor each time they get a migraine headache?) This intermittent leave can be and is sometimes abused, although the magnitude of that abuse is debated.[80] And of course, we expect more abuse with employers who have the most stringent attendance policies. So imagine that an employee who is a single mother works for an employer with a no-fault attendance policy and the employee is

77 Porter 2014d, at 347.

78 29 C.F.R. § 825.114(2) ("Any period of incapacity requiring absence from work, school, or other regular daily activities, of more than three calendar days, that also involves continuing treatment by (or under the supervision of) a health care provider.").

79 29 U.S.C. § 2612(b)(1).

80 Porter 2014d, at 350.

nearing the limited number of absences allowed in a year (sometimes as few as seven). She is certified for intermittent leave for migraine headaches, but she also has a one-year-old daughter. If her daughter is sick with the stomach flu (which is usually of short duration and not something for which you would seek medical care), the employee might call off work and use the migraine headache as the excuse to avoid termination. Given this horrible choice between caring for family members and losing their job, the abuses of the FMLA are frankly not surprising.

The second main objection of employers about the FMLA is that compliance with the short-term and intermittent leave provisions of the statute is very complicated. Compliance with three particular FMLA provisions is complicated: (1) the definition of serious health condition; (2) the notice requirement; and (3) tracking intermittent leave.[81]

First, determining whether an employee or her family member has a serious health condition is difficult. "Serious health condition" is defined as "an illness, injury, impairment, or physical or mental condition that involves inpatient care in a hospital, hospice, or [a] residential medical care facility or continuing treatment by a health care provider."[82] Frequent disputes arise over what constitutes "continuing treatment" and who qualifies as a "health care provider."[83]

Second, the "notice" requirement is vague and therefore, often litigated. Employees are required to give thirty days' notice if possible, or in the case of a sudden illness or injury, as soon as is practicable.[84] In many cases, employees call in at the last minute because they are sick or a family member is sick. Because employees do not have to use any magic language to request leave under the FMLA, managers need to be trained to understand when an employee's absence might qualify for FMLA leave. Mistakes in this regard can lead to frustration by all parties and sometimes costly litigation.[85]

Third, the most difficult provision for employers to comply with is undoubtedly tracking intermittent leave. As discussed, many employees can get certified for intermittent leave if they have a chronic health condition. This allows the employee to take FMLA-protected leave in very small increments of time, equal to the shortest period of time that the employer uses to account for other forms of leave, no greater than one hour. So if an employer tracks other leave in quarter-hour increments, every time an employee takes intermittent leave (such as 1 hour, 45 minutes for a doctor's appointment) the employer has to track how much of the employee's allotted 12 weeks of leave has been used. Employers frequently complain about the record-keeping nightmare caused by intermittent leave under the FMLA.[86]

81 Porter 2014d, at 351.
82 29 U.S.C. § 2611.
83 Porter 2014d, at 351.
84 29 U.S.C. § 2612(e).
85 Porter 2014d, at 352.
86 Porter 2014d, at 352–53.

IV TACKLING TIME OFF

As I have addressed in prior work, I recommend two major reforms to tackle time off. First, the "self-care" provisions of the FMLA should be severed from the statute, leaving the FMLA with only the "care of others" provisions. (It could still be called the "Family and *Medical* Leave Act" because it would deal with caring for family members who have medical needs necessitating care.) Thus, the FMLA would cover the first three enumerated reasons employees qualify for FMLA leave: (1) because of the birth of a child of the employee and in order to care for such child; (2) because of the placement of a child with the employee for adoption or foster care; and (3) in order to care for a spouse, child, or a parent of the employee, if such spouse, child, or parent has a serious health condition.[87] Moreover, my proposal would also amend the FMLA so that it only applies for absences of more than two weeks.[88] Long-term leave for the employee's own medical condition would be covered by the new accommodation mandate, discussed in the next chapter.

The second major reform is that shorter-term absences (less than two weeks) would be covered by a new statute I propose, which I am calling the "Short-Term Absences Act." As discussed in the next section, this would require employers to provide up to two weeks (10 working days) of paid absences.

A *Extended Leaves of Absence under the FMLA*

As stated, the FMLA would still provide up to twelve weeks for the three reasons listed; however, it would no longer cover very short-term absences (fewer than 10 days) for any of these reasons nor would the FMLA cover leave for an employee's own serious health condition (whether the leave needed was long-term or short-term). The FMLA would still require certifications to document the serious health condition of a family member or the arrival of a new baby, although I do not envision as many debates about these longer leaves because any illness or injury that is serious enough to require more than ten days of leave is unlikely to be challenged under the serious health condition provision. Instead, it is most often very short-term absences that are challenged under the FMLA.[89]

The reason for severing care-of-others from self-care and separating out short-term absences is to hopefully garner renewed support for family leave. It is indisputable that most of the criticisms of and challenges under the FMLA deal with short-term absences and most often with employees using the FMLA for self-care. In contrast,

[87] 29 U.S.C. § 2612(a)(1)(A)–(C). I am not addressing the military leave provisions in this project, but I see no reason to modify those provisions.
[88] Porter 2014d.
[89] Porter 2014d, at 355.

there are very few objections to long-term leaves taken by employees with caregiving responsibilities.[90]

Of course, this does not take care of two of the major criticisms of the FMLA from the employee's perspective—that it does not cover enough workers and that the leave is unpaid.[91] Accordingly, the FMLA should be amended to apply to all employers with 15 or more employees (the threshold used by Title VII and the ADA), and the leave should be at least partially paid. There is no need for me to reinvent the wheel here; there are several proposals for paid leave and several states have already enacted paid leave statutes, giving plenty of examples to guide the way.[92]

Importantly, in addition to this leave being partially paid (by contributions from employees, employers, or both), it's important that it keeps the one benefit of the current FMLA—that the leave be job-protected. In at least one study, researchers revealed that low-wage workers with access to paid family leave through California's paid leave program often do not take this leave even though it would offset a substantial part of their lost wages. Their research revealed that many workers (especially lower-income workers) did not take advantage of the partially paid leave California offers because it was not job-protected leave.[93]

B *New Statute: Short-Term Absences Act*

What about absences that are shorter than 10 days? I propose the enactment of a new statute that I call the Short-Term Absences Act (STAA), which would provide up to ten days of paid absences that can be used for any reason. I have deliberately used the word "absences" instead of "leave" to move away from the mindset that routine absences have anything in common with longer leaves to care for a new baby or a seriously ill family member.[94]

Most importantly, the absences could be used for *any* reason. Although most employees will use the absences because they are sick (or a child is sick), or for routine medical appointments, etc., they would not be limited to these reasons. These absences could also be used if an employee has car trouble, wants to attend a child's school performance, for bereavement, to take care of government bureaucratic obligations that are only available during regular business hours (e.g., DMV), or even just for a "mental health" day.[95]

90 Albiston & O'Connor 2016, at 60; Porter 2014d, at 358.

91 Albiston & O'Connor 2016, at 59.

92 Grossman, Joanna 2005; Lester 2005; Malin 1994; Selmi 2000; Widiss 2021a; Widiss 2021b. For instance, California's leave law is paid for entirely by workers with no contributions from employers or the state beyond the administration of benefits. Albiston & O'Connor 2016, at 26.

93 Albiston & O'Connor 2016, at 26, 29.

94 Porter 2014d, at 355. Other scholars have made similar proposals. Befort 2004.

95 Porter 2014d, at 355.

Although employees would be required to give "notice" (meaning they would have to notify their supervisor that they were going to be absent), because all short-term absences except for vacation days would be subsumed into the STAA, employers would no longer have to grapple with the issue of whether the communication provided was sufficient to put the employer on notice that the employee was requesting authorized leave.[96]

This proposed statute will benefit both employers and employees. As for employers, it will likely curb many of the current abuses we see with the FMLA. Recall where I described employees who take longer leaves than necessary to try to get the absence excused as an FMLA absence. Because they do not need to justify their leave to get it excused, they would only take the one day they likely needed. So the parent of the child with an ear infection might only take one or two days off—until the antibiotics have started working and the child is feeling better.[97]

This statute would also benefit employers because it will avoid the difficulty employers have in trying to determine whether a leave qualifies under the complicated definitions in the FMLA or under the employer's other policies.[98] For a non-FMLA example, employers might struggle to determine if a death in an employee's family qualifies for bereavement leave under the employer's policies. Although it is incredibly silly for employers to attempt to determine whether an employee's relative is close enough to justify bereavement leave, some employers do engage in this silliness, and this statute would avoid them having to make these decisions.[99]

Finally, the STAA would benefit employers because it would lead to a dramatic decrease in the costs of record keeping without being more expensive for most employers. Many employers already provide some sick leave and bereavement leave. Some employers provide personal leave. Implementing many of these leave policies requires a great deal of record keeping by human resources professionals. The STAA would avoid the time and effort of that record keeping.[100]

Employees would also benefit from this statute. Although many employees are already entitled to sick leave, many millions of employees are working under very draconian "no fault" attendance policies.[101] Moreover, even if employers have sick leave policies, they often do not allow employees to use that time for caring for a child or because of car trouble, etc.[102] This statute would undoubtedly improve the situation of many workers, without making any employees worse off. Employees also benefit from this proposed statute because it avoids infringing on their privacy.

96 Porter 2014d, at 356.
97 Porter 2014d, at 360–61; Williams, JC 2010, at 82 (absenteeism is reduced by workplace flexibility).
98 Befort 2004, at 635.
99 Porter 2014d, at 361.
100 Porter 2014d, at 361–62.
101 Bakst et al. 2020.
102 Widiss 2021b.

Employees would not need to disclose that they have diarrhea or that their beat-up car has stopped working.[103]

Perhaps most importantly, as discussed in Chapter 7, providing these 10 days of absences without eligibility rules avoids the problem of special treatment stigma. Because the absences under the STAA would be available to *all* employees for *any* reason, special treatment stigma (as it applies to absences from work) should disappear.[104]

Finally, the COVID-19 pandemic has taught us that society as a whole benefits when employees have access to paid days off without penalty. Workers should stay home when they are sick, but historically (and even during the early days of the pandemic), many workers went into work sick and infected their coworkers.[105] If they had job-protected paid time off, they (hopefully) would have stayed home and avoided spreading the infection. The same benefit applies when parents keep sick children home from school. We all know someone who has loaded a kid up on cough syrup, decongestant, pain reliever, etc. and sent the kid to school because the parent could not afford to take a day off. This kind of behavior benefits no one and needs to stop, for the good of society.

C *Addressing the Logistics and Criticisms*

1 Logistics

There are a few logistical issues that require a brief discussion.

First, in an attempt to avoid a frequent criticism of intermittent leave under the FMLA, I propose that employees would take their absences in half-day increments. So a full-time employee would have access to 10 full-day absences or 20 half-day absences (or some combination of the two). This is much easier to track from a record keeping perspective than the current FMLA rules that require employers to track intermittent leave in hours or even partial hours.

Second, part-time or reduced-hours employees should receive a proportional share of these paid days off. So an employee who works half-time (20 hours per week) should get five paid days off.[106]

Third, it is certainly possible (and maybe even likely) that employees will use up their STAA days before the end of the year and then have a truly compelling need to take a day off. In this situation, the employee would either be subject to the employer's regular discipline process or the employee could seek an accommodation pursuant to the individual accommodation mandate in Chapter 9.

[103] Porter 2014d, at 363–64.
[104] Porter 2014d, at 364.
[105] Bakst et al. 2020.
[106] Cox 2022; Williams, JC 2001.

Finally, I am cognizant of the concern of some employers that there might be days where it would be a significant hardship to have many (if any) employees absent from work. Black Friday for retail employers is the most obvious situation, but I am sure there are others. Under this proposal, employers should have the right to designate up to 10 days per year as "No STAA" days. The employer should give employees at least one month of notice (but more is obviously better) that it plans to declare a "No STAA" day. Employees would not be entitled to use one of their STAA days if the employer has declared it a "No STAA" day. This means that if an employee still misses work on a "No STAA" day (and the exception described shortly does not apply), the employer would have the right to discipline that employee.

And yet, there might be situations where a truly unavoidable emergency occurs on one of the "No STAA" days. In that case, the employee would be able to ask for an individual exception under the accommodation mandate discussed in Chapter 9. In other words, imagine an employee or her child ends up in the hospital with a serious illness or injury on a "No STAA" day. The employee has the right to ask for an accommodation—"please do not terminate me for missing work today because I [or my child] was in the hospital." Employers would have to provide this accommodation if it truly is "necessary" (a term I define in great detail in the next chapter). But employers would not have to provide the accommodation if the reason for the absence on a "No STAA" day was not necessary.

2 Anticipated Criticisms

The most obvious criticisms of this proposal are cost and the fact that it takes away some employer discretion. Addressing the second criticism first, it is true that under this proposal, employers will no longer be able to have the draconian attendance policies some employers currently have. But society as a whole is better off not allowing employers to have "no fault" extremely stringent attendance policies. When employers have such policies, employees are often left making the impossibly unfair choice between caring for their children and their jobs. There are plenty of tragic stories where an employee left her young children without adequate supervision because she knew she would be terminated if she did not report to work.[107] And as the pandemic has taught us, draconian policies harm the workplace and society in general because they give employees an incentive to come into work sick.[108]

A related argument is that employers want to have discretion regarding which absences to excuse and which to not excuse. Again, it is true that this proposal would take away this discretion. But I think that's a good thing. Employers often use this discretion in troubling ways, granting favoritism to certain employees for dubious reasons. And what employers don't always realize is that exercising this

[107] Bernstein 2003.

[108] Albiston & Fisk 2021; Bakst et al. 2020.

discretion can get them into trouble. Many discrimination claims are brought (and won) simply because an employer provided some benefit to one employee and not another.[109]

With respect to the cost argument, it is doubtful this proposal will be more expensive than the status quo for a couple of reasons. First of all, most employers already offer a potpourri of days off (sick days, personal days, bereavement leave, etc.). This proposal simply consolidates those days off. Moreover, any increase in costs will likely be offset by decreased record keeping costs. Because there is no need to have human resources personnel making difficult eligibility decisions, employers should see a decrease in the cost of implementing the FMLA and other leave policies. And finally, studies show that when employers have more generous (or at least less draconian) workplace policies, they benefit in terms of increased morale and loyalty and decreased attrition.[110]

V CONCLUSION

The need for time off is universal. Accordingly, this proposal will create a universal right to some job-protected paid time off. In this way, we are attacking one of the structural norms directly—the expectation of perfect attendance. But as discussed, employees need all types of modifications of the workplace environment—both how the job is performed and when and where it is performed.[111] Because these needs vary so greatly, only an individual accommodation mandate will suffice. I turn to that next.

[109] Clarke 2011; Emens 2012; Porter 2014d, at 365; Williams, JC & Segal 2003.

[110] Arnow-Richman 2003, at 382; Flake 2020, at 1722; Jacobs & Gerson 2004, at 1887; Porter 2014d, at 366; Smith 2001, at 1478; Williams, JC 2010, at 77; Williams, JC & Segal 2003.

[111] Williams, JC 2010, at 233 (leave is important, but we need more than leave).

9

The Workplace Reimagined, Part II

Accommodating Our Bodies and Our Lives

I INTRODUCTION

In prior chapters, I laid the groundwork for this last step in reimagining the workplace—a universal accommodation mandate. Chapter 7 explained why universal mandates are superior to targeted mandates, both for ease of administration (which benefits employers) and buy-in from coworkers (which decreases stigma). Chapter 8 proposed mandating one substantive benefit—two weeks of paid, job-protected absences regardless of the reason. Although having access to paid, job-protected absences is vitally important for all workers, it is not the only workplace modification that workers need. Accordingly, this chapter proposes a universal accommodation mandate, which would allow employees to request modifications to the structural norms of the workplace (when and where work is performed) and to request modifications to how the physical tasks of the job are performed. This chapter explains how the mandate would work, discusses various applications of the mandate, briefly addresses logistical issues, and then responds to the anticipated criticisms.

II ACCOMMODATING OUR BODIES AND OUR LIVES

My idea for a universal accommodation mandate grew out of the similarities I saw between people with disabilities and workers with caregiving responsibilities trying to balance work and life. As discussed earlier, both groups frequently need modifications in the workplace, and yet both groups suffer "special treatment stigma" when they request such modifications (regardless of whether the employer grants the request or not). I hope I convinced you in Chapter 7 that accommodating caregivers and people with disabilities is the right thing to do as a matter of policy, and can have tangible benefits for the accommodated employees, their families, their coworkers, their employers, and society at large. But knowing that argument is unlikely to carry the day, a universal accommodation mandate is the best way to improve the lives of marginalized employees.

A *Accommodating Everyone*

What does accommodating everyone mean? It means exactly what you would think it means—all employees would be entitled to request a modification of a workplace policy or the specific manner in which the job tasks are performed, regardless of the reason for the request.

Some examples? First, some obvious ones. A person with diabetes requests more frequent breaks to monitor and manage their blood glucose levels. A mother requests a shift in hours (working from 7–3 instead of 9–5) so she can be home when her children arrive home from school. A pregnant woman asks for a stool to sit on while she is working as a cashier at a grocery store because her pregnancy has caused back pain and swelling. An employee who observes the Sabbath requests a schedule change so that she can adhere to her religious beliefs.

Some less common ones. A short woman requests a modification to a manufacturing process so that she can better reach the machinery, instead of straining to do the job on her toes with her arms overhead. An older worker with chronic back pain (which might be a disability, although it's unlikely the worker would see it that way[1]), requests reassignment to an available vacant position that would be much easier on his back. An obese employee asks for a special chair at his desk so that he is more comfortable.

And some requests that might seem preposterous or at least highly irregular. A marathon runner requests a change in his schedule (working from 7–3 instead of 9–5) for a two-month period in the winter while he is training for a spring marathon so that he can get his training runs in while it's still light outside. Another employee wants to change her hours to allow her to obtain an advanced degree. A worker who just adopted a new dog asks to leave work early once per week for two months (without pay) to take her dog to puppy obedience training. A childless (or child-free) worker is taking care of her school-aged niece for three months and requests to leave work early and work from home in the afternoons so that she can be home when her niece arrives home from school.

The options are almost endless. Two things are worth noting at the outset. First, all of these requests are similar to the requests that people with disabilities have the right to under the ADA, and many of them are similar to requests that many employers might already voluntarily grant for pregnant workers, caregivers, or for religious practices that conflict with work (whether or not Title VII would mandate it). Second, all of the employees making these requests (even those in the third group of uncommon requests) are likely to believe that their request is equally valid

[1] Porter 2022.

as many or all of the other examples listed. At this first stage of the analysis, all requests should be considered equally valid. But the reality is—not all requests are equally valid. Some are *needed* in order to allow the employee to remain employed. Others are *desired* and would be *highly valued*, but are not, strictly speaking, *necessary*. This is where the two-tiered undue hardship comes into play.

B *Two-Tiered Undue Hardship Defense*

As discussed in Chapter 3, the ADA requires employers to provide disabled employees with reasonable accommodations as long as those accommodations do not create an undue hardship. Under the ADA, the undue hardship defense is defined as "an action requiring significant difficulty or expense."[2] The ADA also provides factors for employers and courts to consider when determining whether an accommodation causes an undue hardship. These factors are focused on the costs of the accommodation compared to the resources of the employer.[3]

As I have discussed elsewhere, the undue hardship defense is difficult to meet and rarely dispositive. This is especially true when the defense is being asserted based on actual financial costs. Interestingly (and maybe even surprisingly), the defense is easier to meet when the employer argues that the accommodation is difficult in the sense that it will upend the way tasks are normally performed or will deviate from highly entrenched workplace rules.[4]

Contrast that with the first use of the undue hardship defense, which was in the context of religious accommodations under Title VII. Although Title VII as initially enacted did not contain an accommodation requirement for religion, the EEOC and Congress soon realized that employers could refrain from discriminating against an employee because of his religion and yet refuse to modify workplace policies to allow that employee to practice his religion. Accordingly, in 1972 Congress amended Title VII to include an obligation to accommodate employees' religious practices.[5] The amendment defines religion to include "all aspects of religious observance and practice, as well as belief, unless an employer demonstrates that he is unable to reasonably accommodate to an employee's or prospective employee's religious observance or practice without undue hardship."[6] But unlike the stringent undue hardship defense under the ADA, the undue hardship defense for religious accommodations was defined by the Supreme Court as "anything more than a de minimis expense."[7] This undue hardship defense is considerably more lenient, allowing employers to win much more readily than under the ADA's undue hardship defense.

2 42 U.S.C. § 12111(10)(A).
3 42 U.S.C. § 12111(10)(B).
4 Porter 2019d.
5 Flake 2020, at 1680–81.
6 42 U.S.C. § 2000e(j).
7 Trans World Airlines v. Hardison, 432 U.S. 63 (1977).

Instead of reinventing the wheel and coming up with a completely new and different defense, my proposal would use both of these defenses to differentiate between accommodations that are *necessary* and those that are *desired* or *valued* but not strictly necessary. In case it's not obvious, for those accommodation requests that are necessary, the employer would have to provide the accommodation unless it could establish the more stringent undue hardship defense—that the accommodation would cause significant difficulty or expense. Consistent with case law on the accommodation mandate and undue hardship defense under the ADA, this should be an affirmative defense that the employer has the burden of proving,[8] and it should be just as difficult to prove as it currently is under the ADA.

However, for accommodations that are not necessary, the employer would still have to provide the accommodation unless the accommodation would cause an undue hardship using the more lenient test borrowed from the religious accommodation context, where any accommodation that causes more than a de minimis expense would not have to be provided. Although more lenient, this should also be an affirmative defense that the employer must prove.

Of course, the million-dollar question is which accommodations are necessary and which are not? I will state my proposed rule here and then elaborate on it. Accommodations that are necessary include two types of workplace modifications—(1) those that allow the employee to perform the essential functions of the job; and (2) those that allow the employee to attend to *unavoidable* caregiving obligations. Everything else would fall under the *valued* and *desired* category and would still have to be provided unless the employer could prove undue hardship using the more lenient test—the accommodation causes no more than a de minimis expense.

Although I justify this distinction more in the next section, the basic idea is one of compromise. Some would insist that protecting *everything* is offensive to those who truly need an accommodation in order to remain employed. But the harm flowing from special treatment stigma is why we cannot protect *only* people with disabilities and workers with caregiving responsibilities. Accordingly, allowing all employees to be accommodated but providing slightly more protection for those accommodations that are necessary is a compromise between the two polarized positions of only protecting marginalized employees and protecting everyone equally.

1 Necessary Accommodations

A ACCOMMODATIONS THAT ALLOW AN EMPLOYEE TO PERFORM THE JOB. The first category of accommodation requests that would be considered *necessary* are those that are required to allow the employee to perform the essential functions of the job. The most common (and familiar) reason this would apply would be for

[8] Rodal v. Anesthesia Group of Onondaga, 369 F.3d 113 (2d Cir. 2004).

employees with disabilities who need an accommodation to allow them to perform their job. But, unlike our current legal landscape, where *only* employees with disabilities must be accommodated, there are other situations where an accommodation would be deemed necessary because it allows the employee to perform the essential functions of the job.

First, pregnancy. After the ADA was amended in 2008, there are situations where pregnancy, especially a pregnancy with complications, can be considered a disability. But there are also cases where pregnancy would not be considered a disability, and yet the pregnant employee might still need an accommodation (aside from leave, discussed in Chapter 8). Some of these situations involve preemptive (or protective) accommodations—situations where a pregnant woman's doctor advises her to avoid certain activities because of the risk of complications if she doesn't avoid the activity (such as heavy lifting). In other words, she does not have complications with her pregnancy sufficient to be classified as disabled, but she still *needs* the accommodation so that she can avoid a workplace activity that her doctor has advised her to avoid. Or instead of avoiding an activity, her doctor might advise her to take more frequent breaks or to drink water more frequently.[9] Some of these pregnant women could possibly get an accommodation under the PDA after *Young v. UPS*[10] was decided (discussed in Chapter 3). But as I've discussed elsewhere, there are many problems with the post–*Young* pregnancy accommodation doctrine,[11] and this proposal would eliminate the need for parsing through that complex area of law.

Second, advanced age. The percentage of older Americans still in the workforce is increasing. This is in part due to diminished retirement savings. Many of these older workers will have physical or mental conditions that might affect their ability to do their job. Some who have spent their careers doing arduous physical labor will have back pain, knee pain, or other structural impairments. Some might have diminished senses, such as seeing or hearing. Others might have arthritis that could affect job tasks that require fine motor skills.[12] Although it is certainly possible that many of these older workers' impairments could be considered disabilities under the broadened definition of disability in the ADAAA, proving disability remains complicated. Moreover, many older workers are unlikely to claim a disability either because they don't recognize that their impairment is a disability or because claiming disability is stigmatizing, or both.[13] If they need an accommodation to allow them to perform a function of their job, they would not have to prove they have a disability in order to be accommodated under my proposal.[14]

9 Bornstein 2020; Porter 2020a.

10 Young v. United Parcel Service, Inc., 575 U.S. 206 (2015).

11 Porter 2020a.

12 Harris, S. 2020; O'Brien 2005; Stein et al. 2014.

13 Porter 2022.

14 *See also* Stein et al. 2014.

Third, non-typical height or weight. There are many individuals whose height or weight might make some job tasks difficult or even impossible.[15] For example, because I am 4'11," I know there are many job tasks that I could not perform. But many of those job tasks could possibly be modified in such a way that would allow me to perform them. Machines that are too high off the ground for me to reach could possibly be lowered or made adjustable (which would help everyone) or a stool or platform could be used to allow someone like me to perform the job tasks. My short stature is not a disability, but my inability to perform certain job tasks is simply evidence of how often workplaces (and especially workplace machinery) are designed based on the bodies of average-size men.[16] Under current law, I would not be entitled to an ADA accommodation but under my proposal, I should be able to get an accommodation if one existed that would allow me to perform the functions of the job unless the accommodation would cause the employer an undue hardship under the more stringent definition—significant difficulty or expense.[17] One example of undue hardship in this context involves cockpits of planes that were designed around a norm of a pilot who is at least 5'8"; I assume it would be prohibitively expensive to force an airline employer to modify the cockpits of airplanes.[18] (Of course, moving forward, airline manufacturers should be obligated to design cockpits of new planes to be accessible for a broader range of body sizes and shapes.)

One quick caveat: There might be someone reading this who is thinking that some of these accommodations are not strictly *necessary* because the employee can still perform the job without the accommodation; they simply would be in pain when doing so or putting their health at risk (or the health of their fetus, if pregnant). But "necessary" in this context does not mean that an employee should not get an accommodation if they could do the workplace activity but it would cause them pain, risk of injury, or (in the case of pregnancy) potential threat to the pregnancy. In other words, if a doctor advises you to take frequent breaks for your diabetes, type with an ergonomic keyboard to avoid the worsening of your carpal tunnel syndrome, or avoid lifting more than 20 pounds to make sure your pregnancy remains healthy, these accommodations are *necessary* even if you technically could do the job without them. This is how most courts interpret the accommodation obligation under the ADA, so this should be nothing new.

B UNAVOIDABLE CAREGIVING OBLIGATIONS. The other broad category of accommodations that would be deemed *necessary* under my proposal are accommodations that are required to allow the employee to attend to unavoidable caregiving obligations. What is an unavoidable caregiving obligation? Briefly stated, these are the

[15] Stein et al. 2014, at 697; Williams, JC 2001.
[16] Roberts 2008.
[17] Karlan & Rutherglen 1996 (distinguishing heavy-lifting accommodation for people with disabilities but not for women).
[18] Roberts 2008.

types of caregiving obligations that might cause you to quit or risk getting fired rather than neglect the obligation. In Chapters 2 and 8, I discussed some of the stories of parents having to make impossible decisions between keeping their jobs and attending to their young children. Recall the woman who left her two young children home alone when the babysitter was late because her employer had threatened to terminate her if she missed work one more time. The children died in a fire. Or imagine hearing that your child has had a serious accident at school and is being taken to the hospital.[19] Or, less traumatic but much more common, imagine you wake up to find your two-year-old has a fever and cannot attend day care. You call around to your backup babysitters and no one is available. It would be criminally negligent to leave a two-year-old home alone, and thus, missing work to take care of the child would be an unavoidable caregiving obligation. (To be clear, meeting the "criminal negligence" standard is a sufficient but certainly not necessary factor for characterizing the obligation as unavoidable.)

Many years ago, Peggie Smith discussed accommodating caregiving using a religious accommodation model. Although this book's proposal is significantly different from her proposal, her article does provide a useful framework for determining which caregiving obligations are important enough to be protected. Keep in mind, under my proposal, even if a caregiving obligation is not unavoidable, it should still be accommodated but would be subject to the more lenient undue hardship defense, so we would expect *avoidable* caregiving accommodations to be granted less frequently than *unavoidable* ones. Under Smith's proposal, the result is a binary—either the caregiving obligation is compelling and therefore should be accommodated, or it's not and therefore would not have to be accommodated at all.[20] But her standard for determining which caregiving obligations are significant enough to warrant protection (here, the highest level of protection) is helpful.

Smith suggests using decisions from the unemployment compensation context. As a general rule, employees can only receive unemployment compensation if they were terminated through no fault of their own or they resigned for good reason.[21] Over the years, some employees (usually women) have resigned when their employer modified their hours in such a way that would make it impossible to continue working considering their childcare obligations. Some common examples would be an employer changes the shift of a single mom from day shift to the night shift. If the single mom is not able to find childcare during those hours (which would understandably be very difficult), then it's likely her resignation will be deemed for good reason and she would be able to collect unemployment benefits. Similarly, if an employee is terminated because she leaves work early one shift after learning that her child had an accident and was being taken to the hospital, this

[19] Porter 2014e.
[20] Smith 2001.
[21] Smith 2001, at 1467.

employee would likely be able to collect unemployment insurance.[22] Basically, the standard is whether a reasonable caregiver would have felt compelled to resign because of the caregiving obligation or would have met the caregiving obligation, even knowing it could lead to her termination. If so, then under Smith's proposal, these would be *compelling* caregiving obligations that should be accommodated.[23]

Although I am not suggesting that employers and courts would have to consult the database of unemployment insurance decisions in order to decide whether the caregiving obligation is unavoidable or not, Peggie Smith's proposal does provide a helpful way of thinking about these caregiving obligations.

The test I propose is very similar to hers (although my proposal is part of a larger accommodation mandate): a caregiving obligation should be considered *unavoidable* if: (1) a reasonable person in the caregiver's situation would have felt compelled to miss work (or request a schedule change) because of the significance of the caregiving obligation; and (2) there was not a reasonable alternative for fulfilling the caregiving obligation.

Some easy applications of this test.

First, you learn your child is in the hospital. You go to the hospital. There is no reasonable alternative but for you to go to the hospital when your child is unexpectedly taken to one. I shouldn't have to say this, but just in case, this would apply to both mothers and fathers. But let's change the facts a bit. If the child receives once weekly medical treatment that must take place in the hospital, although the first step would be met (a reasonable person in the parent's situation would feel compelled to miss work to take the child to the hospital for these once-weekly treatments), the second step would have to be scrutinized. Does the child have two parents nearby? If so, in most cases, the parents should trade off who takes the child to the hospital so that one parent (usually the mom) would not have to miss work every week. If both parents are not in the picture, is there another family member (e.g., grandparent) or a trusted nanny/caregiver (not the teenage babysitter used for an occasional date night) who could take the child to the hospital? In many situations, the answer would probably be no.[24] And we certainly should not force parents to allow their occasional teenage babysitter to take the child to the hospital (I imagine the hospital would also object to this). But the point is—with the planned-in-advance weekly visit to the hospital for medical treatment, we would need to scrutinize the second element of the test—whether there was a reasonable alternative for fulfilling the caregiving obligation.

Second, you are a single mom. Your regular babysitter does not arrive on time to care for your two young children and is not answering your phone calls. You have

22 Smith 2001, at 1468–70.

23 Smith 2001, at 1471.

24 Hochschild 1997 (discussing a mom who did not admit at work that she needed to take her son for asthma shots because he was afraid of the shots).

been told you will be terminated if you are late one more time. Although you have no family in the area, as soon as you recognize your babysitter is late, you call your two substitute babysitters, the two parents you sometimes swap childcare with, and the drop-in day care in your city. None of these options work. This is an unavoidable caregiving obligation and your absence should be excused unless the employer can prove that missing work caused "significant difficulty or expense"—a very stringent standard. Contrast this with a situation where the babysitter gives you a two-week warning that she will be unavailable on a particular day you are scheduled to work. In most cases you should be able to find an alternative caregiver and this would not be an *unavoidable* caregiving obligation.

Third, your young child's school has a snow day. Again, after checking in with the children's other parent (if applicable), any relatives in your area, and other backup caregivers (including drop-in day care), this would be an unavoidable caregiving obligation. But it would probably not be considered unavoidable on a day where the school is closed but you had several weeks or months of notice of the pending closure.

One quick word about backup day care. In some situations, it is entirely appropriate to expect an employee to utilize backup childcare options. If you have a typical child who is not sick and you are able to find a trusted adult (or older teen) to care for your child, this would be an *avoidable* caregiving obligation. But in some situations, you would not be expected to use backup childcare. Perhaps your child has a disability that makes caring for him more difficult or makes him more anxious around unfamiliar caregivers. Or your child is sick (with something more than just the sniffles). Or you have just moved to a new town and have not yet had time to research or vet the local drop-in day care. In these situations, requiring the employee to use backup childcare would be unreasonable.[25]

Finally, one word about family. Unlike the current FMLA, which is defined rather narrowly to only include leave to care for a child, spouse, or parent, under my proposal, "family" should be defined broadly. For instance, assume that a childless (or child-free) worker is taking care of her school-age niece for three months. Assume further that the niece has a disability that requires weekly medical treatment. This employee requests one day off per week to take her niece to these weekly medical appointments and offers to make up the hours by working through her lunch hour on the other four days and working remotely in the evenings and on weekends. Despite the fact that this employee is not caring for her own child (biological, adopted, or foster), "family" should be defined broadly enough to include this situation.

This argument has been advanced and discussed by other scholars, including Deborah Widiss and Trina Jones;[26] as stated by Widiss, because only a "sliver of

[25] Williams, JC 2010, at 72 (securing backup childcare is extremely difficult as most day cares do not allow drop-ins).

[26] Jones 2014; Widiss 2021b.

American households consist of a traditional nuclear family, there should be flexibility in defining who you can take leave for."[27] And as argued by Jones, we should not be privileging some relationships over others. Caregiving can take place in many different contexts, for more distant relatives, and for close friends.[28] I agree with Jones that we should not privilege some relationships over other relationships (unless there is some reason to doubt the sincerity of the request).

And speaking of family, I would be remiss to not mention caregiving of elder and/or disabled family members. Many middle-age adults are part of the "sandwich generation," where they are caring for both minor children and aging parents.[29] Some of the most common caregiving situations when caring for elderly family members involve short-term absences, such as taking the family member to doctor's appointments or a longer-term leave of absence to care for an adult family member who is recovering from a surgery or illness. If the entirety of my proposal in Chapter 8 was enacted, longer leaves of absence to care for a loved one would be granted under the expanded FMLA, which would cover all employees who work for employers with 15 or more employees (rather than the current FMLA standard of 50 or more employees). If, however, no changes were made to the FMLA, and an employee worked for an employer with 15–49 employees, they would need to seek a leave using this universal accommodation mandate.

These caregiving issues are more difficult to analyze because what is reasonable in terms of caring for adult family members differs based on the situation. Let's assume that an employee requests a reduced-hours schedule to care for her mom, who is recovering from cancer treatment and surgery. The question is this: If this request was denied, would a reasonable person feel compelled to quit? Part of this analysis might depend on what other alternatives exist (if any) for caring for the employee's mom. Does the employee have one or more siblings who live nearby and could share the care of the mom? Is the mom eligible for any in-home care? Would that be sufficient? Studies show that people have a better recovery when they are being cared for by a loved one.[30] But these questions would have to be analyzed to determine whether this is an unavoidable caregiving obligation that falls under this category or the category discussed next for caregiving obligations that are not strictly necessary.

At this point, you might be thinking to yourself—Wait! Why aren't some of these requests (such as a day off without penalty because the babysitter doesn't show) covered by the Short-Term Absences Act proposed in Chapter 8? In many cases, they would be, and the caregiver would not have to request an accommodation at all. The caregiver would simply use one of their ten allotted days of paid leave to

27 Widiss 2021b.
28 Jones 2014, at 1342.
29 Clarke 2011, at 1367–68; Jacobs & Gerson 2004; Kessler 2001, at 379; Widiss 2021b.
30 Harms 2003, at 83–85.

cover the absence. But there are three scenarios where this inquiry would still be necessary. First, if the employee has used up their 10 days of STAA absences, perhaps because of weekly trips to the hospital with their child, they would need to ask for an accommodation in order to avoid discipline for the absence (assuming the employer has a relatively strict attendance policy). Second, as discussed in Chapter 8, employers are allowed to designate certain days as mandatory attendance days (or "No STAA" days). In this situation, the employee should not be fired for missing work on a No STAA day if the absence was required to comply with an unavoidable caregiving obligation. And third, the STAA does not apply to schedule changes as opposed to absences. So an employee might ask to work four 10-hour days to have the fifth day off each week to take their child to required weekly medical treatment. This would not be an absence under the STAA and would instead be a schedule-change accommodation.

To sum up where we are so far: Under this proposal, if an employee requests an accommodation that is needed to allow the employee to perform their job or to attend to an unavoidable caregiving obligation, that accommodation must be granted unless the employer can establish that the accommodation would cause an undue hardship, defined as "significant difficulty or expense." As discussed here and explored in other work,[31] this is a difficult standard to meet.

2 Accommodations for Everything Else

Accommodations that do not fall into the first category would still have to be provided unless the employer can establish undue hardship. But the difference here is that the employer's undue hardship defense is a more lenient one, which makes it more likely that the employer will be able to prove undue hardship if the accommodation is not *necessary*.

What kinds of accommodations would fall into this category? Some of the accommodation requests are closely related to the ones just discussed, except in this case, they aren't strictly necessary.

Avoidable caregiving obligations. Previously I described the test for *unavoidable* caregiving obligations, which must be accommodated unless the employer can prove undue hardship using the more stringent standard. But there are many routine caregiving obligations that would not meet this test. Many of these would be covered by the Short-Term Absences Act, discussed in Chapter 8, that would provide 10 days of leave for any reason. Parents who want to attend a field trip with their children, watch their children in performances or games, or attend parent/teacher conferences would be able to use their STAA absences for those purposes. In this case, they wouldn't need to request an accommodation unless they have exceeded their 10 days. But if they had exceeded their 10 days of STAA, the accommodation request

[31] Porter 2019d.

would fall into this category and be subject to the more lenient undue hardship test. The reason for this result is that a reasonable worker would not quit their job because they could not get the day off work to attend a school field trip.

As another example, if a parent wants to work reduced hours so that they can be home every day at 3:00 when their children are out of school even though there is a safe and well-respected after-school program, this would not be an *unavoidable* caregiving obligation and would instead fall into this category. Of course, keep in mind that the employer would still be required to provide this accommodation if it could do so without the requested accommodation causing more than a de minimis expense. And in this particular case, the two fewer hours per day (if we assume a 5:00 end of shift) might in fact cause an undue hardship under this standard. But perhaps the employee could come in early, not take a lunch, work from home, or some combination of these to make up those extra hours. In that case, the schedule change might not cause more than a de minimis expense.

Other types of avoidable caregiving obligations might include a short-term change in schedule to allow a parent to coach a child's sports team. Or perhaps a parent wants to work four, 10-hour days and have the fifth day off to manage all of the routine caregiving and household management tasks. Or the employee has a child who has been given an amazing academic or athletic opportunity, but it would involve being in a different state for a two-month period. In all of these cases, the request would fall into this category of avoidable caregiving obligations and would be subject to the more lenient undue hardship test. Again, this does not mean that the accommodations would never be granted. In fact, I expect a great many of them could be granted without an undue hardship even under the more lenient standard, especially requests that involve modifying *when* and *where* the hours are performed rather than *how many* hours are worked.

Disability accommodations to enjoy the benefits and privileges of employment. Imagine an employer hires a new employee who uses a power wheelchair. The employer would be obligated to make sure the main areas of the workplace, including restrooms and break rooms, are accessible. And because the undue hardship defense would be the more stringent one—significant difficulty or expense—all but the smallest employers would be obligated to make the modifications. But now let's imagine that the workplace has a small exercise room in the basement of the building. It has one exercise bike, one rowing machine, and some free weights. It is not strictly necessary for an employee to use this exercise room; accordingly, if there are features of the exercise room that are inaccessible—perhaps the doorway is too narrow for the wheelchair to fit through—the employee could still ask for the accommodation (and be protected against retaliation, discussed shortly). But if it was too difficult or expensive to widen the door, the employer would only be required to prove the easier undue hardship defense. Assuming widening the doorway has more than a de minimis cost (which is likely), the employer would not be required to provide it. Change the facts a bit. Now assume that the employee who uses a wheelchair can get in the exercise room, but the only weight equipment she can use (light dumbbells and resistance bands) is not available in the weight room. Because purchasing some light dumbbells and resistance bands is very cheap, the employer would be required to provide that accommodation.

One might respond to this by arguing that I'm weakening the protections for people with disabilities because they already would be entitled to such accommodations under the ADA and the employer would be subject to the more stringent undue hardship defense. Generally, this is true (or rather, this *should* be true).[32] But when an accommodation is requested to allow an employee to enjoy the benefits and privileges of employment rather than needed to allow the employee to perform the essential functions of the job, courts have not consistently ruled that such accommodations are required under the ADA.[33] The most well-known example of this phenomenon is an earlier ADA reasonable accommodation case, *Vande Zande* v. *Wisconsin Department of Administration*.[34] In this case, the plaintiff was a paraplegic who worked for a large state employer. When the employer was remodeling a new building, she requested to have the sink in the break room placed lower to be at an appropriate height for someone in a wheelchair. The employer refused, even though the cost would have been minimal, arguing that she could use the sink in the bathroom. Judge Posner, writing for the court, agreed with the employer, noting that the sink in the break room was not necessary to allow the plaintiff to perform her job. The court stated that "employers do not have to spend even modest amounts of money to bring about an absolute identity in working conditions between disabled and non-disabled workers."[35] Although this issue is in dispute, it rarely gets litigated. Moreover, even though I am slightly uncomfortable with this result, I could not find a principled way of placing this type of request in the "necessary" category, without sweeping in many other accommodations that are not strictly necessary.

Religious accommodations. Determining how to handle accommodations that are needed to allow an employee to avoid a conflict between work and his religion was one of the most difficult issues I grappled with in writing this book. On the one hand, classifying a religious accommodation as not *necessary* seems to denigrate an employee's sincere religious belief. Although some employees have a choice regarding whether or not to comply with the religious practice (so that if they cannot get the accommodation, they will remain employed without the accommodation), other employees would feel compelled to quit their job if they cannot get an accommodation that would allow them to practice their religious belief.[36]

32 EEOC, Enforcement Guidance on Reasonable Accommodation and Undue Hardship under the Americans with Disabilities Act (2002), https://www.eeoc.gov/policy/docs/accommodation.html.

33 Porter 2020b.

34 44 F.3d 538 (7th Cir. 1995)

35 *Id.* at 545–46.

36 Trans World Airlines, Inc. v. Hardison, 432 U.S. 63 (1977); *see also* Flake 2020.

Moreover, treating religious accommodations similarly to some of the accommodations discussed shortly that will certainly be seen by some as frivolous (e.g., schedule change to train for a marathon or train a puppy) might be seen as though I am insensitive to religion and religious beliefs. As a non-religious person, I admittedly have very little experience with religious beliefs that would conflict with work. However, my decision to place religious accommodations here, rather than above in the *necessary* accommodations category, is simply based on the fact that the undue hardship standard here (no more than a de minimis expense) is the one that already applies to religious accommodations.[37] Although not explicitly stated by the Court when it announced the de minimis standard in *Trans World Airlines v. Hardison*, most scholars agree that the more deferential standard for religious accommodations is because of First Amendment concerns. Specifically, courts are worried that if the statute is read to require employers to provide religious accommodations with a strict undue hardship defense, this might violate the Establishment Clause of the First Amendment.[38] Accordingly, to avoid these concerns, the standard I set here is consistent with religious accommodations under current Title VII jurisprudence. Some scholars have argued for a more stringent undue hardship defense that employers would be required to meet.[39] I am not opposed to such a change, but proposing it is beyond the scope of this project.

Everything else. What else falls into this catch-all category? As the heading of this section indicates, pretty much everything else. Some would be fairly easy to grant and employers likely already consider many of these requests—an ergonomic keyboard (despite not having carpal tunnel syndrome), a different desk chair to fit an atypically small or large body, or a standing desk to work more comfortably. These would all be very inexpensive and should be granted readily.[40]

Some requests might involve workplace modifications that would prove more difficult and expensive. Perhaps an employee is sensitive to certain smells and asks to move her desk or office or to avoid particular tasks that bring her into contact with those smells. (However, keep in mind that if the smell sensitivity was severe enough, it might mean that the employee was unable to perform the job without the accommodation, and the accommodation would be considered necessary.) Or perhaps an employee is sensitive to particular lighting and asks for the lighting to be changed in his office. (Again, a vision impairment that makes someone very sensitive to light might fall into the "necessary" category.) One final example might be someone who is sensitive to the cold or the heat and asks for a space heater for

37 Trans World Airlines, Inc. v. Hardison, 432 U.S. 63 (1977).

38 Karlan & Rutherglen 1996, at 7; Porter 2016b, at 120; Smith, 2001; Sullivan 2019.

39 Flake 2020; Ruan 2008, at 3.

40 Although, interestingly, Jennifer Shinall's study indicates that some employers would be unwilling to hire someone who would need a different chair if the anticipated cost was more than $300. Shinall 2020, at 666.

their office, or to move offices if the one assigned is particularly cold or hot. Space heaters are inexpensive (although can be dangerous) but moving offices might be logistically more difficult.

Some of the examples involving modifications to structural norms were mentioned earlier: A marathon runner requests a change in his schedule (working from 7–3 instead of 9–5) for a two-month period in the winter while he is training for a spring marathon so that he can get his training runs in while it's still light outside. Another employee wants to change her hours (but still work full time) to allow her to attend school for an advanced degree. A worker who just adopted a new dog asks to leave work early once per week for two months (without pay) to take her dog to puppy obedience training. Or an avid hunter wants to work four 10-hour shifts during the two months of hunting season so that he can enjoy three-day hunting weekends. Some people might think some of these things are not important or even frivolous. But everyone has their own definition of what's important to them. And if we keep in mind that one of the main purposes of a universal accommodation mandate is to eliminate (or at least minimize) special treatment stigma, we should not judge how people choose to spend their leisure time. Employees don't just need work/*family* balance; they also need work/*life* balance.[41]

C *Logistics*

To some extent, because this reimagining of the workplace is an academic endeavor rather than an attempt to write a detailed statute, the nitty gritty details of the reform are beyond the scope of this project. However, in part to respond to anticipated questions and critiques, I have given *some* thought to the logistics.

1 Coverage

Similar to Title VII and the ADA,[42] my proposal should apply to all employers (public and private) who have 15 or more employees. I realize that is leaving out some employees who work for very small employers. But I am sympathetic to the plight of very small employers, where one lawsuit can be financially devastating. On the employee side of coverage, I do not support requiring employees to work a certain length of time or number of hours before coverage kicks in (such as the

41 Heyer 2007; Jones 2014; Schultz & Hoffman 2006.

42 I should emphasize here that I believe my proposed legislation could (and should) exist alongside Title VII, the ADEA, and the ADA. Those statutes would continue to prohibit discrimination, harassment, and retaliation on the basis of their respective protected classes—race, color, sex, religion, and national origin (Title VII), age for employees over 40 (ADEA), and disability (ADA). But the accommodation mandates for disability (ADA), religion (Title VII), and pregnancy (PDA) would be subsumed with this proposed legislation.

FMLA requires). It would kick in from day one. As for how to define "employee" and how to deal with the lack of protection for gig workers, who are among the most vulnerable workers in society, I would follow current law with respect to defining employees, warts and all. Much ink has been spilt on the problems caused by the lack of workplace protections for gig workers.[43] I agree with much of what has been said, but rewriting the law of employee versus independent contractor is beyond the scope of this project.

2 Interactive Process

How will employees request accommodations? And what is an employer's obligation once an accommodation has been requested? Although there is no official interactive process for religious accommodations under Title VII, under the ADA, there is a requirement that employers engage in an interactive process with an employee who requests an accommodation in order to determine an appropriate and effective accommodation. There is nothing in the statutory language of the ADA that requires employers to engage in an interactive process. But the EEOC promulgated regulations that, although worded in a permissive way—"To determine the appropriate reasonable accommodation *it may be necessary* for the [employer] to initiate an informal, interactive process" with the disabled employee[44]—have been interpreted by the courts as being mandatory.[45]

Some of the scholarship regarding the interactive process has been very positive. For instance, Steve Befort said:

> [A] revolution … has occurred in the procedural arena. The interactive process contemplated by the ADA is a unique procedural device that has launched untold numbers of successful workplace accommodations.
>
> …
>
> All over the United States, disabled employees and human resources managers are joining together to invent mutually acceptable workplace solutions in the form of reasonable accommodations.[46]

Moreover, when arguing in favor of adopting the interactive process for religious accommodations, Dallan Flake notes that this process is beneficial to employers because it helps them make more informed accommodation decisions, which can decrease the risk of litigation. It also can boost employee morale.[47]

However, there has been some recent criticism of the process. Shirley Lin has argued that employees lack sufficient bargaining power to effectively engage in the

43 *See, e.g.*, Cherry 2016; Zietlow 2020.
44 29 C.F.R. § 1630.2(o)(3).
45 *See, e.g.*, Barnett v. U.S. Air, Inc., 228 F.3d 1105 (9th Cir. 2000).
46 Befort 2004, at 626, 628; *see also* Macfarlane 2021.
47 Flake 2019.

interactive process.[48] Some of this lack of bargaining power is inherent in the information deficits of the parties, and more specifically, of employees. Not surprisingly, there are intersectional dimensions to this lack of bargaining power. Michelle Travis has discussed the bargaining power disadvantage many women suffer from because they have been socialized to not negotiate on their own behalf and because many employers still see women negotiating for themselves as a gender norm violation.[49] Shirley Lin also notes that women are less likely to receive disability accommodations due to the "confluence of disability stigma and ascribed femininity, which clash with negotiating norms that predominately favor masculine attributes."[50] And evidence demonstrates that there are racial disadvantages related to requesting accommodations. Specifically, there is evidence that employers are more hostile to requests for accommodations from minority employees.[51]

Lin has proposed several reforms to improve the interactive process, including: (1) having the government collect information about accommodations so that workers could be armed with knowledge when they seek accommodations; (2) amending the National Labor Relations Act (NLRA)[52] so that seeking an accommodation for yourself or another worker would be considered protected activity; and (3) amending the NLRA to make clear that collective bargaining agreements (CBAs) should be construed to permit deviation from the terms of the CBA in order for employers and unions to comply with the ADA in the event of a conflict between the CBA and the ADA.[53]

Although I think there is merit to some of the critiques of the interactive process (and the proposals to reform it), I do not think it is one of the biggest problems with the ADA. But that doesn't mean it can't be improved at all. Accordingly, my proposed statute would contain an interactive process, and for the most part, it would mimic the process of the ADA, with three relatively small tweaks: (1) the requirement that employers and employees engage in an interactive process should be in the statute itself, and not just the regulations; (2) the statute should make clear that engaging in the interactive process is mandatory (versus the regulation's permissive language); and (3) as some circuits currently hold, if a court finds that an employer failed to engage in good faith in the interactive process, the employer should not be granted summary judgment.[54]

48 Lin 2021.

49 Travis 2017.

50 Lin 2021, at 39–40.

51 Lin 2021; Ribet 2010.

52 29 U.S.C. § 157.

53 Lin 2021. Seth Harris has also proposed requiring employers to report the number of employees who requested and received accommodations. Harris, S. 2020, at 229.

54 *See, e.g.*, Barnett v. U.S. Air, Inc., 228 F.3d 1105 (9th Cir. 2000); Fjellestad v. Pizza Hut of America, Inc., 188 F.3d 944 (8th Cir. 1999); Baert v. Euclid Beverage, Ltd., 149 F.3d 626 (7th Cir. 1998).

3 Determining Essential Functions

One of the most likely criticisms of my proposal is this: Employees with disabilities already have difficulty obtaining the accommodations they need, especially when those accommodations involve the structural norms of the workplace.[55] This is perhaps most evident by the fact that the ADA has not improved the employment rate of people with disabilities, and by the fact that, even after the broadened definition of disability under the ADAAA, the win rate of plaintiffs in ADA lawsuits has not noticeably improved.[56]

The major obstacle is how courts determine the essential functions of the job. As discussed in Chapter 3, in order to be entitled to accommodations under the ADA, employees are required to prove that they are "qualified," which is defined as being able to perform the essential functions of the job with or without reasonable accommodation.[57] Accordingly, determining the essential functions of a job is pivotal to analyzing virtually every disability discrimination claim. If there is no possible accommodation that would allow the employee to perform the essential functions, the employee is not qualified and can be lawfully terminated.

There are two primary problems with respect to how courts analyze these issues. The first is that many courts too readily defer to the employer's judgment regarding the essential functions,[58] especially if the employer has a written job description stating what the functions are. To some extent this deference is understandable, given that the ADA specifically states that an employer's judgment regarding the essential functions should be considered, especially if the employer has prepared a job description before the position is advertised.[59] The EEOC has promulgated regulations that list other factors that courts should consider in determining the essential functions, such as: the amount of time spent performing the function, the consequences of not requiring performance of the function, and the work experience of past or current incumbents in the same or similar job.[60] Unfortunately, some courts merely give lip service to these factors or don't mention them at all. In these cases, the court simply agrees with the employer regarding the essential functions even if there is little evidence to support the fact that the employer's alleged essential functions are truly "essential."[61]

55 Albiston 2010; Porter 2014b; Travis 2005.
56 Befort 2013; Shinall 2022.
57 42 U.S.C. § 12111(8).
58 Albiston 2010; Kanter 2022; Travis 2005.
59 42 U.S.C. §12111(8).
60 29 C.F.R. § 1630.2(n)(3).
61 *Compare* Knutson v. Schwan's Home Service, 711 F.3d 911 (8th Cir. 2013) (giving deference to employer's judgment that driving trucks requiring DOT certification was an essential function of manager's job even though plaintiff seldom was required to drive a delivery truck), *with* Samson v. Federal Express Corp., 746 F.3d 1196 (11th Cir. 2014) (declining to defer to

The second problem with how courts analyze the essential functions inquiry is specifically with respect to the structural norms of the workplace. Instead of viewing essential functions as the job tasks that must be completed, many courts also consider an employer's policies regarding when and where work is completed as essential *functions* of the job. As Michelle Travis has argued, it makes little sense to consider when and where work is performed as an essential function of the job. Functions of the job are job tasks, not when and where those tasks are performed. The EEOC agrees with that view, stating that policies regarding when and where work is performed are not essential functions. Instead, if an employee can perform the actual job tasks but is asking for a modification of when or where that work is performed, the inquiry should turn on whether the accommodation would cause an undue hardship.[62]

To make matters worse: If an employer designates a policy regarding when and where is performed as an essential function, there is usually no possible accommodation. Consider these contrasting examples. Assume an employee's disability prevents the employee from lifting more than 50 pounds. Even if lifting more than 50 pounds is considered an essential function, there might be accommodations that would allow the employee to perform that function. There might be pneumatically assisted lifting devices, or the employee could possibly get assistance with the lifting. But now let's assume that the employer states that an essential function of the job is to work rotating shifts, one week on day shift and then one week on night shift. If an employee cannot work rotating shifts because of a disability, there is no possible accommodation that would allow the employee to work rotating shifts. Accordingly, if the court gives deference to the employer's judgment that rotating shifts is an essential function, the employee will be deemed unqualified and can be lawfully terminated.[63]

In order to fix both of these problems, my proposal would do two things. First, the EEOC's factors for determining essential functions should be in the statute itself, not only in the regulations, and language should be added to make clear that courts are required to analyze *all* the factors and not merely give deference to the employer's judgment regarding the essential functions. Second, statutory language should be added that makes clear that employers' rules regarding when and where work is performed are not considered essential functions of the job. Instead, only the actual job tasks can be considered essential functions. If the employee is asking for a modification to the hours/shifts/schedules required, the issue would be (1) whether the accommodation is reasonable under the circumstances (e.g., it is not reasonable for someone who works on an assembly line to work from home); and (2) whether the accommodation would cause an undue hardship.

employer's judgment that driving trucks requiring DOT certification was an essential function of a mechanic's job because the plaintiff seldom test-drove trucks). *See also* Albiston 2010.

62 Travis 2005, at 48–49.

63 Porter 2014b, at 70.

4 Defining "Reasonable"

Another issue that is often litigated in ADA cases is how to define "reasonable." As I discussed in Chapter 3, I previously proposed a test for how we should define the boundaries of the reasonable accommodation obligation.[64] Because I still agree with what I said then, my proposal should include the definition of "reasonable" that I proposed in my prior work. This is a two-part test.

First, accommodations would be unreasonable if they fundamentally alter the employer–employee relationship. In order to apply this test, we need to know which accommodations fall within the employer–employee relationship. As discussed in Chapter 3, there are four types of accommodations that fall within the ambit of employer–employee relationship and therefore would be deemed reasonable and have to be provided (absent an undue hardship): (1) accommodations to make the physical structure of the workplace accessible; (2) accommodations to make the work environment accessible, including acquisition of tools and equipment; (3) modifications to shifts and schedules; and (4) accommodations to remedy the subtle barriers in the workplace—the rules and structures built around the assumption of able-bodied employees.[65] Accommodations that do not fall into one of these categories would be unreasonable, such as requiring an employer to monitor an employee's medications.

Second, accommodations are unreasonable if they give the employee with a disability an unfair advantage over his coworkers. Many accommodations have little or no effect on the employer at all but rather, only affect coworkers. Most notably, this includes reassignment to a vacant position in situations where other employees are interested in the same vacant position. But it can also include situations where providing an accommodation to an employee might make coworkers perform different tasks (some tasks might be more onerous or less pleasant) or work different shifts (some shifts might be less desirable).[66] Applying this test provides answers for most of these issues. Any accommodation that requires an employer to prefer a disabled applicant over a more qualified non-disabled applicant when hiring or promoting employees is unreasonable. Bumping an employee to provide that position to an employee with a disability would also be unreasonable. Both of these situations would give an unfair advantage to the employee with a disability over his non-disabled coworkers.[67]

But what about accommodations that might make other employees perform different tasks or work different shifts? As long as the accommodation does not give the employee with a disability an unfair advantage—that is, it simply allows the

64 Porter 2013.
65 Porter 2013, at 570.
66 Porter 2007.
67 Porter 2013.

disabled employee to remain employed—the accommodation would be reasonable. Even in cases of reassignment, where a non-disabled employee has more seniority or is arguably more qualified, reassigning the qualified employee with a disability (assuming there are no other possible accommodations) would still be reasonable because it is necessary to allow the disabled employee to remain employed.[68] The non-disabled employee is also still employed and has the opportunity to apply for other vacant positions in the future.[69]

Finally, there are a couple of rules surrounding ADA accommodations that I agree with and would apply to this proposal. First, I would keep the rule that an employer does not have to provide an employee his *preferred* accommodation.[70] As long as the accommodation is effective and reasonable, the employer can choose the accommodation that best serves the employer's needs. Second, I would keep the burden of proof rules outlined in the Supreme Court decision of *U.S. Airways v. Barnett*. In that case, the Court announced the appropriate burdens of proof as follows. It's the employee's burden to establish that the accommodation is reasonable, in the ordinary run of cases. (Under my proposal, employees would do this using the definition of "reasonable" I've described.) Assuming the employee can prove this, then the burden shifts to the employer to try to establish that, in this particular case, the accommodation would cause an undue hardship.[71]

On the other hand, there are some troubling trends in the case law that I do not agree with and that I would change for this proposal. First, there is a circuit split among the courts regarding whether a long-term leave of absence is a reasonable accommodation under the ADA. A troubling trend has developed where courts have held that a leave of absence cannot be a reasonable accommodation because leave from work is solely the province of the FMLA.[72] There are two problems with this. First, for many disabilities, the 12 weeks of leave allowed per year under the FMLA is not sufficient to allow the employee to return to work. If an employer can hold open a job while an employee takes additional *unpaid* leave without this causing the employer an undue hardship, the employer should be required to provide such leave. Moreover, under the current FMLA, many employees are not entitled to FMLA benefits because the threshold for coverage under the FMLA is 50 employees, rather than the 15 employees for ADA coverage. In Chapter 8, I proposed severing the self-care provisions of the FMLA from the care-of-others provisions. This means that long-term, job-protected leave must be considered a reasonable accommodation under this proposed statute.

[68] Stone 2011, at 550.

[69] Porter 2013; Porter 2007; *see also* Stone 2011, at 550 (the true purpose of the reasonable accommodation provision is to keep qualified employees employed).

[70] Porter 2020b, at 17–21; *see, e.g.*, Hoffman v. Caterpillar, Inc., 256 F.3d 568 (7th Cir. 2001).

[71] U.S. Airways, Inc. v. Barnett, 535 U.S. 391 (2002).

[72] *See* Befort & Porter, at 161–62.

A second troubling reasonable accommodation issue is when courts hold that a request for part-time or reduced hours is a request to create a new position, which is not required under the ADA.[73] Because schedule changes are very clearly within the scope of the employer–employee relationship, they should be considered reasonable accommodations, which means that employers would be required to provide them unless they result in an undue hardship.

5 Proving Undue Hardship

Because my proposal borrows the undue hardship tests for both religious accommodations under Title VII and disability accommodations under the ADA, the statutory language and case law for both of these provisions would serve as persuasive authority for my proposed statute.

As discussed earlier, the ADA defines undue hardship as "an action requiring significant difficulty or expense."[74] The factors are primarily cost-based. Although there was (and to some extent, still is) a fear of very expensive accommodations, it is actually very rare for a court to hold that an accommodation causes an undue hardship based on costs. Although some courts have found undue hardship in cases where the accommodation was not costly but perhaps had an effect on other employees, it is my hope that clarifying the essential functions and reasonable accommodations issues in the prior sections would put a stop to courts finding undue hardship even when the accommodation is not at all costly.

Regarding the undue hardship defense for religious accommodations (which under my proposal would apply to all accommodation requests that are not strictly *necessary*), it has traditionally not been too difficult for employers to prove undue hardship. As stated, the Supreme Court defined undue hardship under the religious accommodation provision to mean anything more than a de minimis expense.[75] Employers have been able to prove undue hardship by demonstrating that an accommodation would cost money, hurt productivity, compromise safety, or conflict with corporate image.[76] Some courts have held that even if an accommodation only partially alleviates the conflict between work and a religious practice, it is still reasonable. For instance, in one case, an employee asked for Sundays off work because of her Catholic faith. The employer instead required her to work Sundays still but scheduled her in a way that allowed her to attend religious services.[77] A corollary to this in the context of my proposal would be an employee asking to leave work early two days each week during their child's sporting season so they can attend every game, and the employer instead permits the employee to leave early

[73] Travis 2005.
[74] 42. U.S.C. § 12111(10)(A).
[75] Trans World Airlines, Inc. v. Hardison, 432 U.S. 63 (1977).
[76] Flake 2015; *see also* Sullivan 2019.
[77] Flake 2020, at 1686.

only one day per week, allowing the employee to attend half of their child's games. This would be permissible under my proposal.

Moreover, courts have not required employers to accommodate employees' religious beliefs if those accommodations would force other employees to work shifts that they would otherwise not have to work.[78] The most common way religious accommodations are granted is through other employees voluntarily swapping shifts.[79] I imagine many non-necessary accommodations under my proposal could also be granted by allowing employees to voluntarily swap shifts. So using the example of leaving early to attend a child's sporting events, perhaps one employee's child plays a fall sport and another employee's child plays a spring sport. These two employees might voluntarily agree to cover each other during their respective absences. Employers should allow this accommodation if possible. Not only is it unlikely to cause an undue hardship under traditional religious accommodation jurisprudence, but it also furthers a communitarian spirit of employees helping each other.

6 Retaliation Protection

An employment law is only as effective as its anti-retaliation protection. It does no good to give employees a right to be free from discrimination or to request and obtain an accommodation if that employee can be terminated for complaining about the discrimination or for asking for the accommodation. Accordingly, my proposed statute would have an anti-retaliation provision that mirrors the ADA's anti-retaliation provision.[80] A plaintiff must prove three elements in an ADA retaliation claim: (1) that she engaged in protected activity (opposition or participation); (2) that she suffered a materially adverse action; and (3) the existence of a causal connection between the protected activity and the adverse action.[81]

Although some argue that retaliation plaintiffs do better than discrimination or harassment plaintiffs, that is not necessarily true under the ADA. In a prior study I conducted (of post-ADAAA cases), plaintiffs litigating ADA retaliation claims had their cases dismissed (either on a motion to dismiss or a motion for summary judgment) more than 74 percent of the time.[82] Accordingly, I repeat here suggestions I've made to strengthen the ADA's anti-retaliation protections.

When bringing a retaliation claim, the first element a plaintiff needs to establish is that she engaged in protected activity. This can include participating in a lawsuit or filing a charge with the EEOC. But it more often includes what is called "opposition" activity. This is more informal activity, such as when an employee complains to a supervisor or human resources about discrimination they experienced. Two

78 Flake 2015, at 190–91; *see also* Sullivan 2019.
79 Smith 2001.
80 42 U.S.C. § 12203(a).
81 Porter 2019b; *see, e.g.*, Proctor v. UPS, 502 F.3d 1200 (10th Cir. 2007).
82 Porter 2019b, at 836.

problems might arise at this step. First, although most courts have held that requesting an accommodation under the ADA is considered protected activity, the Supreme Court has never so held.[83] Moreover, a recent case involving a request for a religious accommodation under Title VII held that requesting an accommodation is *not* protected activity.[84] Thus, my proposed statute would make perfectly clear that requesting an accommodation *is* protected activity.

The second problem that arises with this first element of the retaliation claim (engaging in protected activity) is that courts require plaintiffs to have a "reasonable belief" that they are complaining about activity that violates the law or, in the case of requesting an accommodation, a reasonable belief that they are entitled to the accommodation.[85] This problem arises quite frequently under the ADA, but because everyone is entitled to request accommodations under my proposal for any reason, it should not pose any difficulty at all.

The second element of a retaliation claim is that the plaintiff suffered a materially adverse employment action.[86] ADA retaliation cases borrow this standard from Title VII retaliation cases, where the Supreme Court case of *Burlington Northern v. Santa Fe Railway v. White* held that in order to prove an adverse action, the plaintiff needed to demonstrate that the action "would have been materially adverse to a reasonable employee ... [; that it would] well dissuade a reasonable worker from making or supporting a charge of discrimination."[87] This seems like a pretty deferential standard, but as I have discussed in both the ADA context[88] and the Title VII context,[89] the lower courts do not appear to be following this standard and have found many actions not adverse that most reasonable people would think *were* materially adverse. I'm not sure there is an easy fix to this, except perhaps to only require that the action be *subjectively* adverse to the plaintiff. In other words, if the plaintiff in good faith asserts (most likely during deposition testimony) that she perceived the action as materially adverse, that should be good enough to survive summary judgment.

Finally, the third element is that the plaintiff establishes that their protected activity caused the adverse employment action. Because there is rarely a "smoking gun" where a supervisor explicitly states that he is terminating an employee because they requested an accommodation, this element is most often proven with circumstantial evidence, usually the temporal proximity between the protected activity and the adverse employment action. Unfortunately, courts have required a very close

83 Porter 2019b.
84 Sullivan 2019, at 401–02 (discussing EEOC v. North Memorial Health Care, 908 F.3d 1098 (8th Cir. 2018).
85 Porter 2019b, at 837–40.
86 Porter 2019b, at 840–41.
87 548 U.S. 53, 57 (2006).
88 Porter 2019b.
89 Porter 2018d.

temporal proximity, which is inconsistent with what we know about human behavior. Any savvy employer, especially one who is being advised by counsel, will know that they cannot take an adverse action against a complaining employee right away because it will be perceived (rightfully so) as retaliatory. These employers often just bide their time, waiting three months or more before taking the adverse action. Courts then hold that the causal link has been broken.[90] My proposal would make clear that no dispositive inference can be drawn from a delay between the protected activity and the adverse employment action.

III ADDRESSING THE CRITICISMS

The anticipated criticisms of this proposal will likely come from both sides of the aisle, so to speak. In other words, there will be those siding with employers, arguing that this proposal is much too burdensome or costly (or both). But criticisms will also be lobbed from the left—that my proposal does not go far enough in one way or another. I discuss each of these in turn.

A *Employers' Concerns*

Employers will likely have three concerns regarding my proposal: (1) that it's too expensive; (2) that it's too administratively burdensome; and (3) there is a potential for abuse.

With regard to the first concern, studies consistently show that accommodations are not expensive. There have been several studies on the costs of ADA accommodations and although the details vary, the bottom line is that ADA accommodations are usually very cheap, and often free.[91] The common figures used are that the majority of accommodations cost less than $500, and no more than 5 percent of accommodations cost more than $5,000.[92] Another study demonstrates that two-thirds of all accommodations cost nothing, the average cost is $120, and 70 percent cost less than $500, with only 3 percent costing more than $1,000.[93] There are also tax credits for small businesses for expenditures related to workplace accessibility.[94] Of course, some will argue that there will be far more individuals requesting accommodations and this will dramatically increase the costs for employers. This argument was made at the time the ADA was passed. Some commentators argued that basing the ADA's undue hardship defense on Section 504 of the Rehabilitation

90 Porter 2019b; 2018d.

91 Burgdorf 1991; Colker 2005; Harris, S. 2007, at 6; Hoffman 2011, at 1543; Jolls 2000, at 277; Lin 2021; O'Brien 2005, at 119; Pendo 2002; Schartz 2006b; Schur et al. 2014, at 612; Shinall 2020; Stein 2003; Wendell 1996.

92 Colker 2005; Lin 2021; O'Brien 2005; Schartz et al. 2006a; Schur et al. 2013, at 76; Stein 2003.

93 O'Brien 2005, at 140.

94 Schur et al. 2013, at 81.

Act (which applies only to governmental entities and those private entities that receive federal financial assistance) was a mistake because there would be far more accommodations requested under the ADA than were requested under Section 504.[95] It is undoubtedly true that there are many more requested accommodations under the ADA. But it is *not* true that the additional accommodations have proven overly costly for employers.[96]

Moreover, when analyzing costs, we should also look at the benefits of accommodations.[97] As detailed in Chapter 7, there are both direct and indirect benefits of providing disability accommodations that often outweigh the costs.[98] It's also important to remember that the undue hardship defense does serve as a stop gap for overly expensive accommodations.[99] And for accommodations that are not strictly necessary, the undue hardship standard is much easier to meet. For religious accommodation claims under Title VII (upon which my more lenient standard is based), there is no evidence at all that complying with the religious accommodation provision in Title VII has been expensive.[100]

To the extent that costs remain a concern, the law could (and perhaps *should*) include tax incentives for compliance, based on number of accommodations granted as a percentage of accommodations requested (the higher the better), or based on the number of lawsuits filed under the proposed statute (the lower the better). Several scholars have also proposed tax incentives. Rather than starting from scratch, their sound proposals should be explored.[101]

With regard to the second concern, that administering or implementing this proposal would be too burdensome on employers, there is no doubt that, at least in its initial stages, there would be growing pains as employers learn how to deal with a new employment mandate. However, in most cases, the burdensome questions are minimized, not expanded. For instance, determining who has a disability has proven to be extraordinarily difficult over the years. Even though the definition has expanded after the Amendments, the statutory and regulatory language surrounding the definition is more complicated.[102] Determining whether an accommodation must be granted for pregnant women after the *Young v. United Parcel Service* case is also complicated.[103]

95 Porter 2019d, at 127–28 (citing sources).

96 Anderson 2000, at 145; Pendo 2002.

97 Clarke 2017, at 153; Pendo 2002.

98 Emens 2008, at 842–43; Harris 2007; Hickox & Case 2020; Karlan & Rutherglen 1996, at 23; Lin 2021; Schartz et al. 2006a; Schartz et al. 2006b; Schur et al. 2013; Stein 2003; Travis 2009b, at 377–78; Wendell 1996, at 51.

99 Linton 1998, at 80; Stein 2004c, at 645.

100 Flake 2015; Flake 2020; Smith 2001; Sullivan 2019.

101 Hochschild & Munger 2012; Jacobs & Gerson 2004; Lin 2021; Smith 2001, at 1486; Schur et al. 2013; *see also* Shinall 2020 (proposing government-subsidized accommodations).

102 Porter 2019a.

103 Porter 2020a.

Under this proposal, employers would only have to determine whether an accommodation is *necessary* or not, either because it allows the employee to perform a job task that they would otherwise not be able to perform or because it allows an employee to fulfill an unavoidable caregiving obligation. I acknowledge that these decisions might not be simple (although I doubt they are more difficult than determining who meets the definition of disability). Employers could make the decision-making process even easier by first asking whether the request poses an undue hardship *at all*, regardless of which undue hardship standard applies.[104] Most accommodations do not pose a hardship even under the more lenient undue hardship defense that applies to religious accommodations. So accommodations like flexible start/end times (but still working the same number of hours), or occasional time off (that is otherwise not covered by the STAA discussed in Chapter 8) will likely not cause any hardship at all. If that's the case, the employer does not even need to determine whether the request falls under the *necessary* category or not. This will minimize the administrative burden of implementing this proposal.

Finally, what about the potential for abuse? Some commentators will argue that because many of the requests cannot (as a practical matter) be supported by documentation, there is a potential for abuse.[105] I have several responses to this concern. First, to the extent we are referring to the wants/desires category, it should not matter what reason the employee has for the accommodation request. The employer should only be considering whether it is feasible given the more lenient undue hardship standard.

However, with respect to the accommodations that fall into the *necessary* category (and are therefore subject to the more stringent undue hardship standard), I acknowledge that there could be some efforts by employees to try to abuse this benefit, knowing that their accommodation is more likely to be granted if it falls into the necessary category. For accommodation requests involving the inability to perform the job, the employer would still be entitled to ask for medical documentation.[106] For example, regardless of whether the employee cannot lift heavy weights because of a disability, old age, or pregnancy, the employee would submit a doctor's note that verifies this limitation (although the doctor's note should not have to indicate what the specific impairment is that caused the doctor to limit the employee's lifting). With respect to unavoidable caregiving obligations, some of these

[104] Travis 2009b; Williams, JC 2001, at 75.

[105] Smith 2001. *But see* Kaminer 2004, at 358 (arguing that parents will not likely abuse a mandate allowing them to request accommodations for caregiving).

[106] I recognize this is a hotly contested issue. Macfarlane 2021; *see also* Bakst et al. 2020. Although I agree with many of Katherine Macfarlane's arguments, I believe having no documentation requirement at all might lead to abuse or the perception of abuse, which might undermine an accommodation mandate. But in agreement with Macfarlane, the documentation requirement should be very minimal.

obligations will be related to the medical needs of the family members who need care. In these cases, it is possible for employees to obtain documentation confirming the need for the accommodation (such as a doctor's note confirming that the parent took the child to the doctor). To the extent such confirmation is impossible, and the employer has good reason to suspect abuse, it can always take steps similar to those taken when it suspects FMLA or workers compensation abuse—it can use an investigator to determine if the employee is being truthful. If an employee reports that she must stay home because her toddler is sick and she cannot find alternative care, and an investigator sees her getting a pedicure, this deception would warrant discipline.

Finally, it is important to remember that we more often see employees abuse employer-provided and/or legally-mandated benefits when they have few options. For example, as discussed in Chapter 8, most abuses of FMLA leave arise because employers have very stringent attendance policies, so employees are forced to characterize the leave as FMLA leave even when it doesn't technically meet that standard. Because these two proposals are designed to make the workplace a more hospitable place for all employees, abuses should be minimal.

B *Employees' Concerns*

With regard to employees' concerns (or more specifically, scholars advocating on behalf of employees), I anticipate four arguments: (1) that protecting everyone will dilute the rights of those employees who are most marginalized; (2) on the complete opposite side of the spectrum, that all accommodations should be treated equally; (3) that my proposal does not address head-on the fact that women still do the vast majority of caregiving and they likely will continue to do so under my proposal; and (4) that my proposal does not address many of the reforms that would be particularly valuable to lower-income workers, many of whom are single moms and/or racial minorities.

1 Dilution of Rights

Some scholars are opposed to universal solutions because they threaten to dilute the rights of disadvantaged groups by trivializing the more serious harms of discrimination and undermining support for anti-discrimination in general.[107] Jessica Clarke argues that allowing protections for everyone trivializes the needs of caregivers and individuals with disabilities and "water[s] down protections like parental leave."[108] According to Clarke, a truly universal accommodation mandate that would allow for granting accommodations for "frivolous" things like

[107] Linton 1998.
[108] Clarke 2011, at 1278; *see also* Nelson & Stein 2022; Selmi 2008, at 543.

"manicures, fantasy football, and tropical vacations" would "undermine the entire project."[109] She notes that when scholars argue in favor of universal mandates, they give examples like military service or volunteering because these look like caregiving in that they contribute to the "reproduction and preservation of American life and culture."[110] But a truly universal accommodation mandate, Clarke recognizes, would also protect the worker who just wants to spend more time watching television. This, in turn, might dilute the protections of those who need them the most: "[I]f all employees were entitled to request leave for any reason … then a worker who needed the day off to take an elderly parent to a doctor's appointment would have the same chance of getting that accommodation as a worker who wants the day off to go fishing."[111]

This is a legitimate concern regarding my proposal. I have several responses. First, using her last example, it is quite possible that both accommodations could be granted without any hardship at all on the employer. Second, if the caregiving request was because of an "unavoidable caregiving obligation," which would likely include caring for elderly family members, then the caregiving request would be given priority because it would be subject to the more stringent undue hardship test. Third, in the unlikely scenario that an employer received both requests on the same day and concluded that it could only grant one without causing an undue hardship, I imagine the employer would naturally favor the caregiving employee, even if the caregiving obligation was not unavoidable.

I recognize that there might be situations where an employer is granting accommodations for reasons that most of us might think are unworthy of protection. I personally would be bothered by someone who seeks a modification of normal workplace hours to watch television. (Although, in this example, the employee would likely use one of their STAA days so this issue would never arise.). More importantly, there are all kinds of accommodation requests that would help an employee better balance their work life and home life that have nothing to do with caregiving or a medical condition, and yet are valuable for that employee's personal well-being. Whether that involves volunteering, community service, entrepreneurial efforts, continuing one's education, or achieving a physical fitness goal like running a marathon, all of these allow an employee to be renewed and refreshed, which will make that employee more productive as well as happier and more loyal.[112] I am admittedly troubled by some of the more frivolous reasons for seeking an accommodation, but if we start prioritizing some reasons over others, we are right back to where we started, with the stigma that accompanies special treatment. In other words, the only way to eliminate special treatment stigma is to accommodate

[109] Clarke 2011, at 1278.
[110] Clarke 2011, at 1278.
[111] Clarke 2011, at 1279.
[112] Jones 2014.

everyone, for all reasons (subject, of course, to the accommodation not causing an undue hardship).

2 *All Accommodations Should Be Treated Equally*

This next anticipated criticism is the polar opposite of the argument just made. Some commentators will undoubtedly argue that my universal accommodation mandate should treat all accommodations equally; in other words, that it should dispense with the two-tier undue hardship test. After all, if the goal is to eliminate special treatment stigma, we won't be able to completely eliminate it as long as some requests are treated more favorably than others.[113]

This is also a legitimate concern. However, my goal is to strike a compromise between the argument just made, that accommodating everyone will dilute the rights of those who most need accommodations, and the argument that the two-tier hardship defense will exacerbate special treatment stigma. I believe my two-tier undue hardship defense strikes the appropriate balance between the two positions.

I also think that even the most individual-rights-oriented employees can understand the difference between *needs* and *wants*. Employees who need the accommodation in order to perform the essential functions of the job or to comply with unavoidable caregiving obligations would likely lose their job without the accommodation. The employees who are denied a desired (but not necessary) accommodation will not suffer the same consequences. If we consider the disastrous consequences of unemployment[114]—especially to already marginalized workers, such as those with disabilities, older workers, pregnant workers, single mothers, and lower income workers—we can hopefully convince those who don't *need* their accommodation to stay employed why the necessary accommodations should be prioritized.[115]

Another reason for prioritizing necessary accommodations is because most of the necessary accommodations are needed for reasons that are not within the control of the individual requesting the accommodation. People with disabilities do not *choose* to be disabled.[116] People do not choose to age (although it's better than the alternative). People like me who are very small (and might need accommodations for certain job tasks) did not choose to be this small.

[113] Goldberg-Hiller & Milner 2003.

[114] Porter 2007.

[115] Porter 2016b.

[116] Choice is probably not the best word here. What we are really talking about is causation and fault. Was the disability caused by reckless behavior, such as someone who has lung cancer from years of smoking? We have a tendency to blame people for their disability or disease because we do not want to acknowledge that we might become disabled no matter how careful we are. Wendell 1996. But even when a disability was caused by voluntary behavior, we don't generally refuse to consider the person disabled or refuse to offer the ADA's protection. Cox 2019, at 335; Porter 2018c.

Admittedly, some people might argue that some accommodations that I'm classifying as *necessary* are actually based on voluntary choices, and therefore I'm privileging some life choices over other life choices.[117] Pregnant women often choose to become pregnant. People who have children and therefore have unavoidable caregiving obligations often choose to have children.[118] But certainly not everyone chooses to become pregnant or have children.[119] And no one chooses to have a spouse, parent, or other adult family member become ill, injured, or disabled and need care. Even someone who plans to remain child-free might end up having caregiving obligations that need to be accommodated.[120]

Moreover, as discussed in Chapter 7, even when having children is a voluntary choice, caring for them is not a choice—it's a responsibility.[121] Fulfilling that responsibility benefits not only the accommodated employees (usually women) but also their children, their spouses, and society.[122] No one benefits when employees are forced to choose between unavoidable caregiving obligations or termination.

3 Changing Gender Norms

Another criticism I anticipate is that my proposal does nothing to change gender norms. By this I mean that it does nothing to get men to take on more of the caregiving-related obligations. Proposals that have attempted to do that usually include mandatory leave for men with the thought that, if men take more leave when a baby is born, they will be more active caregivers for the rest of their children's lives.[123] Similarly, some might argue that even though my proposal allows all employees to seek accommodations, if women and people with disabilities continue to disproportionately seek those accommodations, some special treatment stigma will remain.[124]

These concerns are valid. I have two responses. First, it's my hope that *all* employees will start to seek accommodations, especially easy-to-grant accommodations like working from home (when feasible) or flextime. As the COVID-19 experience has taught us, having many employees requesting accommodations is how we dismantle entrenched workplace norms. And second, as I've discussed elsewhere, changing long-standing gender norms is incredibly difficult, and perhaps

[117] Jones 2014.

[118] Albiston 2010 (discussing cases focused on this concept of choice).

[119] This will be especially true after the Supreme Court's abortion decision in 2022. Dobbs v. Jackson Women's Health Organization, slip op. 19–1392 (June 24, 2022).

[120] Lester 2005, at 44.

[121] Eichner 1998; Kaminer 2004; Kessler 2001.

[122] Finley 1986.

[123] Selmi 2000, at 773; Selmi & Cahn 2006.

[124] Schoenbaum 2017a. *But see* Areheart 2017 (arguing that the advantages of providing benefits to all remain even if only some use the benefits, as long as the employer believes that all groups make at least some use of the law).

impossible.[125] Despite the arguments made by commentators such as Mike Selmi,[126] the reality is that most men still do not believe they should contribute equally to household labor, even when both spouses work full time, and surprisingly, even when the woman makes more than the man.[127] Moreover, changing gender norms does nothing to help single parents, many of whom are lower-income and/or racial minorities.[128]

4 *Not Enough Help for Lower-Income Workers*

The final anticipated criticism of this proposal is that it doesn't go far enough to help lower-income workers. Many commentators have criticized the proposals of work/family scholars who are focused on freeing up more time for caregiving.[129] These commentators rightly note (as I discussed in Chapter 2) that some caregivers don't need more time; they need more predictable working hours with better pay, and they need support that will allow them to work those hours.[130] These proposals generally include subsidized day care, longer school days, and better paying jobs.[131] Admittedly, I have not proposed or advocated for some of these proposals. Instead, my focus has been to propose reforms that are focused on the workplace and that are specific and feasible. Instead, most reforms that will benefit lower-income workers would require government funding or are too nebulous to be included here. Examples of the first include subsidized day care, longer school hours, or more general government financial assistance. A proposal that is too vague for me to include here would be attempts to increase the pay for low-income workers.[132]

Having said this, it is not the case that my proposals do nothing for low-income workers. All workers will occasionally need workplace flexibility or modifications to how they perform their job.[133] Low-income workers will benefit from the STAA proposed in Chapter 8, where they will be entitled to two weeks of job–protected paid days off. And low-income workers often have disabilities, at higher percentage rates than higher-income workers,[134] and therefore might need accommodations without the stigma that currently accompanies receiving accommodations under the ADA. Finally, low-income workers might need to vary their working hours because of childcare obligations, which the universal accommodation proposal allows them to do.

[125] Porter 2011a; Williams, JC 2010; *see also* Schultz 2010 (noting that allowing everyone to work similar hours does not guarantee equality).
[126] Selmi 2007.
[127] Hochschild 1997; Hochschild & Munger 2012; Travis 2009a.
[128] Kessler 2001, at 421.
[129] Dowd 2004.
[130] Albiston & O'Connor 2016, at 28–29; Jacobs & Gerson 2004; Selmi & Cahn 2006.
[131] Kessler 2001; Jacobs & Gerson 2004; Selmi & Cahn 2006; Williams, JC 2010.
[132] *But see* Albiston & Fisk 2021.
[133] Jacobs & Gerson 2004.
[134] Schur et al. 2013.

IV CONCLUSION

I'm sure there are other criticisms that will be lobbed at the proposals in this book. This is true of any wide-reaching, ambitious reform. And I realize I have thus far ignored the biggest criticism of all, which is simply that none of what I've suggested here is practical from a political feasibility perspective. This might be true, but it is not because it would not work; it's because employers, policy makers, and politicians have not yet imagined how we could go about broadly restructuring the workplace. It's my hope that this book will help everyone realize just how possible it is to reimagine the workplace to accommodate our bodies and our lives.

Bibliography

A

Catherine Albiston, *Institutional Inequality*, 2009 WIS. L. REV. 1093 (Albiston 2009).

INSTITUTIONAL INEQUALITY AND THE MOBILIZATION OF THE FAMILY AND MEDICAL LEAVE ACT: RIGHTS ON LEAVE (Cambridge Univ. Press 2010) (Albiston 2010).

Catherine Albiston & Catherine Fisk, *Precarious Work and Precarious Welfare: How the Pandemic Reveals Fundamental Flaws of the U.S. Social Safety Net*, 42 BERKELEY J. EMP. & LAB. L. 257 (2021) (Albiston & Fisk 2021).

Catherine Albiston & Lindsey Trimble O'Connor, *Just Leave*, 39 HARV. J. L. & GENDER, 1 (2016) (Albiston & O'Connor 2016).

Cheryl L. Anderson, *"Deserving Disabilities": Why the Definition of Disability under the Americans with Disabilities Act Should Be Revised to Eliminate the Substantial Limitation Requirement*, 65 MO. L. REV. 83 (2000) (Anderson 2000).

Ideological Dissonance, Disability Backlash, and the ADA Amendments Act, 55 WAYNE L. REV. 1267 (2009) (Anderson 2009).

ANTI-DEFAMATION LEAGUE, A *Brief History of the Disability Rights Movement* (2005) (Anti-Defamation League 2005).

Bradley A. Areheart, *When Disability Isn't "Just Right": The Entrenchment of the Medical Model of Disability and the Goldilocks Dilemma*, 83 IND. L.J. 181 (2008) (Areheart 2008).

Disability Trouble, 29 YALE L. & POL'Y REV. 347 (2011) (Areheart 2011).

The Symmetry Principle, 58 B.C. L. REV. 1085 (2017) (Areheart 2017).

Rachel Arnow-Richman, *Accommodation Subverted: The Future of Work/Family Initiatives in a Me, Inc. World*, 12 TEX. J. WOMEN & L. 345 (2003) (Arnow-Richman 2003).

Public Law and Private Process: Toward an Incentivized Organizational Justice Model of Equal Employment Quality for Caregivers, 2007 UTAH L. REV. 25 (Arnow-Richman 2007).

Incenting Flexibility: The Relationship between Public Law and Voluntary Action in Enhancing Work/Life Balance, 42 CONN. L. REV. 1081 (2010) (Arnow-Richman 2010).

B

Samuel R. Bagenstos, *Subordination, Stigma, and "Disability,"* 86 VA. L. REV. 397 (2000) (Bagenstos 2000).

"Rational Discrimination," Accommodation, and the Politics of (Disability) Civil Rights, 89 VA. L. REV. 825 (2003) (Bagenstos 2003).

The Future of Disability Law, 114 YALE L.J. 1 (2004) (Bagenstos 2004).

LAW & THE CONTRADICTIONS OF THE DISABILITY RIGHTS MOVEMENT (Yale Univ. Press 2009) (Bagenstos 2009).

Disability, Universalism, Social Rights, and Citizenship, 39 CARDOZO L. REV. 413 (2017) (Bagenstos 2017).

Disability Rights and the Discourse of Justice, 73 SMU L. REV. FORUM 26 (2020) (Bagenstos 2020).

Dina Bakst, Elizabeth Gedmark, & Christine Dinan, *Misled & Misinformed: How Some U.S. Employers Use "No Fault" Attendance Policies to Trample on Workers' Rights (And Get Away with It)*, A BETTER BALANCE (June 2020), https://perma.cc/75SM-BHR8 (Bakst et al. 2020).

Carlos A. Ball, *Looking for Theory in All the Right Places: Feminist and Communitarian Elements of Disability Discrimination Law*, 66 OHIO ST. L.J. 105 (2005) (Ball 2005).

Kevin Barry, *Toward Universalism: What the ADA Amendments Act of 2008 Can and Can't Do for Disability Rights*, 31 BERKELEY J. EMP. & LAB. L. 203 (2010) (Barry 2010).

Arianne Renan Barzilay, *Labor Regulation as Family Regulation: Decent Work and Decent Families*, 33 BERKELEY J. EMP. & LAB. L. 119 (2012) (Barzilay 2012).

Stephen F. Befort, *Accommodation at Work: Lessons from the Americans with Disabilities Act and Possibilities for Alleviating the American Worker Time Crunch*, 13 CORNELL J.L. & PUB. POL'Y 615 (2004) (Befort 2004).

An Empirical Examination of Case Outcomes under the ADA Amendments Act, 70 WASH. & LEE L. REV. 2027 (2013) (Befort 2013).

STEPHEN F. BEFORT & NICOLE BUONOCORE PORTER, DISABILITY LAW: CASES & MATERIALS (West Academic, 2d ed. 2021) (Befort & Porter 2021).

Nina Bernstein, *Daily Choice Turned Deadly: Children Left on Their Own*, N.Y. TIMES, Oct. 19, 2003, at N1 (Bernstein 2003).

Robert C. Bird & Niki Mirtorabi, *Shiftwork and the Law*, 27 BERKELEY J. EMP. & LAB. L. 383 (2006) (Bird & Mirtorabi 2006).

SUSAN BISOM-RAPP & MALCOLM SARGEANT, LIFETIME DISADVANTAGE, DISCRIMINATION AND THE GENDERED WORKFORCE (Cambridge Univ. Press 2016) (Bisom-Rapp & Sargeant 2016).

Stephanie Bornstein, *The Politics of Pregnancy Accommodation*, 14 HARV. L. & POL'Y REV. 293 (2020) (Bornstein 2020).

Robert L. Burgdorf Jr., *The Americans with Disabilities Act: Analysis and Implications of a Second-Generation Civil Rights Statute*, 26 HARV. C.R.-C.L. L. REV. 413 (1991) (Burgdorf 1991).

"Substantially Limited" Protection from Disability Discrimination: The Special Treatment Model and Misconstructions of the Definition of Disability, 42 VILL. L. REV. 409 (1997) (Burgdorf 1997).

Restoring the ADA and Beyond: Disability in the 21st Century, 13 TEX. J. C.L. & C.R. 421 (2008) (Burgdorf 2008).

C

Devon W. Carbado & Cheryl I. Harris, *Intersectionality at 30: Mapping the Margins of Anti-essentialism, Intersectionality, and Dominance Theory*, 132 HARV. L. REV. 2193 (2019) (Carbado & Harris, C. 2019).

ALLISON C. CAREY, PAMELA BLOCK, & RICHARD K. SCOTCH, ALLIES AND OBSTACLES: DISABILITY ACTIVISM AND PARENTS OF CHILDREN WITH DISABILITIES (Temple Univ. Press 2020) (Carey et al. 2020).

MARTHA CHAMALLAS, INTRODUCTION TO FEMINIST LEGAL THEORY (Aspen Publishing 1999) (Chamallas 1999).

Miriam A. Cherry, *Beyond Misclassification: The Digital Transformation of Work*, 39 COMP. LAB. L. & POL'Y 577 (2016) (Cherry 2016).

Jessica Clarke, *Beyond Equality? Against the Universal Turn in Workplace Protections*, 86 IND. L.J. 1219 (2011) (Clarke 2011).

Protected Class Gatekeeping, 92 N.Y.U. L. REV. 101 (2017) (Clarke 2017).

RUTH COLKER, THE DISABILITY PENDULUM: THE FIRST DECADE OF THE AMERICANS WITH DISABILITIES ACT (New York Univ. Press 2005) (Colker 2005).

The Mythic 43 Million Americans with Disabilities, 49 WM. & MARY L. REV. 1 (2007) (Colker 2007).

Speculation about Judicial Outcomes Under 2008 ADA Amendments: Cause for Concern, 2010 UTAH L. REV. 1029 (Colker 2010).

Joanne Conaghan, *Time to Dream? Flexibility, Families, and the Regulation of Working Time*, in PRECARIOUS WORK, WOMEN, AND THE NEW ECONOMY: THE CHALLENGE TO LEGAL NORMS, Judy Fudge & Rosemary Owns, eds. (Hart Publishing 2006) (Conaghan 2006).

Jeannette Cox, *Pregnancy as "Disability" and the Amended Americans with Disabilities Act*, 53 B.C. L. REV. 43 (2012) (Cox 2012).

Disability Law and Gender Identity Discrimination, 81 U. PITT. L. REV. 315 (2019) (Cox 2019).

Work Hours and Disability Justice, 111 GEO. L.J. 1 (2022) (Cox 2022).

Marion Crain, *Feminizing Unions: Challenging the Gendered Structure of Wage Labor*, 89 MICH. L. REV. 1155 (1991) (Crain 1991).

Kimberlé Crenshaw, *Demarginalizing the Intersection of Race & Sex: A Black Feminist Critique of Antidiscrimination Doctrine, Feminist Theory and Antiracist Politics*, 1989 U. CHI. LEGAL FORUM 139 (Crenshaw 1989).

Mary Crossley, *The Disability Kaleidoscope*, 74 NOTRE DAME L. REV. 621 (1999) (Crossley 1999).

D

Theresia Degener, *Disability in a Human Rights Context*, 5 LAWS 35 (2016) (Degener 2016).

David Dominguez, *Just Cause Protection: Will the Demise of Employment at Will Breathe New Life into Collective Job Security?*, 28 IDAHO L. REV. 283 (1991) (Dominguez 1991).

Doron Dorfman, *Disability Identity in Conflict: Performativity in the U.S. Social Security Benefits System*, 38 THOMAS JEFFERSON L. REV. 47 (2015) (Dorfman 2015).

Re-claiming Disability: Identity, Procedural Justice, and the Disability Determination Process, 42 LAW & SOC. INQUIRY 195 (2017) (Dorfman 2017).

Fear of the Disability Con: Perceptions of Fraud and Special Rights Discourse, 53 LAW & SOC'Y REV. 1051 (2019) (Dorfman 2019).

Disability as Metaphor in American Law, 170 PENN. L. REV. 1757 (2022) (Dorfman 2022).

Nancy E. Dowd, *Work and Family: The Gender Paradox and the Limitations of Discrimination Analysis in Restructuring the Workplace*, 24 HARV. C.R.-C.L. L. REV. 79 (1989) (Dowd 1989).

Work and Family: Restructuring the Workplace, 32 ARIZ. L. REV. 431 (1990) (Dowd 1990).

Bringing the Margin to the Center: Comprehensive Strategies for Work/Family Policies, 73 U. CIN. L. REV. 433 (2004) (Dowd 2004).

E

EEOC, ENFORCEMENT GUIDANCE: UNLAWFUL TREATMENT OF WORKERS WITH CAREGIVING RESPONSIBILITIES (2007), https://www.eeoc.gov/laws/guidance/enforcement-guidance-unlawful-disparate-treatment-workers-caregiving-responsibilities (EEOC Enforcement Guidance 2007).

Maxine Eichner, *Square Peg in a Round Hole: Parenting Policies and Liberal Theory*, 59 OHIO ST. L.J. 133 (1998) (Eichner 1998).

KATIE ELLIS, ROSEMARIE GARLAND-THOMSON, MIKE KENT, & RACHEL ROBERTSON, INTERDISCIPLINARY APPROACHES TO DISABILITY: LOOKING TOWARDS THE FUTURE: VOLUME 2 (Routledge Press, 2019) (Ellis et al. 2019).

Elizabeth F. Emens, *Integrating Accommodation*, 156 U. PA. L. REV. 839 (2008) (Emens 2008).

Disabling Attitudes: U.S. Disability Law and the ADA Amendments Act, 60 AM. J. COMP. L. 205 (2012) (Emens 2012).

LIFE ADMIN: HOW I LEARNED TO DO LESS, DO BETTER, AND LIVE MORE (HarperOne 2019) (Emens 2019).

Getting It: The ADA after Thirty Years, 71 SYRACUSE L. REV. 637 (2021) (Emens 2021).

DAVID M. ENGEL & FRANK W. MUNGER, RIGHTS OF INCLUSION: LAW AND IDENTITY IN THE LIFE STORIES OF AMERICANS WITH DISABILITIES (Univ. Chi. Press 2003) (Engel & Munger 2003).

AMITAI ETZIONI, THE SPIRIT OF COMMUNITY: RIGHTS, RESPONSIBILITIES, AND THE COMMUNITARIAN AGENDA (Crown 1993) (Etzioni 1993).

Katie Eyer, *Claiming Disability*, 101 B. U. L. REV. 547 (2021) (Eyer 2021).

F

Benjamin Fearnow, *83 Percent of Americans Support Wearing Masks, but Only Half Wear Them: Poll*, NEWSWEEK (Jan. 23, 2021), https://www.newsweek.com/83-percent-americans-support-wearing-masks-only-half-wear-them-poll-1563944 (Fearnow 2021).

Martha Albertson Fineman, *Cracking the Foundational Myths: Independence, Autonomy, and Self-Sufficiency*, 8 AM. U.J. GENDER SOC. POL'Y & L. 13 (2000) (Fineman 2000).

Equality, Autonomy, and the Vulnerable Subject in Law & Politics, in VULNERABILITY: REFLECTIONS ON A NEW ETHICAL FOUNDATION FOR LAW & POLITICS, Martha Albertson Fineman & Anna Grear, eds. (Routledge Press 2013) (Fineman 2013).

Lucinda M. Finley, *Transcending Equality Theory: A Way Out of the Maternity and the Workplace Debate*, 86 COLUM. L. REV. 1118 (1986) (Finley 1986).

Joseph Fishkin, *The Anti-bottleneck Principle in Employment Discrimination Law*, 91 WASH. U. L. REV. 1429 (2014) (Fishkin 2014).

Dallan F. Flake, *Bearing Burdens: Religious Accommodations That Adversely Affect Coworker Morale*, 76 OHIO ST. L.J. 169 (2015) (Flake 2015).

Interactive Religious Accommodations, 71 ALA. L. REV. 67 (2019) (Flake 2019).

Restoring Reasonableness to Workplace Religious Accommodations, 95 WASH. L. REV. 1673 (2020) (Flake 2020).

G

ELLEN GALINSKY, JAMES T. BOND, & KELLY SAKAI, NATIONAL STUDY OF EMPLOYERS (Families and Work Institute 2008) (Galinsky et al. 2008).

Jonathan Goldberg-Hiller & Neal Milner, *Rights as Excess: Understanding the Politics of Special Rights*, 28 LAW & SOC. INQUIRY 1075 (2003) (Goldberg-Hiller & Milner 2003).

Joanna L. Grossman, *Job Security without Equality: The Family and Medical Leave Act of 1993*, 15 WASH U. J.L. & POL'Y 17 (2004) (Grossman, Joanna 2004).

Joanna L. Grossman & Gillian Thomas, *Making Sure Pregnancy Works: Accommodation Claims after Young v. United Parcel Service, Inc.*, 14 HARV. L. & POL'Y REV. 319 (2020) (Grossman & Thomas 2020).

Jonathan Grossman, *Fair Labor Standards Act of 1938: Maximum Struggle for a Minimum Wage*, 1 MONTHLY LAB. REV. 22 (1978), https://www.dol.gov/general/aboutdol/history/flsa1938# (Grossman, Jonathan 1978).

Angelica Guevara, *The Need to Reimagine Disability Rights Law because the Medical Model of Disability Fails Us All*, 2021 WIS. L. REV. 269 (Guevara 2021).

H

Harlan Hahn, *Accommodations and the ADA: Unreasonable Bias or Biased Reasoning?*, 21 BERKELEY J. EMP. & LAB. L. 166 (2000) (Hahn 2000).

SARAH COTE HAMPSON, THE BALANCE GAP: WORKING MOTHERS AND THE LIMITS OF THE LAW (Stanford 2017) (Hampson 2017).

K. Nicole Harms, *Caring for Mom & Dad: The Importance of Family-Provided Eldercare and the Positive Implications of California's Paid Family Leave Law*, 10 WM. & MARY J. WOMEN & L. 69 (2003) (Harms 2003).

Jasmine E. Harris, *The Frailty of Disability Rights*, 169 U. PA. L. REV. ONLINE 29 (2020) (Harris, J. 2020).

Reckoning with Race & Disability, YALE L.J. FORUM 916 (2021) (Harris, J. 2021a).

Taking Disability Public, 169 U. PA. L. REV. 1681 (2021) (Harris, J. 2021b).

Seth D. Harris, *Law, Economics, and Accommodations in the Internal Labor Market*, 10 U. PA. J. BUS. & EMP. L. 1 (2007) (Harris, S. 2007).

Increasing Employment for Older Workers with Effective Protections against Employment Discrimination, 30 CORNELL J. L. & PUB. POL'Y 199 (2020) (Harris, S. 2020).

Katharina Heyer, *A Disability Lens on Sociolegal Research: Reading Rights of Inclusion from a Disability Studies Perspective*, 32 LAW & SOC. INQUIRY 261 (2007) (Heyer 2007).

Stacy A. Hickox, *Bargaining for Accommodations*, 1 U. PA. J. BUS. L. 147 (2016) (Hickox 2016).

Stacy A. Hickox & Keenan Case, *Risking Stigmatization to Gain Accommodation*, 22 U. PA. J. BUS. L. 533 (2020) (Hickox & Case 2020).

Stacy A. Hickox & Chenwei Liao, *Remote Work as an Accommodation for Employees with Disabilities*, 38 HOFSTRA LAB. & EMP. L.J. 25 (2020) (Hickox & Liao 2020).

ARLIE RUSSELL HOCHSCHILD, THE TIME BIND: WHEN WORK BECOMES HOME AND HOME BECOMES WORK (Metropolitan Books 1997) (Hochschild 1997).

ARLIE HOCHSCHILD WITH ANNE MACHUNG, THE SECOND SHIFT: WORKING FAMILIES AND THE REVOLUTION AT HOME (Penguin Books 2012) (Hochschild & Machung 2012).

Sharona Hoffman, *The Importance of Immutability in Employment Discrimination Law*, 52 WM. & MARY L. REV. 1483 (2011) (Hoffman 2011).

I

Samuel Issacharoff & Justin Nelson, *Discrimination with a Difference: Can Employment Discrimination Law Accommodate the Americans with Disabilities Act*, 79 N.C. L. REV. 307 (2001) (Issacharoff & Nelson 2001).

J

JERRY A. JACOBS & KATHLEEN GERSON, THE TIME DIVIDE: WORK, FAMILY, AND GENDER INEQUALITY (Harv. Univ. Press 2004) (Jacobs & Gerson 2004).

SANFORD M. JACOBY, EMPLOYING BUREAUCRACY: MANAGERS, UNIONS, AND THE TRANSFORMATION OF WORK IN THE 20TH CENTURY (Psychology Press 2004) (Jacoby 2004).

Return of the Repressed: Will the Coronavirus Bring a Great Transformation to America?, 41 COMP. LAB. L. & POL'Y J. 503 (2020) (Jacoby 2020).

Christine Jolls, *Accommodation Mandates*, 53 STAN. L. REV. 223 (2000) (Jolls 2000).

Antidiscrimination and Accommodation, 115 HARV. L. REV. 642 (2001) (Jolls 2001).

Jeffrey M. Jones, *Majority in U.S. Supports Biden COVID-19 Vaccine Mandates*, GALLUP (Sept. 24, 2021), https://news.gallup.com/poll/354983/majority-supports-biden-covid-vaccine-mandates.aspx (Jones, J. 2021).

Trina Jones, *Single and Childfree! Reassessing Parental and Marital Status Discrimination*, 46 ARIZ. ST. L.J. 1253 (2014) (Jones 2014).

K

Debbie N. Kaminer, *The Work-Family Conflict: Developing a Model of Parental Accommodation in the Workplace*, 54 AM. U.L. REV. 305 (2004) (Kaminer 2004).

Arlene S. Kanter, *The Law: What's Disability Studies Got to Do with It or an Introduction to Disability Legal Studies*, 42 COLUM. HUM. RTS. L. REV. 403 (2011) (Kanter 2011).

Remote Work and the Future of Disability Accommodations, 107 CORNELL. L. REV. (forthcoming 2022), https://ssrn.com/abstract=3895798 (Kanter 2022).

ALISON KAFER, FEMINIST, QUEER, CRIP (Indiana Univ. Press 2013) (Kafer 2013).

Marcy Karin, Lara Bollinger, & UDC Law Staff, *Disability Rights: Past, Present, and Future: A Roadmap for Disability Rights*, 23 UDC L. REV. 1 (2020) (Karin et al. 2020).

Pamela S. Karlan & George Rutherglen, *Disabilities, Discrimination, and Reasonable Accommodation*, 46 DUKE L.J. 1 (1996) (Karlan & Rutherglen 1996).

Tammy Katsabian, *The Telework Virus: How the COVID-19 Pandemic Has Affected Telework and Exposed Its Implications for Privacy and Equality*, (Sept. 1, 2020), https://ssrn.com/abstract=3684702 (Katsabian 2021).

Mark Kelman, *Market Discrimination and Groups*, 53 STAN. L. REV. 833 (2001) (Kelman 2001).

Laura T. Kessler, *The Attachment Gap: Employment Discrimination Law, Women's Cultural Caregiving, and the Limits of Economic and Liberal Legal Theory*, 34 U. MICH. J. L. REFORM 371 (2001) (Kessler 2001).

Keeping Discrimination Theory Front and Center in the Discourse over Work and Family Conflict, 34 PEPP. L. REV. 313 (2007) (Kessler 2007).

Nina A. Kohn, *Vulnerability Theory and the Role of Government*, 26 YALE J.L. & FEMINISM 1 (2014) (Kohn 2014).

Dezimey Kum, *Fueled by a History of Mistreatment, Black Americans Distrust the New COVID-19 Vaccines*, TIME (Dec. 28, 2020), https://time.com/5925074/black-americans-covid-19-vaccine-distrust (Kum 2020).

L

James Leonard, *The Equity Trap: How Reliance on Traditional Civil Rights Concepts Had Rendered Title I of the ADA Ineffective*, 56 CASE W. RES. L. REV. 1 (2005) (Leonard 2005).

Gillian Lester, *A Defense of Paid Family Leave*, 28 HARV. J.L. & GENDER 1 (2005) (Lester 2005).

Jennifer L. Levi & Kevin M. Barry, *Transgender Tropes & Constitutional Review*, 37 YALE L. & POL'Y REV. 589 (2019) (Levi & Barry 2019).

Shirley Lin, *Bargaining for Integration*, 96 N.Y.U. L. REV. 1826 (2021) (Lin 2021).

SIMI LINTON, CLAIMING DISABILITY: KNOWLEDGE AND IDENTITY (NYU Press 1998) (Linton 1998).

MY BODY POLITIC: A MEMOIR (U. Mich. Press 2007) (Linton 2007).

Christine Littleton, *Reconstructing Sexual Equality*, 75 CAL. L. REV. 1279 (1987) (Littleton 1987).

M

Katherine A. Macfarlane, *Disability without Documentation*, 90 FORDHAM L. REV. 59 (2021) (Macfarlane 2021).

Martin H. Malin, *Fathers and Parental Leave*, 72 TEX. L. REV. 1047 (1994) (Malin 1994).

Ann C. McGinley & Frank Rudy Cooper, *Intersectional Cohorts, Dis/Ability, and Class Actions*, 47 FORDHAM URB. L.J. 293 (2020) (McGinley & Cooper 2020).

Miranda Oshige McGowan, *Reconsidering the Americans with Disabilities Act*, 35 GA. L. REV. 27 (2000) (McGowan 2000).

Terrence M. McMenamin, *A Time to Work: Recent Trends in Shift Work and Flexible Schedules*, MONTHLY LAB. REV. (Dec. 2007), https://www.bls.gov/opub/mlr/2007/12/art1full.pdf (McMenamin 2007).

Paul Steven Miller, *Disability Civil Rights and a New Paradigm for the Twenty-First Century: The Expansion of Civil Rights Beyond Race, Gender, and Age*, 1 U. PA. J. LAB. & EMP. L. 511 (1998) (Miller 1998).

Katherine L. Moore, *Disabled Autonomy*, 22 J. HEALTH CARE L. & POL'Y 245 (2019) (Moore 2019).

N

Camille A. Nelson, *Racializing Disability, Disabling Race: Policing Race and Mental Status*, 15 BERKELEY J. CRIM. L. 1 (2010) (Nelson 2010).

Ryan H. Nelson & Michael Ashley Stein, *Ability Apartheid and Paid Leave*, 120 MICH. L. REV. 1247 (2022) (Nelson & Stein 2022).

O

RUTH O'BRIEN, BODIES IN REVOLT: GENDER, DISABILITY, AND A WORKPLACE ETHIC OF CARE (Routledge Press 2005) (O'Brien 2005).

Ann O'Leary, *How Family Leave Laws Left Out Low-Income Workers*, 28 BERKELEY J. EMP. & LAB. L. 1 (2007) (O'Leary 2007).

Angela Onwuachi-Willig, *What About #UsToo? The Invisibility of Race in the #MeToo Movement*, 128 YALE L.J. FORUM (2018) (Onwuachi-Willig 2018).

P

Kimani Paul-Emile, *Blackness as Disability?*, 106 GEO. L.J. 293 (2018) (Paul-Emile 2018).

Elizabeth A. Pendo, *Disability, Doctors and Dollars: Distinguishing the Three Faces of Reasonable Accommodation*, 35 U.C. DAVIS L. REV. 1175 (2002) (Pendo 2002).

LEAH LAKSHMI PIEPZNA-SAMARASINHA, CARE WORK: DREAMING DISABILITY JUSTICE (Arsenal Pulp Press 2018) (Piepzna-Samarasinha 2018).

Nicole Buonocore Porter, *Sex Plus Age Discrimination: Protecting Older Women Workers*, 81 DENV. U. L. REV. 79 (2003) (Porter 2003).

Re-defining Superwoman: An Essay on Overcoming the "Maternal Wall" in the Legal Workplace, 13 DUKE J. GENDER L. & POL'Y 55 (2006) (Porter 2006).

Reasonable Burdens: Resolving the Conflict Between Disabled Employees and Their Coworkers, 34 FLA. ST. U.L. REV. 313 (2007) (Porter 2007).

Why Care about Caregivers? Using Communitarian Theory to Justify Protection of "Real" Workers, 58 KAN. L. REV. 355 (2010) (Porter 2010a).

Synergistic Solutions: An Integrated Approach to Solving the Caregiver Conundrum for "Real" Workers, 39 STETSON L. REV. 777 (2010) (Porter 2010b).

Embracing Caregiving and Respecting Choice: An Essay on the Debate over Changing Gender Norms, 41 SW. L. REV. 1 (2011) (Porter 2011a).

Relieving (Most of) the Tension: A Review Essay of Samuel R. Bagenstos, Law and the Contradictions of the Disability Rights Movement, 20 CORNELL J. L. & PUB. POL'Y 761 (2011) (Porter 2011b).

Nicole Buonocore Porter & Jessica Vartanian, *Debunking the Market Myth in Pay Discrimination Cases*, 12 GEORGETOWN J. GENDER & L. 159 (2011) (Porter & Vartanian 2011c).

Nicole Buonocore Porter, *Martinizing Title I of the Americans with Disabilities Act*, 47 GA. L. REV. 527 (2013) (Porter 2013).

A Defining Moment: A Review of Disability & Equity at Work, Why Achieving Positive Employment Outcomes for Individuals with Disabilities Requires a Universal Definition of Disability, edited by Jody Heymann et al., Oxford Univ. Press, 18 EMP. RTS. & EMP. POL'Y J. 289 (2014) (Porter 2014a).

The New ADA Backlash, 82 TENN. L. REV. 1 (2014) (Porter 2014b).

Caregiver Conundrum Redux: The Entrenchment of Structural Norms, 91 DENV. U. L. REV. 963 (2014) (Porter 2014c).

Finding a Fix for the FMLA: A New Perspective, a New Solution, 31 HOFSTRA LAB. & EMP. L.J. 327 (2014) (Porter 2014d).

Mutual Marginalization: Individuals with Disabilities and Workers with Caregiving Responsibilities, 66 FLA. L. REV. 1099 (2014) (Porter 2014e).

The Difficulty Accommodating Health Care Workers, 9 ST. LOUIS U. J. HEALTH L. & POL'Y 1 (2015) (Porter 2015).

Special Treatment Stigma after the ADA Amendments Act, 43 PEPP. L. REV. 213 (2016) (Porter 2016a).

Accommodating Everyone, 47 SETON HALL L. REV. 85 (2016) (Porter 2016b).

Mothers with Disabilities, 33 BERKELEY J. GENDER L. & JUST. 75 (2018) (Porter 2018a).

An Ambitious Approach: A Review of Lifetime Disadvantage, Discrimination and the Gendered Workforce, Susan Bisom-Rapp & Malcom Sargeant, 22 EMP. RTS. & EMP. POL'Y J. 125 (2018) (Porter 2018b).

Cumulative Hardship, 25 GEORGE MASON L. REV. 753 (2018) (Porter 2018c).

Ending Harassment by Starting with Retaliation, 71 STAN. L. REV. ONLINE 49 (2018) (Porter 2018d).

Explaining "Not Disabled" Cases Ten Years after the ADAAA: A Story of Ignorance, Incompetence, and Possibly Animus, 26 GEO. J. POVERTY L. & POL'Y 383 (2019) (Porter 2019a).

Disabling ADA Retaliation Claims, 19 NEV. L.J. 823 (2019) (Porter 2019b).

Mixed Signals: What Can We Expect from the Supreme Court in This Post-ADA Amendments Act Era, 35 TOURO L. REV. 435 (2019) (Porter 2019c).

A New Look at the ADA's Undue Hardship Defense, 84 MO. L. REV. 121 (2019) (Porter 2019d).

Accommodating Pregnancy Five Years after Young v. UPS: *Where We Are & Where We Should Go*, 14 ST. LOUIS U. J. HEALTH L. & POL'Y 73 (2020) (Porter 2020a).

Adverse Employment Actions in Failure-to-Accommodate Cases: Much Ado about Nothing, 95 NYU L. REV. ONLINE 1 (2020) (Porter 2020b).

Working While Mothering during the Pandemic and Beyond, 78 WASH. & LEE. L. REV. ONLINE 1 (2021) (Porter 2021).

Disclaiming Disability, 55 UC DAVIS L. REV. 1829 (2022) (Porter 2022).

R

Beth Ribet, *Surfacing Disability through a Critical Race Theoretical Paradigm*, 2 GEO. J. L. & MOD. CRITICAL RACE PERSP. 209 (2010) (Ribet 2010).

Jessica L. Roberts, *Accommodating the Female Body: A Disability Paradigm of Sex Discrimination*, 79 U. COLO. L. REV. 1297 (2008) (Roberts 2008).

Victoria M. Rodriguez-Roldan, *The Intersection between Disability and LGBTQ Discrimination and Marginalization*, 28 AM. U. J. GENDER SOC. POL'Y & L. 429 (2020) (Rodriguez-Roldan 2020).

Laura Rothstein, *Would the ADA Pass Today? Disability Rights in an Age of Partisan Polarization*, 12 ST. LOUIS U. J. HEALTH L. & POL'Y 271 (2019) (Rothstein 2019).

Elizabeth Roush, *(Re)entering the Workforce: An Historical Perspective on Family Responsibilities Discrimination and the Shortcomings of Law to Remedy It*, 31 WASH. U. J.L. & POL'Y 221 (2009) (Roush 2009).

Nantiya Ruan, *Accommodating Respectful Religious Expression in the Workplace*, 92 MARQ. L. REV. 1 (2008) (Ruan 2008).

S

Adam M. Samaha, *What Good Is the Social Model of Disability?*, 74 U. CHI. L. REV. 1251 (2007) (Samaha 2007).

Ani B. Satz, *Disability, Vulnerability, and the Limits of Antidiscrimination*, 83 WASH. L. REV. 513 (2008) (Satz 2008).

Helen A. Schartz, D.J. Hendricks, & Peter Blanck, *Workplace Accommodations: Evidence Based Outcomes*, 27 WORK 345 (2006) (Schartz et al. 2006b).

Helen A. Schartz, Kevin M. Schartz, D.J. Hendricks, & Peter Blanck, *Workplace Accommodations: Empirical Study of Current Employees*, 75 MISS. L.J. 917 (2006) (Schartz et al. 2006a).

Naomi Schoenbaum, *It's Time That You Know: The Shortcomings of Ignorance as Fairness in Employment Law and the Need for an "Information-Shifting" Model*, 30 HARV. J. L. & GENDER 99 (2007) (Schoenbaum 2007).

The Case for Symmetry in Antidiscrimination Law, 2017 WIS. L. REV. 69 (Schoenbaum 2017a).

Towards a Law of Coworkers, 68 ALA. L. REV. 605 (2017) (Schoenbaum 2017b).

Vicki Schultz & Allison Hoffman, *The Need for a Reduced Workweek in the United States*, in PRECARIOUS WORK, WOMEN, AND THE NEW ECONOMY: THE LEGAL CHALLENGE TO LEGAL NORMS, Judy Fudge & Rosemary Owens, eds. (Hart Publishing 2006) (Schultz & Hoffman 2006).

Vicki Schultz, *Feminism and Workplace Flexibility*, 42 CONN. L. REV. 1203 (2010) (Schultz 2010).

Lisa Schur, Douglas Kruse, & Peter Blanck, *Corporate Culture and the Employment of Persons with Disabilities*, 23 BEHAVIOR SCI. LAW 3 (2005) (Schur et al. 2005).

Lisa Schur, Douglas Kruse, Joseph Blasi, & Peter Blanck, *Is Disability Disabling in All Workplaces? Workplace Disparities and Corporate Culture*, 48 INDUS. REL 381 (2009) (Schur et al. 2009).

PEOPLE WITH DISABILITIES: SIDELINED OR MAINSTREAMED? (Cambridge Disability Law and Policy 2013) (Schur et al. 2013).

Lisa Schur, Lisa Nishii, Meera Adya, Douglas Kruse, Susanne M. Bruyere, & Peter Blanck, *Accommodating Employees With and Without Disabilities*, 53 HUM. RESOURCES MGMT. 593 (2014) (Schur et al. 2014).

Michael Selmi, *Family Leave and the Gender Wage Gap*, 78 N.C. L. REV. 707 (2000) (Selmi 2000).

Is Something Better than Nothing? Critical Reflections on Ten Years of the FMLA, 15 WASH U. J. L. & POL'Y 65 (2004) (Selmi 2004).

Michael Selmi & Naomi Cahn, *Women in the Workplace: Which Women, Which Agenda*, 13 DUKE J. GENDER L. & POL'Y 7 (2006) (Selmi & Cahn 2006).

The Work-Family Conflict: An Essay on Employers, Men and Responsibility, 4 U. ST. THOMAS L.J. 573 (2007) (Selmi 2007).

Interpreting the Americans with Disabilities Act: Why the Supreme Court Rewrote the Statute, and Why Congress Did Not Care, 76 GEO. WASH. L. REV. 522 (2008) (Selmi 2008).

Jennifer Bennett Shinall, *The Substantially Impaired Sex: Uncovering the Gendered Nature of Disability Discrimination*, 101 MINN. L. REV. 1099 (2017) (Shinall 2017).

The Pregnancy Penalty, 103 MINN. L. REV. 749 (2018) (Shinall 2018).

Anticipating Accommodation, 105 IOWA L. REV. 631 (2020) (Shinall 2020).

Without Accommodation, 97 IND. L.J. 1147 (2022) (Shinall 2022).

D'Andra Millsap Shu, *Remote Work Disability Accommodations in the Post-Pandemic Workplace: The Need for Evidence-Driven Analysis*, TEMPLE L. REV. (forthcoming 2023), https://ssrn.com/abstract=4190092 (Shu 2023).

Peggie R. Smith, *Accommodating Routine Parental Obligations in an Era of Work-Family Conflict: Lessons from Religious Accommodations*, 2001 WIS. L. REV. 1443 (Smith 2001).

Parental-Status Employment Discrimination: A Wrong in Need of a Right, 35 U. MICH. J.L. REFORM 569 (2002) (Smith 2002).

Michael Ashley Stein, *The Law and Economics of Disability Accommodations*, 53 DUKE L.J. 79 (2003) (Stein 2003).

Under the Empirical Radar: An Initial Expressive Law Analysis of the ADA, 90 VA. L. REV. 1151 (2004) (Stein 2004a).

Generalizing Disability, 102 MICH. L. REV. 1373 (2004) (Stein 2004b).

Same Struggle, Different Difference: ADA Accommodation as Antidiscrimination, 153 U. PA. L. REV. 579 (2004) (Stein 2004c).

Michael Ashley Stein, Anita Silvers, Bradley A. Areheart, & Leslie Pickering Francis, *Accommodating Every Body*, 81 U. CHI. L. REV. 689 (2014) (Stein et al. 2014).

Kerri Stone, *Substantial Limitations: Reflections on the ADAAA*, 14 N.Y.U. J. LEGIS. & PUB. POL'Y 509 (2011) (Stone 2011).

Charles A. Sullivan, *Retaliation and Requesting Religious Accommodation*, 70 CASE W. RES. L. REV. 381 (2019) (Sullivan 2019).

T

Michelle A. Travis, *Equality in the Virtual Workplace*, 24 BERKELEY J. EMP. & LAB. L. 283 (2003) (Travis 2003).

Recapturing the Transformative Potential of Employment Discrimination Law, 62 WASH. & LEE L. REV. 3 (2005) (Travis 2005).

The Future of Work-Family Policy: Is "Choice" the Right Choice? Review of Women and Employment: Changing Lives and New Challenges, 13 EMP. RTS. & EMP. POL'Y J. 385 (2009) (Travis 2009a).

Lashing Back at the ADA Backlash: How the Americans with Disabilities Act Benefits Americans without Disabilities, 76 TENN. L. REV. 311 (2009) (Travis 2009b).

Gendering Disability to Enable Disability Rights Law, 105 CAL. L. REV. 837 (2017) (Travis 2017).

A Post-Pandemic Antidiscrimination Approach to Workplace Flexibility, 64 WASH. U. J. L. & POL'Y 1 (2020) (Travis 2020).

Bonnie Poitras Tucker, *The ADA's Revolving Door: Inherent Flaws in the Civil Rights Paradigm*, 62 OHIO ST. L.J. 335 (2001) (Tucker 2001).

V

J. H. Verkerke, *Disaggregating Antidiscrimination and Accommodation*, 44 Wm. & Mary L. Rev. 1385 (2003) (Verkerke 2003).

W

Michael Waterstone, *The Untold Story of the Rest of the Americans with Disabilities Act*, 58 Vand. L. Rev. 1807 (2005) (Waterstone 2005).

The Costs of Easy Victory, 57 Wm. & Mary L. Rev. 587 (2015) (Waterstone 2015a).

Backlash, Courts, and Disability Rights, 95 B.U. L. Rev. 833 (2015) (Waterstone 2015b).

Michael E. Waterstone & Michael Ashley Stein, *Disabling Prejudice*, 102 Nw. U. L. Rev. 1351 (2008) (Waterstone & Stein 2008).

Susan Wendell, The Rejected Body: Feminist Philosophical Reflections on Disability (Routledge 1996) (Wendell 1996).

Deborah A. Widiss, *Changing the Marriage Equation*, 89 Wash. U. L. Rev. 721 (2012) (Widiss 2012).

Equalizing Parental Leave, 105 Minn. L. Rev. 2175 (2021) (Widiss 2021a).

Chosen Family, Care, and the Workplace, 131 Yale L.J. Forum 215 (2021) (Widiss 2021b).

Shirley Wilcher, *The Rehabilitation Act of 1973: 45 Years of Activism and Progress*, Insight into Diversity (Sept. 17, 2018), https://www.insightintodiversity.com/the-rehabilitation-act-of-1973-45-years-of-activism-and-progress (Wilcher 2018).

Jamillah Bowman Williams, *Beyond Sex-Plus: Acknowledging Black Women in Employment Law and Policy*, 25 Emp. Rts. & Emp. Pol'y J. 13 (2021) (Williams, JB 2021).

Joan Williams, Unbending Gender: Why Family and Work Conflict and What to Do About It (Oxford Univ. Press 2001) (Williams, JC 2001).

Reshaping the Work-Family Debate: Why Men and Class Matter (Harv. Univ. Press 2010) (Williams, JC 2010).

Joan C. Williams & Nancy Segal, *Beyond the Maternal Wall: Relief for Family Caregivers Who Are Discriminated against on the Job*, 26 Harv. Women's L.J. 77 (2003) (Williams, JC & Segal 2003).

Joan C. Williams & Stephanie Bornstein, *Caregivers in the Courtroom: The Growing Trend of Family Responsibilities Discrimination*, 41 U.S.F. L. Rev. 171 (2006) (Williams, JC & Bornstein 2006).

Z

Rebecca E. Zietlow, *The New Peonage: Liberty and Precarity for Workers in the Gig Economy*, 55 Wake Forest L. Rev. 1087 (2020) (Zietlow 2020).

Index

For EU product safety concerns, contact us at Calle de José Abascal, 56–1°,
28003 Madrid, Spain or eugpsr@cambridge.org.

www.ingramcontent.com/pod-product-compliance
Lightning Source LLC
LaVergne TN
LVHW011814200926
848484LV00005B/1190
* 9 7 8 1 0 0 9 3 4 7 4 2 6 *